God's

Human

Future

Seminar on God

and the

Human Future

David Galston, series editor

Vol. 1: *The Folly of God,* John D. Caputo
Vol. 2: *God's Human Future,* David Galston

God's Human Future

The Struggle to Define Theology Today

David Galston

POLEBRIDGE PRESS
Salem, Oregon

Polebridge Press is the publishing arm of the Westar Institute, a non-profit, public-benefit research and educational organization. To learn more, visit westarinstitute.org.

Cover and interior design by Robaire Ream

Library of Congress Cataloging-in-Publication Data

Names: Galston, David, 1960- author.
Title: God's human future : the struggle to define theology today / by David
    Galston.
Description: Farmington, Minnesota : Polebridge Press, 2016. | Series: God
    and the human future ; Vol. 2 | Includes bibliographical references and
    index.
Identifiers: LCCN 2016005217 | ISBN 9781598151732 (alk. paper)
Subjects: LCSH: Religion--Philosophy. | Theology.
Classification: LCC BL51 .G323 2016 | DDC 202--dc23
LC record available at http://lccn.loc.gov/2016005217

10   9   8   7   6   5   4   3   2   1

Contents

Introduction 1

1. What Is the Bible? 7

2. What Is Religion? 23

3. Enlightenment Theology 43

4. Covenant Theology 61

5. Jesus the Teacher of Nothingness 77

6. Creating God in 325 93

7. Meet the New Jesus, a Christian Avatar 111

8. When God Stopped Working 127

9. Religion and the God Who Almost Is 145

10. Saving Apocalypticism 161

11. Theology and the Opening of Time 175

Epilogue 195

Notes 199

Bibliography 213

Index 217

Acknowledgments

In the course of writing a book, every author has many supportive people to thank. In this particular case the community of people involved is quite diverse. Many of the chapters were written in my office in Westdale, a community in Hamilton, Ontario. Each morning as I faced the task of thinking and writing, I first made a short trip to the local Second Cup coffee shop. Many of the staff there came to know about this project, talked to me about it, and encouraged me, all while making the best large latte around. I want to thank Tijana and her staff at the Second Cup in Westdale for their interest, conversations, and kindness.

The main idea of this book was conceived in the context of a Westar Jesus Seminar on the Road event (called a JSOR). I experimented with the idea of two types of theology, which were initially called avatar and royal theology. I attempted this distinction first in Fort Wayne, Indiana, and tried it in a revised way in Minneapolis, Minnesota. I want to thank both communities who hosted the JSOR programs and who invited me as a speaker. It is important to try out ideas in a public forum to see whether they work or do not work. I have always held that we do not know what we know until we have to explain ourselves. I thank the people of these communities for giving me the opportunity to explain myself and to find out whether I knew what I was talking about.

I recently made a trip to New Zealand and Australia in relation to *Embracing the Human Jesus* and because of my position as the Academic Director of the Westar Institute. In Auckland, Perth, and Melbourne I had the occasion to try yet another version of two types of theology, which I then distinguished as epistemological and ontological theology. The people there received this distinction with inquiring and questioning minds, and this resulted in many interesting conversations during which I learned things I did not know before. I want to thank Dick Carter for making this trip possible and all the many people I met who made my visit a wonderful, memorable time.

I speak a couple of times a month in a community known as the Quest Learning Centre for Religious Literacy in Hamilton, Ontario. Every time I get a chance to speak in this context, I try to address a topic that will challenge both myself and the community members. The habit of pushing myself with the community into new ideas and new fields of inquiry has meant that my theological experience has expanded in many directions over time. The people of this community are learned and hold several different kinds of expertise, so their desire to be challenged further has always help me think, re-think, and then question what I have learned and what I need to learn. Quest is a special community, very hard to describe, and I have never been in one like it. I thank the people of this community very much.

Through the Westar Institute I have met many great scholars involved in different fields. From each I have learned so many things and, I hope, I have made a decent contribution in return. It is impossible to name all the friends that I have been lucky to meet and make, but I do want to mention some folks who have had a great influence on me. I thank Don Cupitt, Lloyd Geering, Lane McGaughy, Roy Hoover, Perry Key, Stephen Patterson, Robert Miller, Art Dewey, Brandon Scott, Hal Taussig, John Caputo, Joe Bessler, John Kelly, and Jarmo Tarkki. I have learned much in the way of biblical and theological scholarship, and with the two Johns, Joe, and Jarmo I was happy to join in the launch of the Westar Institute's Seminar on God and the Human Future. There are many more friends and scholars whom I am privileged to know through the Westar Institute and its mission of religious literacy. A list of names would be very long, but I thank the Westar Institute as a whole and all the members who compose it for giving me great experiences on the level of both friendships and academic growth.

I want to thank some of my co-workers at the Westar Institute who are also my friends and who have been extremely kind to me and my family: Cassandra Farrin, Bill Lehto, Robaire Ream, and Char Matejovsky. Cassandra and Char were involved in the production of this book as well and have a hand in the ideas here contained. I thank Cassandra for her insightfulness in the many conversations we held and Char for her persistent encouragement of my work and her concern that I express the ideas clearly and accessibly. Char in particular was the first person to encourage me to write, so I will always remain grateful to her for her support. Bill Lehto and I share a love for Nietzsche, and our conversations in this regard have often been about how to push the question further. I am and am not a Nietzschean, but to the extent that I am I owe thanks to Bill for directing my reading.

Larry Alexander is the immediate person who asked, after I had spoken on Descartes in a Westar context, that I consider expanding some of my comments into a book. Naturally, the expansion soon became about everything but Descartes. The few words in this text concerning Descartes arose from whatever comments I made on that occasion some time back. Still, I thank Larry for approaching me about another book and then for reading every word as this project changed its shape, content, and direction. I must also thank Larry for his straightforward way of telling me to rethink and rewrite what were to be chapters 8, 9, 10, and 11. I had written these chapters quickly before leaving for New Zealand and Australia, and upon return I had to agree with Larry that they were indeed too quickly written.

I want to thank my students at Brock University in St. Catharines, Ontario. During the early work on this book I was giving a special seminar class on the critical study of the Christian New Testament. The seminar was extremely small, making the conversations highly stimulating and incredibly honest. Each student, in his or her own way, contributed to the writing of this book through interest, conversation, and excitement. I thank Jennica, Casey, Matthew, and

Collin for their sincere efforts to understand and challenge theology with critical thinking skills and concern for the future of religion.

I want finally to thank Barbara, my partner and best friend. She holds a broad understanding of English literature and a deep appreciation for the arts. We hold a common mind when we think about the nature of religion and when we question its potential value or loss of value for humanity. Barbara inspires me, and I hope I return the favor to her. She is also an excellent copy editor and worked in this capacity through this book. I owe her thanks for the many ways she improved this text and I hold thankfulness for her as her partner.

Regretfully every book holds an error in some form or another. Even more regretfully the sincere help and inspiration of everyone above did not prevent me from making some, whether in the judgment of a subject or in the explanation of an idea. All errors herein contained are mine. I hope that, despite errors or misjudgments, this book makes a contribution to thinking about theology and its value today.

Introduction

The writing of these pages is intended to be popular in style, which means equally accessible to anyone. This accessibility, though, is somewhat modified by technical terms and abstract thoughts. In an effort to soften these two aspects of the book, I offer here some comments of orientation and a few explanations.

In much of the text I rely on two types of theology, called Enlightenment and Covenant theology, that loosely derive from two Western cultural experiences of language and religion. The first is the tradition commonly called the Proto Indo-European tradition (PIE). Basically, Western traditions that arose in Europe and were transported to North and South America share a deep history with traditions that arose in India and were (eventually) called Hinduism. The archaeological link is found in the roots of languages that share common histories and deep cultural memories. The word "much" in English is a simple example, for it appears in cognate forms in ancient Latin (*magnus*), Greek (*megas*), Celtic (*maige*), Persian (*mazant*), and Sanskrit (*mahant*). In fact, it even occurs in ancient Hittite (*mekkis*), which also arises from the PIE tradition.[1] The common linguistic relationships do not translate directly into shared religious beliefs, but neither do they isolate the people of these languages. One common denominator is the manner in which gods are portrayed as interactive beings who represent a hidden, stable reality behind the appearance of the chaotic and stormy fluctuations of nature. This could be called "Avatar" theology because it is about the individual worshiper finding divine qualities behind natural fluc-tuations and within the self.

The second tradition identifies those cultures of the Ancient Near East (ANE) which, though distinct, have always mixed with the Indo-European tradition. The ANE cultures include Canaanite

1

populations like the ancient Israelites and dominating populations like the Amorites, Assyrians, and Babylonians. These peoples also shared linguistic characteristics broadly named the Afro-Asiatic linguistic family and held certain religio-cultural features, like the imagery of cherubs, in common. Cherubs in particular hovered around kings and represented the blessings of the deity upon the governing royal figure. But of course royal figures do not always carry out the divine will, so here also are the great prophets of the Bible who courageously speak out against their governments in the name of the divine who is no longer recognized in the halls of power.

There is some merit in this very basic and deeply historical division, and some books depend on its existence. Thorleif Boman's highly regarded and now classical book *Hebrew Thought Compared with Greek* is an example.[2] Avatar theology seemed like a good name for the PIE tradition because, with the popularity of the same-named movie, it was bound to strike a chord. An avatar is an incarnation of the divine, but it is also the realization of the divine essence in wise individuals. Still, though perhaps this analysis is loosely accurate, Ancient Near Eastern cultures and Indo-European cultures have mixed together at least since the days of the Sumerian city-states found along the Tigris dating to 3000 BCE and earlier. Accordingly, though I name two types of theology, I do not mean a hard distinction. What I intend is to discuss models of theology that I hope will prove to be constructive when it comes to thinking about the history of theological understanding as it developed in the Western experience.

Covenant theology arises from the Bible, particularly the Torah, with the image of God in an agreement or covenant with a nation and a people. The agreement is quite mutual, as later rabbis expanded it, in that both God and the people are accountable to the Torah (or Law) and its interpretation.[3] Enlightenment theology arises from the wisdom tradition in which the actualization of the divine reality happens in the lifestyle of individuals or communities.

The influence, in Christianity, of Greek philosophy is strong here, but biblical examples can be found in Job and Ecclesiastes as well as, for Christians particularly, the parables of Jesus. The Torah in these instances effectively becomes incarnate through a vision of a re-imagined world (as in parables) or in the question of the meaning of life (as in Ecclesiastes) or even in the problem of justice before the face of suffering (as in Job). In Greek philosophy, it is a matter of the principle of the divine realized in the life and practices of an individual or community. In the Bible the enlightenment image is also present when the Torah is ingested by prophets like Ezekiel (3:3) and Jeremiah (15:16) to become part of the very breath of the individual. When it comes specifically to Christianity and generally to the question of the future of religion in the West, one must deal with and name the background and, often, the combination of the biblical tradition and Greek philosophy. The way I have chosen to contemplate this combination is to use the words Covenant and Enlightenment theology.

The concerns of the opening chapters, I sincerely hope, are not too difficult to follow. But later chapters that address concerns about the future of Western theology do rely upon abstract thoughts. The early chapters on what is the Bible and on types of theology serve to set up some operating assumptions that handle bigger questions. The bigger questions arise when considering how a human being that we know as Jesus of Nazareth became God, and not just any God at that. Jesus became the Avatar or Incarnate God of Christianity who is the divine principle of the universe at the same time as he is busy in common life. There is no definitive way to understand how this metamorphosis happened. But it is incredibly important to understand the structure of what happened and why it made sense. My attempt to present the comical nature of the historical Jesus in contrast to the Church's creation of Jesus Christ occurs in the middle part of this book. The key idea here is to address how God, following the Roman era, was understood as the ontological principle of the universe. This is a difficult word, but it means that God was related to the order of beings in the cosmos from the upper echelons of angels to the lower strata of peasant farmers and all things in between. Everything had its place in the order of being.

The ideas that sustained Jesus as the principle of creation and the same identity with God could not survive the Enlightenment period. Every time the world changes, God changes, and when an old world stops working so does God. It is hard to talk about the future of theology if the conversation does not include recognizing why the old idea of God in heaven no longer works. It does not make sense anymore to think that at the end of history a Messiah will return to clean up the mess human beings have made and to restore the stasis or perfect order of the universe. This old idea was God understood as fullness. We could say that in the old idea God was the biggest being around who had a hand on a light switch called time. But this God does not exist anymore, and in its place there is a poetic role for God that I call the God who almost is. What I am saying with this expression I hope will be clear, but it does lead to two points.

The first point is that theology betrays itself when it holds on to the old version of God and thereby emphasizes a closed version of religion. I will try to show that both types of theology, Covenant and Enlightenment, have "closed" or time-controlling expressions. To close theology is to limit the theological expression to final aims and ultimately unquestionable conclusions. The closure of theology is the silencing of theology and its removal from the human scene. Most often the techniques used to accomplish such closure are the extreme understanding of the apocalypse or end of time and the common use of allegory as a way to interpret parables. In contrast to these tempting ways to understand theology, I will offer, in the end, open ways to engage theology as Covenant and as Enlightenment.

The open form of theology will rely almost exclusively on the parables of the historical Jesus as insightful ways to remember that theology is poetic vision and reconfigured meaning in the midst of the situation of life now. Theology does not answer the question, what is the meaning of life? In parable, theology raises the problem of meaning in life but also awakens the problem or re-presents it as the creative task of life. This does not mean that every theologian must tell parables, but it does mean something like this: the act of theology is a parable. With such an act as its foundation, the task of theology is to re-imagine, re-create, and even permanently re-cast the world with engaging hope. This task requires, and even is in itself, an open form of expression. It requires a new and open way to understand Covenant and Enlightenment theology.

As the reader travels through these pages, my hope is to encourage the consideration of the value of religion for the human future. In the course of expressing this hope I will certainly uphold the understanding that religion is a human creation, but I will definitely resist the temptation to regard it as a human waste of time. Indeed, I attempt to end this work with the understanding that God's future and the human future are the same thing and that, as such, when we speak about theology we are speaking about God's human future.

1

What Is
the Bible?

Socrates was regarded as the wisest person of his time, but like the Jesus of history, no one really knows that much about him. Socrates is mostly legend. Life is like that. We think we know a lot about a subject until the time comes to talk about it. Then we realize we do not actually know that much after all. Socrates, at least as legend has it, thought that this peculiar human predicament was an advantage. It is best to know that we do not know; only on this score can we claim a modicum of wisdom.

It is not an easy task answering the question, what is the Bible? even though at first glance, it should be obvious. The Bible is a book. That is one thing assumed to be commonly known. Everyone knows that the Bible is at the very least a book, and, through our collective cultural experiences, we all know that the Bible is more than just a book. The Bible holds uncommon authority in Western history and everyone presumably needs to know at least a little bit about it if for no other reason than to appreciate great Western literature like Shakespeare. Still, once the surface is scratched, it turns out that underneath the cultural level basic knowledge about the Bible is piecemeal, even among the well educated and, more surprisingly, especially among Bible fundamentalists. Before it is possible to talk about God and the Western tradition of theology, the presupposition of that tradition, which is the Bible and its authority, must be encountered. It is important to know all that we commonly do not know about the Bible.

The first commonly unknown thing about the Bible is that it is not a book, not at all. The word Bible is from the Greek plural for book, *biblia* or books, which is also the same in Latin. The Latin *biblia* is at the root of the French word *bibliotheque*, which means library. The Bible is a collection of books. It is a book of books, not singular but plural. In fact, in many instances, even individual books in the Bible are not single but compiled texts of diverse authors and materials. The "book" of Genesis, the first in the Bible, has several detectable authors whose stories have been woven together as one. Genesis is more like an anthology than a book, and the Bible as a whole is like a library.

The Bible, then, is better called a collection, holding different points of view and different forms of writing. In relation to any given topic the Bible can say many different things. The authors of the Bible did not know each other and never thought, in their lifetimes, that their writings would exist clustered together in something commonly regarded as sacred. So, it is entirely understandable why we can encounter the speculative philosophical writing of Ecclesiastes and the serious legislative writing of Deuteronomy in the same collection. The Psalmist (69:24) calls for the cursing of one's enemies, and the Apostle Paul says to bless those who curse you (Romans 12:14). These contradictory sayings exist in the same assortment because they come from different writers, different situations, and different times. Neither the Psalmist nor Paul, the Genesis authors nor the writer of Ecclesiastes, ever thought that they would all be in the same commonly regarded "book."

Parables, like a famous Jesus parable or the lesser-known one stated before King David by Nathan the prophet (2 Samuel 12:1–4), are not the same kind of writing as *narratives* about Jesus or David found in the Christian Gospels or the Books of Samuel. The legends of Moses recorded in Exodus are not the same style of writing as Proverbs and do not hold the same intention. If we ask a provocative question like, what does the Bible say about sex? there is no single answer and there cannot be. Because the Bible is a library, the answer to the question, of course, is lots of different things. The Apostle Paul raised his concerns about "immorality" (1 Corinthians 6:9–10), listing several items but not sex before marriage—a fact that bothered the Protestant reformer John Calvin (1509–1564). Calvin might have, but did not, understand that preferred marriage customs in sixteenth-century Geneva were a different kettle of fish from what concerned Paul. Meanwhile, at Proverbs 5:19 we read about the delights and infatuations of great love, including the writer's joy in the female body.[1] To ask what the Bible says about sex is like asking what a library says about sex. Unlike Calvin, we must recognize that it will say lots of things and not assume that it will say what we want or think it should say.

When a preacher holds a Bible in hand and proclaims that the "Bible says" something definitive about salvation or family or sex, the preacher only demonstrates ignorance. The Bible cannot be reduced to a single idea or a few catchy phrases. Modern Christians who extol "biblical family values" have probably never read the Bible. The Bible tells lots of stories about families, but exemplary moral families are hard to find in its pages. Additionally, the prudent and largely fabricated notion of "family values" is not a biblical concept. No such expression is to be found anywhere in the Bible. In relation to the Bible one can talk about ancient family practices, structures, obligations, and indebtedness, but not values. The saying attributed to Jesus to the effect of hating your family (Luke 14:26) indicates that "family" here is quite different from what we mean today. To Jesus, the family was a set of economic obligations that one must leave behind, which is something both liberating and risky.

The Bible has almost only dysfunctional families in its content who get caught up in incest, polygamy, lying, and overall drunkenness. Even Mother Mary of the holy family does not get off the hook. When the gospel writer Matthew recounts the genealogy of Jesus, the writer deliberately mentions women of questionable background. Recounting the family line, Matthew includes Tamar (the woman who had children with her father-in-law at Genesis 38:15–17); Ruth (a Moabite woman who provocatively enters a mixed marriage with a Jewish man against the prohibition of Deuteronomy 23:3); Uriah's wife (the Hittite Bathsheba whom David forced into adultery and whose husband he then arranged to have killed at 2 Samuel 11:2–17); and finally Mary (with Joseph called at Matthew 1:16 "the husband of Mary," indicating Jesus was not the son of Joseph but a child of an unknown father). Matthew's point in this genealogy (Matthew 1:1–16) is to address rumors about the reputed dishonorable birth of Jesus. Matthew's idea is to prod the reader into recognizing that women of apparent dishonor, like Tamar[2] or Ruth, and their children are no barrier to the work of God.[3] It is actually terrific theology, but it is not based on family values.[4]

Neither is the Bible primarily nor even particularly a moral work. Again, only those who have never read the Bible could think otherwise. The Bible is supposed to be holy: a symbol of purity and spiritual authority, full of inspired words. Its integrity is so beyond reproach that it is commonly used to swear an oath. But this imagined sacredness attached to "The Bible" does not really exist. The Bible has outlandish stories of revenge, of common brutality, of genocide, of prejudice, and of seething hatred. In Exodus 6 God declares the divine intention to bring the people to the land "I swore to give to Abraham, Isaac, and Jacob," stating, "I will give it to you for a possession" (6:8), but when Moses is before Pharaoh the words are hidden and misleading. God tells Moses to say to the Pharaoh, "Let my people go that they may worship me in the wilderness" (7:16). This latter request is an ambiguous not liberating statement. Does it mean that permission is being sought to leave Egypt but then come back? A bit later in the reading Moses clarifies that what he really wants to do is to undertake a three-day journey (8:27). Pharaoh imagines that this might be fine, saying, "I will let you go to sacrifice to the Lord your God in the wilderness, provided you do not go very far away." The Pharaoh even adds, "Pray for me" (8:28). This account is not really history but storytelling with a bit of sleight of hand mixed in at the Pharaoh's expense. Still, it cannot be upheld as an example of truth-telling, even though this is what the Bible is supposed to be.[5]

The strange and misleading interactions of diplomacy mixed with lies between Moses and the Pharaoh might compose only petty incidences in the Bible, but around this same story are gathered dismal tragedies and immoral acts like genocide. Remarkably, in the Bible God issues the first threat of genocide against the Jewish people (Exodus 32:10). Following the making of a golden calf, God is so angry with the people as to be moved to "destroy" them. The fearless Moses has to indicate how embarrassing such an act will be for God. After all, the Egyptians will think that God is crazy, having just delivered the people from slavery. In the book of Numbers, the story is retold with Moses being even more blunt, asking God, "what will the gentiles think" of a deity so frustrated at not being able to fulfill a promise (Numbers 14:15–16)? Moses has to compromise God before the nations in an effort to remind the deity that godliness involves holding the qualities of love (14:18).

There are incidences in the Bible where God lacks even a hint of moral fiber. Again, in Numbers, the people complain that God is causing the loss of life, but God's response is to send a plague and take even more lives (16:41–49). God advises on many occasions to destroy the cities of one's enemies, including the indiscriminate murder of all men, women, and children regardless of innocence; at Joshua 6:20–21 all the animals of Jericho are added to the list of indiscriminate slaughter. The Christian Bible ends with the book of Revelation where God celebrates getting even with humanity through a final bloodbath of executions and plagues. There are many examples of immorality in the Bible, and the greatest ones are reserved for God. Still, the record of violence is not really by or about "God." It is the human beings who wrote these texts who bear responsibility for their content. For the modern reader, though we cannot simply change these historic texts, we can be responsible for how we chose to interpret and use them.

Many people who grew up in the Western cultural setting gained the basic idea that the Bible is a book of truth and authority. The idea arrives almost automatically as if by cultural osmosis, by the act of absorbing impressions about the Bible in the way people talk of and use it. These impressions express common assumptions about the Bible as a symbol of integrity, but they do not arise from actually reading the Bible. The real content of the Bible betrays its humanity in both its beautiful and disparaging prose. The Bible holds the prejudices of ancient cultures and through them invokes the many tragedies of modern life when people take it too seriously as supernaturally revealed truth. These comments do not discount the amazing things that can be found in the Bible, such as stories of forgiveness, of courage, of compassion, of justice seeking, and of peace. Inasmuch as some biblical writers relay the narrow-mindedness of their time, others rise above their time to express images of everlasting inspiration like swords being beaten into ploughshares (Micah 4:3), like the poetic call to let justice roll down like a river (Amos 5:24), and like the amazing vision of a time when a lion will lie down with a calf and when a child shall lead us (Isaiah 6:11).

The writers of the Bible were human beings like us, and, what is more, the Bible is a human creation, arising as it did over centuries as an amalgamation of writings and oral traditions. In its pages, the Bible mixes ancient poetry with epic narratives, wisdom writing, and prophetic announcements. Sometimes its pages are inspiring and sometimes outrageous. They are so, and are both, because they are the creation of human beings. Again, no writer of the Bible could ever have imagined his or her effort one day would form part of a sacred collection. The Apostle Paul never imagined, and never could have, that his sometimes pedestrian letters and private comments would end up as sacred writing; the prophets loved to pronounce "thus says the Lord," but even they would be shocked to know that the context of their words are often given absolute and timeless authority. It was only with the passing of eras, over the long stretch of Western cultural history, that *biblia*, the assorted collection, became Bible, the authoritative book.

The "real" Bible, which is a collection of books, is neither a retelling of historical facts nor a record of biographical information. The Bible is an amalgamation of genres. This is likely the most significant point when understanding the Bible today. Our contemporary culture is highly literalistic due to our constant use of technology based on numerical patterns, expected repetitions, and reliance on automation. In antiquity, there were forms of technology, but the forms, like threshing wheat, were labor intensive. Mathematics was also in use, but nowhere near the level that relativity or quantum mechanics or string theory demands today. Nothing like the idea of gravity or an expanding universe existed. Darwin, of course, was unknown. As a consequence, the ancient world did not live with the assurances of predictability or the expectations of the automated recurrence of things. Ancient people had no technical means to assume such comfort, and this meant that the ancient mind could not take things literally. No promise could be made that a journey from Alexandria to Rome would be on schedule. You could certainly take such a trip, but you certainly could not count on a schedule. Life was shorter, harder, and largely outside among the natural elements, in the market, and within the open porticoes, large amphitheaters, and courtyards. The uncertain nature of daily life meant that the fleshly body was not supervised with the careful attention we hold today. Instead, the physical world, which was full of daily challenges and changes, acted like an untrustworthy surface hiding things unseen, unchanging, and unambiguous. To convey this unseen world to a reader and hearer, the writers of the Bible relied on genres, that is, on different "kinds" of writing to open up the horizon of the unseen.

This attempt to open up the horizon of the unseen means that biblical writers used heroic forms of writing in place of our contemporary idea of facts. Someone like Moses is not a historical figure—though Moses may well have lived—but a hero. The writer of Deuteronomy provides Moses with several oratory speeches that easily compare to typical ancient hero speeches like those found in Thucydides.[6] The important thing about the speeches is not that they contain facts but that they relay a writer's theology, that is, the writer's theo-centric view of the world.

The writers of the Bible used stories to open up different views of the horizons, whether those horizons are, positively, about the promises of a peaceful world or, negatively, about the vengeance of an angry God (let the reader beware); every writer of the Bible relayed in heroic narratives about great figures, like Abraham, expressions of theology—those elements of life that inspired the ancient reader or hearer who lived in a changing and unpredictable world. Such vision was not, then or now, meant to be "literal" as a fact but more like a metaphor of hope or a symbol of character. The heroes inspired artistic conceptions found in wisdom literature that questioned, for example, as in the book of Job, whether or not belief in the promises of God spills out as blessings in life. Job answers that question negatively: even great belief in God does not mean an end to or explanation of suffering. For others, like the prophet Isaiah, heroic stories inspired visions of God's universal compassion for humanity. Isaiah speaks of Israel, the people who know the Torah, as the light to the nations. This very task of showing the way of God to the world, of being the light, comes from the cache of heroes found in Jewish tradition. But again, none of these forms of writing, these genres like narrative writing, biographical writing, wisdom writing, and prophetic writing, are literally true. They are inspirationally true in the sense that they project a vision for the future—both positive and negative—from the heroic past. If a modern reader turns to the Bible looking for facts about history, the spirit of the biblical writers will be missed and the Bible will become something easily mocked. A literal, modern mind will conclude that the Bible means to state a fact when recounting the creation of the earth in six days. This conclusion is way off base, for the point of that myth is theology, not science. The six day creation story serves to orient or focus the attitudes of human beings. The story places the audience in the world as those who bear responsibility for it. It places human beings in the picture of nature and orients their concept of life accordingly. It is once again heroic writing, but this time in the form or genre of a cosmogony or originating myth about the world.

The Bible then, from its historic narratives to its aphoristic parables, is a collection of forms of writing. Each form of writing is heroic in nature; that is, each form is a project or vision of life rather than a literal explanation about how things work. Each form of writing expresses the imagination of a writer who projects against the incertitudes of nature something conceived as meaningful and directive. It is not necessary, consequently, to believe anything a biblical writer says in order to understand what a biblical writer means. Only the latter focus correctly understands the Bible as an amalgamation of genres, as a collection of writings, and as assorted expressions of theology.

If the first key to reading the Bible involves understanding genres, the second involves being aware of sources. What sources did biblical writers draw upon to write in the genres they did? Identifying sources helps us understand another commonly un-known thing about that Bible, which is that the authors of the Bible did not write the Bible. The authors of the Bible used sources or previous writings and various preexisting oral traditions to put their stories together. Biblical scholars today have well over 250 years of hard work behind them when identifying the evident sources used by the ancient writers of the Bible. Although there are always so-called "merchants of doubt"[7]—scholars of dubious authority who deny such sources ever existed—in real scholarship there is no sub-stantial controversy over the fact that biblical writers used previously existing sources. The E source, which refers to the earlier Elohist writer and teller of tales, is an example of a preexisting source used throughout the books of Genesis to Numbers.[8]

For devout Christians it can be shocking, at least where the Bible is concerned, to discover that each Christian gospel is not the writing of an individual but a cut-and-paste amalgam of sources used to create a theology. A gospel is more accurately understood as a theological presentation than a retelling of history. A "theology" in this sense is an arrangement of beliefs, and each New Testament gospel arranges the material of the sources to favor one form of belief over others. Each gospel writer put together a theology from preexisting sources that were either written or oral. Only for the sake of convenience have the names of Matthew, Mark, Luke, and John been attached to each gospel in the Christian Bible, but in fact no one knows who compiled these gospels. We do not know if each gospel was the work of an individual or a community. What we do know is this: each gospel addresses the concerns of a different community, and each community drew upon preexisting sources.

The most famous or infamous source, depending on one's point of view, for the Christian gospels is called the Q Document or, more appropriately, the Q Sayings Gospel. Q is the common written material found when comparing Matthew and Luke. These two gospels share many verses not found in Mark. The common material used by Matthew and Luke obviously predates these two gospels that use it, and the material is called Q from the German word for source, which is *Quelle*.[9] Matthew and Luke relied neither on eyewitness accounts nor divine inspiration when recording sayings of Jesus. They relied on Q, a document that they could modify for their own purposes. Then, like Q, the Gospel of Mark can also be found in the pages of Matthew and Luke, which means that Mark, too, already existed as a source when the authors of Matthew and Luke, whoever they were, compiled the pages of their accounts. So Matthew and Luke copied from their sources, Mark and Q, adding things in and taking things out as their judgments dictated and their theological reasons demanded. Both Matthew and Luke created their gospels from Mark and Q, which means both gospels are collections rather than books. Both are compositions of theology rather than records of history. Meanwhile the Gospel of Mark had its own set of sources, which means that Mark was not an eyewitness to the life of Jesus either but, like Matthew and Luke, was a composing theologian. Mark's sources are certainly harder to detect, for there is little to compare Mark to. Instead, one has to draw out from Mark the traces of preexisting written and oral traditions. Still, like Matthew and Luke, Mark is a collection turned into a theology.

The Gospel of John is its own kind of problem, for it is so different in style and content from the three other gospels of Matthew, Mark, and Luke. This distinction, however, does not grant John a different status. Like the other gospels, it uses sources, is not an eyewitness account, and is a theology rather than a biography. In the case of the Gospel of John, the major source is the Signs Gospel, which was a collection of seven signs or miracles performed by Jesus. It is possible to isolate the seven signs of Jesus in the Gospel of John and, from this act, reconstruct with significant success the source that John used to relay the "miracles" of Jesus and the point of them. The miracles, a modern reader must constantly remember, are not history but theology; the signs show the identity of Jesus, which acts to secure the belief of Christians. Jesus' turning water into wine (John 2:1–11) is the first of the signs, but it is not a miracle in the literal sense. It is a story or theology used to express the glory of Jesus and to show the reader that, like the disciples, their belief in Jesus is secure. To reduce the miracles in John to debate about whether Jesus factually performed the signs is silly because such debate ignores exactly what John is writing about, which is theology. Theology is a creative, interpretive presentation of an author who uses and modifies stories to make a point. In the Gospel of John, signs make the point, but it is amazing how in our time many readers of the Gospel insist on missing the point due to reading a story literally.

When it comes to the study of the Christian gospels, then, the right question does not involve asking about accuracy. To be sure, the gospels hold the remnants of earlier traditions that presumably relate to the historical Jesus, even if tangentially, but the sources are not collected in order to establish facts about Jesus. The gospels are theologies about Jesus, which means that the right question is always about the theology the gospel writers hold. There is no command from Jesus that goes like this: "Remember in particular this saying and favor it over others." Instead, a modern reader has to figure out what sources a gospel writer used and what editorial biases a gospel writer held. These two observances help identify the theology of the gospel writer.

Since Jesus never left behind a saying about what to remember or what to ignore, three points are easily made. First, the gospel writers got to choose out of their sources what they thought was the important point. We can only read the consequences of their choices. We don't know why the gospel writers made the choices they did, but we can ask about the theology their choices represent. This leads to point number two. The gospel writers were as human as we are, and, in the dilemmas of their lives, had to make choices to form theologies. Looking back, we don't have to agree with their theologies but we do have an obligation to understand them as best we can. The third point is that the central focus on beliefs about Jesus is a phenomenon of Christian history. Beliefs about Jesus are confessions that arose after the lifetime of Jesus and are not things that Jesus believed himself. We can be assured that Jesus did not confess beliefs about himself. Confessions about Jesus assume nascent theologies held by the gospel writers within the context of emerging Christianity. Just as it is not necessary to agree with the gospel writers, it is not necessary to restrict Christian theology to only one set of confessions about Jesus.

A last word concerns the practice of using the historical critical method to understand the Bible. Historical criticism is a general term that identifies the use of modern critical (tested) methods to understand how the Bible is compiled and how it employs the genres and theologies we have discussed. The criticism itself is often criticized somewhat categorically just for being a "method," for using a method always assumes a certain degree of bias built in to the way it is employed. Still, historical criticism clearly remains a primary way to understand the Bible. Even though every critic must account for the biases he or she brings to the subject, the point of historical criticism is to block the biases of our modern world in order to enter the mindset (or biases) of the ancient world. I certainly have my biases, but my biases are my problem. They are not a problem for Mark, for example, or Matthew. My question needs to be what is Mark's bias or Matthew's or Luke's, etc.? And in order to have a chance at answering that question, I have to block the biases I bring to the text. That is the aim of the historical critical method. It is not about criticizing the Bible as if it were something insufficient. It is about blocking the modern worldview so that the ancient text and worldview can be seen as it is, which is a compilation of genres and theologies. Historical criticism demands that the Bible not hold unquestionable authority but that it be allowed to hold its own biases, which of course it will have because it is a diverse collection of writings. Naturally we can question how successfully the historical critical method achieves its aim, but we cannot question the fact that it holds outstanding value when it comes to understanding the Bible in the appropriate context of its own world.

After we recognize that the Bible is a collection of diverse writings, does it still have authority? The answer is twofold: yes it does, and no it does not. The Bible has authority not because it is a policy manual or a set of bylaws about life. It has authority, rather, because it is symbolic of the virtues of a particular cultural experience. In Western history, that symbol is quite powerful due to the historic authority the Christian Church held in the European experience. With the rise of modernity, of nation-states, and of citizen rights, the authority of the Bible as a document representing human knowledge and divine power has passed away along with the centrality of Christianity. Technical science has replaced the Bible as official "knowledge," and the Bible can hardly stand up to science anymore. Still, this does not mean that the power of the Bible as a symbol has passed away. It still represents, and perhaps always will because of its history and in spite of its content, the honor of truth, commitment, and integrity.

Yet, the Bible should not, since it never really did, have authority in the matter of normative human behavior. The reason why the Bible contains ancient laws governing the practices of Israelite males, for example, is because the males did things they ought not to do. There is no need to have laws for things that nobody does. For instance, there is no need for laws about living at the bottom of the ocean since no one can do that. There is only a need for laws to govern what people do but shouldn't do. Laws are negotiated within community settings and according to the activities in which people engage. In our time the internet has brought forward new and complex questions about society and the rights of individuals in relation to the collective well-being of a nation. As the electronic age continues to evolve, laws continue to be modified, negotiated, and legislated. The Bible was (is) no different. In its pages God's mind can change either through negotiation or with new information. How many righteous people are necessary to save a city from destruction? In Genesis, God initially thought fifty was the right answer, but Abraham negotiates with the deity. An agreement was struck at ten (Genesis 18:22–33). Or, compare Exodus to Deuteronomy. The second book is later than the first and it changes or modifies laws accordingly. In Exodus the Ten Commandments are given at 20:1–17, and they start off quickly with, "I am the LORD your God who brought you out of the land of Egypt, out of the house of bondage. You shall have no other God before me." This command suggests that even though there are many gods out there, Israel shall not have another one ahead of or higher than the Lord God. Deuteronomy 5:1–21 records this same law but modifies the effect of its meaning. It uses a preamble that involves Moses telling the people that these laws are a covenant that shall be learned and carefully observed. These warnings are given prior to the command to have no other god. It is clear that for the Deuteronomist the concern is pitched more intensely. Apparently people liked having other gods, maybe not "before" but certainly after, and in addition to the Lord God, so the Deuteronomist is far more serious. In Deuteronomy the Ten Commandments are modified and slight revisions are made. The emphasis is on God commanding (verses 5:12, 15, and 16) with the warning that obedience means blessing and implying here—but explicit elsewhere in Deuteronomy—that disobedience means a curse (16). The Deuteronomist uses repetition to underline the fact that the Sabbath is for both menservants and maidservants and that when we say "cattle" we mean "your ox, your ass, or any of your cattle" (14). These differences are clarifications that address new challenges and relay a new, and somewhat more stringent, theology. Throughout Deuteronomy we can observe these adaptations of Exodus and recognize that a different time and context has influenced a different rendition of what the law says and means. So, does the Bible have authority such that it should not be challenged or changed? Not even the Bible thinks so.

The modern problem of the authority of the Bible arose with the advent of science and evidence-based explanations about the world. Before the seventeenth century, the Bible was the only book of "science" around. It was used to explain the origin of language (supporting the erroneous conviction that Hebrew was the first human language), the geographical age of the earth (thought to be about six thousand years), the origin of life (*ex nihilo* at creation), and medical treatments (practices of social exclusion, bloodletting, and casting out demons). These forms of knowledge, which today are more like superstitions, do not pass any test of evidence. Each conviction, once assumed to be "knowledge," fell to the level of nonsense with the advent of science. Today, no one would claim there is an original human language, and in any case the Western base languages of Latin and Greek are Indo-European languages, not Afro-Asiatic ones (as Hebrew is). No one anymore would try to link English organically to Hebrew. No modern physician would recommend casting out demons as a serious treatment for disease.

Not even modern Christian fundamentalists, or at least very few, obey the Bible literally when it comes to serious health care. Then, there is so much evidence for the 4.5 billion-year-old earth and the evolution of life upon it that it has become a form of comedy to oppose these obvious facts. The Bible is not able to hold authority like it once did in the Middle Ages. As such it is extremely important in our time that people of a progressive mind allow the Bible to turn the page, so to speak, from being a book of authority to being a collection of ancient writings that witness to the trials of human history and the struggles for human wisdom.

In light of the Bible being a compilation of ancient genres and theologies that witnesses to humanity's creative and troubling struggles for truth, there remains today a deep and necessary need to promote a new age for religion. Such a need exists precisely because the Bible no longer holds, beyond the symbolic level, the moral, scientific, and legislative authority it once did. The Bible no longer serves the Western tradition in this fundamental way. In place of literalistic debates over the authority of the Bible there can be a new age of realism and honesty that seeks to understand its contents. The spirit of such an inquiry sees religion as a human creation and thus raises the question about religion as a human value. The question does not concern whether or not the Bible, or a religion, is true. That question is now obsolete. The question is the value of religion. Does religion as a human creation have a value for humanity and for our collective future?

2

What Is
Religion?

Religion is philosophy. Let's get this straight. Religion is not technical philosophy. It does not involve understanding Plato or Aristotle or the legacy of these two classical thinkers spelled out in the thoughts of hundreds of others who followed. Beyond technical philosophy, however, religion is philosophy because it involves the love (*philos*) of wisdom (*sophia*). Whereas technical philosophy, out of its love, studies wisdom in the form of questions about human knowledge, religion—at least historically—involves living out wisdom in the practices of economic and social relationships. Religion is about how wisdom plays out in life. This is why religion is more deeply related to cultural practices, cultural superstitions, sacrificial systems, symbolic systems, and the like than philosophy, properly speaking, has been. Religion is so decisively embedded in societal practices precisely because its history is *the history of systems concerning how to be in the world*. A "system" that relates "to how to be in the world" refers to a way of reflecting on and practicing a certain lifestyle. Because religion as a lifestyle and set of beliefs is so personal, it is exceptionally good at attracting superstitions to its core and insisting on certain disciplinary customs.

Religion has always involved superstition, that is, the act of "standing over" (Latin, "*super-stare*") an issue or event with awe inspired by fear and incomprehension. Superstition is the act of dealing with such fear or awe by integrating these feelings into a system of representation and negotiation. This general system that handles

ways to represent fear and awe and that attempts to negotiate or
relate to these feelings symbolically in both personal and communal
ways is what I call religion.

Accordingly, from the modern perspective, explaining human
suffering and death through a story about a fall from the grace of
God in the Garden the Eden is superstition. It's not really an explanation of suffering and death but a form of negotiating with and
accounting for suffering and death when there are few other options
available. But religion is not just the "superstition" involved in a belief but also the discipline related to it. If the fall from grace remains
an example, then the practices related to this belief can be varied.
They appear most certainly in the practice of confession, for confession is a way of both admitting the fall has occurred and receiving
instructive practices to handle its stigma. Or again, the Christian
communion (or Eucharist) is a practice built on the idea of the fall
since its aim is to reconcile an alienated or distant relationship between the human and divine worlds. Indeed, communion is a pre-
cursor, a taste, of an ultimate reconciliation in a time to come. Or
again, in a severe way, the practice of self-flagellation popularized
in the thirteenth century was a way of dramatically rehearsing the
damnation one deserves as a sinner and anticipating the release from
pain found in God. None of these practices make sense except that
they express a basic, inexplicable, underlying belief, which here I am
calling a superstition but which might otherwise be called religion.

It is not the case that "superstition" has to be understood in a pe-
jorative way. A baseball player might practice a discipline like always
tapping the bat in a certain way before receiving the first pitch. The
act is a "superstition" based on the batter having hit a home run
the first time he did the tapping. The discipline of the tapping has
nothing to do with the home run, but the act, nevertheless, has the
psychological effect of calming the mind and enhancing concentra-
tion. Religion can be a superstition and a practice in this positive
sense, too. It can enact a practice that has nothing to do with reality
except that it helps the individual be in reality according to a certain

way of feeling or a certain way of thinking. It is often the case that religious people feel a deep gratitude for life and are able to celebrate life as a miracle even though this "feeling" is not really based on any fact of biology. So, a superstition and a practice related to it are not necessarily bad things. It is as if, in spite of hard biology, the superstition allows for an artful way of thinking about how to be in the world. However, superstitions can certainly become bad things. This happens when they stand in place of and become understood as facts and absolute truths. When religion stands in place of facts and becomes an absolute truth, it ends up having very little value to offer humanity. There is no point to religion if it simply becomes the denial of reality.

To sharpen, then, the opening statement that religion is philosophy, we can say that religion is a type of philosophy that expresses or relies on psychology, that is, on certain feelings about life and how one should live. In the broadest view of Western history religion has functioned as a way to justify how one should live. The Romans of the ancient world were largely superstitious and used religious practices, like reading the entrails of sacrificed animals, to negotiate both choices in daily life and political decisions about war. Though such practices now seem foolish, they were, nevertheless, popular versions of philosophy exercised as common, if not national, forms of psychology. The soothing rituals of religious customs often address the psychological need for reassurance, which then can surface as knowledge or wisdom about the world. When Octavian defeated the forces of Mark Antony and Cleopatra at Actium in 32 BCE, it was not just a military victory but the victory of one set of gods over another. Effectively, one system of being in the world won over another, one economy over another, one religion over another, and one psychology over another. With the victory came the right to rule, but it was not just the ruler or form of government that earned the right. It was a set of gods that won the right to be supreme over all others. The gods were the "psychology" of Octavian and his system. They were the affirmation of his truth and the encouragement of his purpose. They were the justification of his form of philosophy brought down to the level of social and economic practices.

When we understand that religion is the philosophical expression of our psychology, we can begin to understand why it is both a tragic and inevitable part of human life. Religion can easily go awry, as noted above, when the authority given to it exceeds the actual function it plays. If its function is to help people or even a culture deal with life in all its unpredictable forms then, when it gets fixed as unquestionable authority, it becomes alien to its own primal origin and is, instead, tragically intolerant and often violent. Rather than helping our human frame, it becomes the bulwark of our prejudices and the expression of our desires for control because its symbolic life has been fixed to a supposed absolute, supernatural truth. Religion, when so fixed, establishes divides between the insiders and outsiders, the privileged and alienated, the patriotic and unpatriotic, and the superior and inferior. Religion can convince a group and even a nation that certain people should not only be on the outside but, in fact, deserve to be by nature. Because religion holds such psychological power, it is often assumed to be a truth set beyond critical judgment.

To answer the question about how religion can escape critical judgment, it is necessary to recall how the symbolic functions of religion, such as Christian communion, can address the psychological need for reassurance. To state this in a slightly technical way, we can say that religious symbols correlate to the basic need for approval. The symbols of religion are like a key to a lock, and the lock is the deeply felt human need for meaning. Though religion, precisely because it is a symbolic system, is fictional—that is, it is "made up" in and through the history of cultural systems—a religion, nevertheless, in its symbols reflects the human quest for meaning. A religion is set against our true and absolute fate, which is the knowledge of our eventual death and meaninglessness. The powerful symbol of the Christian savior who, in his sacrificial death, takes upon himself humanity's finite and sinful nature and then delivers this nature in his resurrection to an eternal renewal is aimed directly at our anxious feelings about death and meaninglessness. The symbol is powerful because it is psychological, that is, because it addresses the *psyche* or anxious soul. Of course, even as this Christian symbol is powerful at the level of psychology, it is fictional at the level of history. The Jesus of history was human like anyone and held, at a personal level, no belief in himself as a savior and no control over the fate of his reputation following his cruel death. If Jesus had a "savior" at a psychological level, it was his god whom the Romans were trying to show was certainly a false god and totally helpless before their real ones.

Religion, then, is a philosophy applied in specific practices and beliefs to the psychological task of dealing with life. Sometime the practices are cruel, tied to political ideologies and customs built on various forms of prejudice. Religion is in no way innocent of human corruption and many times arises from it, which is why people of any one religion can act as poorly as those of any other religion or no religion at all. Still, religion also has a built-in generosity. Because it is a fundamental way to address human psychology, when it encourages trust and peaceful existence in the world, and when it provides practices to remember and enhance these traits, it is one of the greatest gifts humanity has to share.

In addition to these opening remarks about the nature of religion, it still remains important to define religion technically. It is useful in this task to remember that when asked what is the first thing to do, Confucius said, "What is necessary is to rectify names" (*Analects*, 3, section 13). Somewhat like Socrates of ancient Greece, Confucius believed that there is no point in talking about a subject if we do not agree on its definition: its rightful or rectified name. This sage advice takes the question from the nature of religion, where psychology can be talked about, to the definition of religion where the question is the origin and meaning of the word.

The advice of Confucius is a prime directive for many occasions, but of course like every form of good advice it, too, holds various problems. The problem is that words change over time. They combine and recombine with other words and appear through history in different political and cultural value systems. By the time a word has taken its journey from Latin through French to land in English, it's meaning more often than not has changed. The Latin word *addictus* was a person who became a slave of another due to debt. It never held the English meaning of drug or alcohol *addiction* as it does today. One word can also impinge its meaning on another, sharing a basic root but evolving along a different path. As Jacques Derrida famously indicated, consider difference (as two different things), deferring (as putting off or postponing), and différance (a made-up word indistinguishable from difference but still not the same).[1] Derrida was demonstrating how words slide through history and change as they go, but there is another problem, as Confucius knew, which is who is in control of the definition? When someone of royal power decrees a definition about what is or is not proper, the subject of that power is supposed to listen. However, major social movements in history arise from the grassroots when whatever the aristocracy means by justice and equality is not what the masses mean with the same words. If the situation is extreme, the power of the aristocracy to say "you better listen" evaporates in the face of the fearlessness and overwhelming numbers of the oppressed. Rectifying names may sound simple but it is no easy task!

Religion is one of those words that might be impossible to rectify. It has had different meanings over time, and for many today it means very little. In Western universities, the study of religion is carried out on an academic level as an objective and independent undertaking, but many non-Western traditions do not isolate "religion" in this way. In many places there is no such thing as a "religion" since religion and culture (religion and government) are the same thing. This makes the question about religion a bit strained. In Muslim majority countries Islam is most often both the religion and the political system; it is both the culture and the law. In such conditions people of other religions are at best tolerated, but hold few social rights. Being Zoroastrian in Iran today is no easy task; being Christian in Pakistan is at times not even safe. Accordingly, if Islam is the only system permissible in an Islamic country, does Islam really exist in that country? For something to be distinctive, it must be compared to something else. If I want to understand what a fruit is, I can't reach that understanding if the only possibility is to see oranges. What makes an orange distinct if there are not apples or other fruit for comparison? If there is no other choice but to be Muslim in an Islamic State, then can Islam, which is or is supposed to be all about choice, actually exist?[2]

This was the predicament of Christianity in the Middle Ages. Christianity was not really a "religion" then since it was both culture and politics. Indeed, Christianity did not really "exist" in the Middle Ages since there was no other religion against which it stood. If you were not Christian, then your only other option was to be a sort of social problem, which was unfortunately how non-Christians were both viewed and handled. The philosopher Søren Kierkegaard (1813–1855) understood this situation quite well when he stated that if objectively everyone has to be a Christian then subjectively no one can be a Christian because there is no genuine choice.[3]

Still, the word religion has a history and seemingly a meaning in the English language. Its roots sink deeply into the Latin *religio*, which is also the Old French form that came into English as "religion." Presumably the word is derived from the Latin *religare*, and here begins its troubling definition. I say "presumably" because it is genuinely uncertain how the word *religio* emerged and to what root it should be connected. Many people associate *religio* with *ligare*, which means "to bind," and see religion as a type of spiritual "re-coupling" or linking up with God. The fragments and images of that word reside in the English "ligament." They are also present in "lianas," those long-stemmed vines rooted in the ground that use tree branches for support and that Tarzan liked to swing on. It seems like "religion" means to connect with the divine world, a meaning that has both popular appeal[4] and the status of Augustine

(354–430 CE), who believed the same,[5] behind it. Though common, this meaning remains only one option. Cicero might be a better, though not frequently cited, option when it comes to the Latin origin of the word religion. Here is the problem. Augustine had a lot at stake for making religion mean something like salvation. Augustine was about proving Christianity was true religion, which for him meant true salvation. Cicero (106–43 BCE),[6] on the other hand, had no such concern. A lawyer and philosopher, the multi-talented Cicero also happened to be a Roman Priest before such a thing as Christianity existed. He associated religion with reading, memorizing, and practicing. Thus it was about *relegendo* (*relego*), to read again. *Religio* is the conduct of public ceremony for which a priest is well rehearsed. It might also be said, following Cicero's line, that religion has a lot to do with study and practice and not so much with belief and faith.

This, however, does not end the quest to define religion because, in its history, "religion" took a turn inward, in the Middle Ages, as if to enter a cloistered life, and then at the end of the Middle Ages took an outward turn as if to leave the monastery for university ivory towers. Commonly in the Middle Ages a "religious" was a cloistered monk distinguished from a "secular" priest, who lived among the people. The difference between being religious and being secular, oddly, had nothing to with religion as we mean it today or seem to mean it. Rather the distinction was between religious life in the monastery and religious life in the world. To be secular meant to be religious "out there" in the *seculum* or the generation of our age. Meanwhile, to be religious meant to be committed to the monastic life. Then in the late fourteenth-century "religion" left the monastery, so to speak, when it attained its modern definition of an identifiable system of beliefs. Throughout the twelfth to fourteenth centuries the Christian West had considerable and consistent contact with Islam. This was especially so with Muslims in Spain, with crusaders in the Levant, and with various wars at the edge of the Byzantine Empire before its fall in 1453. The knowledge of

Islam as a separate but monotheistic faith comparable to but distinct from Christianity created a situation in which "religion" meant an identifiable system of beliefs that could be studied as an objective phenomenon. In some ways, Christianity as a world "religion" was born from the Western encounter with Islam as a distinct religion. After this era, religion as a subject of study entered into the universities of the Enlightenment.

Since the Enlightenment period (1700–1900 CE) it has become easy to define religion as a set of identifiable beliefs. A religion is a family of adherents who hold to common symbols and believe or confess common dogmas. All religions have varieties of dogma and plurality among followers, but each can be identified by certain central figures, texts, or beliefs such as Jesus in Christianity, the Qur'an in Islam, the Four Noble Truths in Buddhism, or the "Atman is Brahman" lesson in Hinduism.[7] It might be easy, then, to say what religion is. We can point to churches and crosses and conclude most assuredly that Christians gather at such locations. However, none of any religious sentiment would be happy with the conclusion that their religion is simply an identifiable system of beliefs.

As Kierkegaard observed, and as noted above, the objective definition of religion actually says very little about a religion or the spirit of religion in general. No one would gather in a synagogue, church, or mosque just to go through the motions of "an identifiable system of beliefs." The purposes for gathering within the boundaries of a religion are rarely reasonable and, as I have argued above, almost always psychological. The great philosopher Thomas Aquinas (1225–1274 CE), in his medieval way, understood this well enough. There are many ways to use reason to argue for the truthfulness of one proposition over another, but religious propositions do not easily fall under the category of reason. Aquinas thought that certain religions' propositions, like the Christian Trinity, were neither reasonable nor unreasonable but were beyond both as revelation. Even though Aquinas believed reason could point to what, to him, was the likely existence of God, this really made no difference to the experience of religion, which resided in revelation. Today it is possible to translate Aquinas in a secular fashion by saying, like Friedrich Schleiermacher (1768–1834 CE) did, that religion is not a logical conclusion drawn from physical evidence. It is rather a "feeling" (intuition); it is, as Aquinas would more likely have said, an experience of the "Holy Spirit."[8] Arguments against religious beliefs based on the claim that such beliefs are not reasonable or lack scientific evidence actually matter little. Most folks, even when ardently arguing in favor of religion, do not actually think religious claims are in the same category as scientific propositions. We argue for or against religion on the basis of our emotions and our instincts about whether or not such beliefs are beneficial to the experience of life. Religion is really and finally a question about values, which is why it is a problem for humanity.

Even though today many new atheists argue against the reasonableness of religion, many people nevertheless persist in belief, even when the belief in question is as ridiculous as a six thousand-year-old earth. On this fact alone, the problem of religion is obviously not related to reason, which means religion is impossible to define with adherence to the Confucian dictum of rectifying names. This returns the problem of religion to the psychological level and relates it to something like "art" in the human experience. Art is emotional experience represented through music, poetry, or even philosophical ideas about meaning and significance. (Of course, it is also sometimes just plain comedic fun). Religion is that dimension of life represented in symbol. So, despite the ability to study religion academically as an identifiable system of beliefs, in practice religion is not a system but a feeling, as Schleiermacher noted, or something like intuition. It is the outward expression of an instinctive desire for orientation, otherwise known as meaning, in the world.

This brings up a final point about religion, which is that as a form of psychology it ties itself deeply and historically to cosmology. Religion throughout its time with humanity has walked hand in hand with theories about the universe. Once, human beings believed in a three-tiered universe. The heavens, with gods in them, were not very far "up there," and sheol or hades (or more extremely, hell) was "down" below the earth's surface. We spent our lives in the third realm, which is on the earth itself. All this seemed perfectly reasonable. It is not difficult, then, to imagine an ancient person looking at the sky and asking, who are we human beings, where have we come from, and why on earth would those great gods up there care about us at all (Psalm 8:4)? But that set of ancient questions assumed there were windows in the sky and mountains here on earth from which gods watched and sometimes engaged the mortal world. When it was thought human beings came from gods or in some way were their creation, religions of the world could easily answer the profoundest questions about our nature. What is human nature? Why are we here? The answer was that since we came from the gods, we hold within ourselves a divine remnant—an image as in Genesis 1:27—of an intended reality from which we are presently in exile. Religions of the world offered diverse ways to overcome the exile, to find reunification with a hidden reality that was or is our true or intended self. This might explain the attractiveness of linking religion to *ligare* and proposing that it is a linking up with a lost self, but the point is that all these metaphors were fabricated in a context in which the gods explained how things worked and why we are the way we are. That world has passed away.

In contemporary understanding the universe does not have any particular reason for existence; indeed, we don't really have a clue why there is anything at all instead of nothing—though we keep working on such questions—nor are we fully convinced that the best model for the universe is the open (expanding forever), closed (expanding from the Big Bang and returning to a Big Crunch), or flat (accelerating and finally burning out) model.[9] To answer these mysteries today with the word "God" rings both of shallow and reductive reasoning. God is not really an answer to the questions of science but only works to silence such questions. Recognizing the deep mystery of the cosmos and labelling it God is like placing a stop sign in the middle of an endless highway. There is no real reason for the stop sign and, in any case, no compulsion to obey it. Secondly, using God as a kind of ultimate silencer prevents human beings from facing and dealing with significant problems on our finite planet. God is often the face put on the denial of reality. The universe probably does not have a meaning, though in a relative way it may have many meanings. God is not an answer to the question of the universe but only a question, a symbolic representation of a question, that dwells in the human psyche as the quest for meaning. God is not really a mystery, either, but rather a form of "humanism," by which I mean a form of human art. The universe invokes the question of meaning in human experience because its very existence leaves us searching for land in a vast sea of stars. Out of this basic cosmic quandary, religion is born. This, however, is no guarantee that religion has a value for the human future.

Religion in a general sense can have two reactions to the mystery of life that imitate two theories about the universe, opened and closed.[10] These words describe ways of relating to the world that surrounds us. In 2002 Rick Warren published *A Purpose Driven Life*, which is the perfect metaphor for religion understood as a closed system.[11] When the universe has a purpose it has a specific goal, an end time, and life within such a system accordingly has its place and reason to be. In a closed form of religion, that purpose is expressed in apocalypticism: that pattern of belief in which life moves toward a determined target as if according to a great plan. It is a very attractive form of religion because it supplies a meaning not only for an individual but also for a nation as much as a universe. The trouble of course is that big plans often eliminate a lot of small people along the way. But religion has always had its other option, the second of its two natures, beside its purpose-driven one. Religion is not limited to being a closed system. It struggles within itself to hold also an open option. As an expression, "open religion" might sound romantic, like an easy flowing sense of life as a great adventure. This, though, is too simplistic. By open religion I refer to a metaphor that is not about finding a purpose. It is about valuing religion without introducing an apocalypse. The saying, "Whoever clutches and grabs after life will lose it," arguably an aphorism of the historical Jesus, indicates the impossibility of joy in life if the psychological relationship to life is apocalyptic-styled control.[12] Apocalypticism is about control because it is the final and absolute way to tell another that he or she is wrong.

The philosopher Friedrich Nietzsche (1844–1900) claimed that a religion based on control is a religion based on resentment.[13] He meant that religion as a closed system is about "sameness," about reducing or eliminating variety with forceful ideas like truth, purity, and authenticity. He saw these themes in opposition to the heroic virtue of courage. Since ideas like truth are meant to be eternal and unchanging, and since what cannot change cannot be living, Nietzsche understood religion and Christianity particularly to be primarily about death, both physically and psychologically. When religion is conceived as a system of control based on sameness it becomes—and here Sigmund Freud (1856–1939) helps—a religion of *thanatos*: that gentle Greek god whom we love despite his being a god of death. Nietzsche called this "thanatos" element (this drive to death) in religion "resentment." Wherever religion flexes its power in order to shame people who walk on alternate paths Nietzsche saw not morality but resentment. It is like thanatos because the act of resentment is to shut down the opposition, to eliminate or isolate others through the shaming of their difference. To put this even more dramatically, Nietzsche felt that the power of religion resided in its immorality, not its morality. It is this kind of power that is apocalyptic in nature because it is, in the end, about control.

It is not just that an open system of religion is opposite to a closed system. It is that an open religion is a different psychology. It is religion set on a different mode of being from those emphasizing resentment or the drive to death. Instead of closing things down, an open religion, as an open psychology, affirms difference because difference opens the horizon both to choice and to change. The elements of choice and change can be threatening to be sure, but an open religion holds the ethic of trust in place of the ethic of resentment. In this way, open religion is more about comparing different things and cultivating wisdom, rather than reducing different things to one choice only and cultivating doctrine.

The words open and closed can be translated into Christianity as weak and strong. Theologians like the word "weak." It is admittedly a fruitful way to counteract the history of Christian theology as a control system and the Christian God as a control freak. The word weak is startling. God is supposed to be strong; how can God be weak? God is "weak" in the sense that God is something like hope: a faint vision that nevertheless has the power to draw us forward. In Process Theology, which understands God in deep relation with the universe, God is like a verb that is actively "persuasive" of things rather than a noun that is unchangingly set apart from things. God in this sense is a weak force. Even more interesting, though, is that weakness as a metaphor for God is actually drawn from the Bible; it is the image that the Apostle Paul stood up against the pretentions of human power (1 Corinthians 1:25).[14]

The weakness of God in an age when the question of the existence of God is often on the table is a radical image that can renew theological metaphors for God. What I want to do, though, is indicate that the words weak and strong can be looked at differently based on the different ways the Apostle Paul used them. There is a certain way, in contrast to our expectation, that in his letters Paul means open when he says strong and closed when he says weak. Another though paradoxical way to say this is to say that when put in our modern context Paul means weak when he says strong and strong when he says weak. This is so because Paul identifies the weak in his communities as those who cannot tolerate difference. They want instead definitive rules and controlled behavior. They exhibit what we now call a strong theology that seeks control.

Meanwhile, the opposite party that Paul calls strong exhibit what we now hold as "weak" qualities. They do tolerate difference. They entertain skepticism. They adapt customs to circumstances. So they are the weak theologians in the modern sense. Following Paul's lead, we can explore his strong and weak expressions in terms of the open and closed models of religion used above.

Paul used the metaphor of the strong and the weak a few times in the letters of Romans and Corinthians. At Romans 14:1–2 the weak are those who believe community members should only eat vegetables while the strong are community members who believe one can eat anything. Similarly, in the Corinthian correspondence[15] the distinction between weak and strong involves food. The strong in Corinth state that Greek and Roman gods do not really exist, so it is perfectly fine to eat meat sacrificed to an idol. Since idols have "no existence," it's the same as eating meat sacrificed to nothing. Paul agrees. "We know that idols have no existence" (1 Corinthians 8:4). Paul is not worried about the reasoning of the strong; in fact, he accepts that they are right and even admires their wit (8:8). His concern, though, is that the weak, who are in a different category, will not get it. They still think that the idols must hold a certain power and that, accordingly, eating meat sacrificed to an idol recognizes the validity of the idol. Paul worries that the actions of the strong will be a stumbling block to the weak and cause their conscience to be wounded (8:9–12). A little bit later at 9:22 Paul indicates that the strong have the ability to become the weak and thus "win the weak" (bring them over) to the body of Christ. Going the other way, the weak are not able to become like the strong because they are just too narrow minded and intolerant. So, it's a one-way street. The weak cannot "win" the strong; only the strong are flexible enough to become like the weak for the sake of winning them over.

In Paul's reflections it is easy to lose track of his basic agreement with the so-called strong. It is certainly understandable to focus on the weak and to care particularly for the people he describes here.

In this act, though, one can forget that Paul is actually perfectly fine with the position of the strong. Paul agrees that eating meat sacrificed to an idol causes no harm. He indicates that he is among the strong precisely because he is capable of being "like the weak" himself. His concern, though, is that if the strong do not hold solidarity with the weak, then the weak will not be capable of standing. Around the weak the strong should make some concessions in their activities for the sake of a greater good. They are capable of doing so. They have the flexibility and understanding to make it happen. To Paul, then, the strong know things that the weak do not, and among the things that the strong know are the liberties of an open lifestyle. The strong can circulate in the common Roman culture without losing their identity. The strong know emerging Christianity as an open system; the weak know it as a closed system. Paul, again, understands himself to be among the strong.

People involved in religion who are liberal or progressive can relate to what Paul calls the weak and the strong. In religious communities, the weak are horrified by the strong. The strong come across as "non-believers" and "atheists"; they threaten the security of the weak who have invested in the sureties of dogma. Out of fear, the weak often guard against the intrusion of other customs or beliefs mixed into their own; the strong often love difference and can't wait to learn something new. The weak are suspicious; the strong are intrigued. The problem with Paul is that in the midst of this great and troubling distinction his advice is poor. Paul admits that the strong are right, but claims that they must make concessions. The results of such concessions, though, can only be one thing: the strong will find little fulfillment in the church. After all, their strength includes not needing religion in order to be spiritual. Instead of the weak being challenged by the strong or being asked seriously to reconsider their position, Paul condescendingly tells the so-called strong to look down upon the weak as if they were children who cannot handle the truth. Yet, how can a person progress in the openness that Paul seems to sincerely admire if those who know the door is open never challenge those bent on closing it? What becomes of the weak if the strong never challenge but bend to their position? Put in another context, what good is all the scholarship we now have about religion if such knowledge never leaves the university to mix with and challenge popular life? Though he lived in the ancient world, Paul seems to be the prototype against which Nietzsche aimed his devastating critique of religion. Resentment to Nietzsche is the sentiment the weak aim at the strong. It is the driving force that interprets religion as the mechanism to convert joy to guilt. Paul used his weak and strong argument to defend the weak. This we can admire. Still, in doing so, did Paul inadvertently set down the resentment of the weak as the cornerstone of Christianity?

Resentment is that awful feeling of recognizing in another what you would wish for yourself and then becoming angry or jealous that you do not have it. In Nietzsche's way of thinking, the weak see in the strong what they would be but cannot be, and out of the energy of this resentment create religion so that the strong are driven underground by guilt and shame. Though Nietzsche knew little about the historical Jesus, he did know and understand the workings of Christian dogma. He could point to "love your enemies" as one such expression of dogma. To Nietzsche only the "weak" have enemies, who emerge from the hard feelings of resentment. The strong do not have enemies because they are the ones who overcome or pass beyond such tiny feelings. Nietzsche, of course, could have understood Jesus differently. The historical Jesus probably meant "love your enemies" ironically, since loving your enemies means not having enemies (for the one you love is not an enemy), but Nietzsche's critical point should not be missed. Nietzsche did not mean that venerated religious aims, like peace and justice, should be ignored but that they should not be founded on resentment. Justice based on resentment is about getting even, not healing, which is the difference in the Western tradition between punitive and restorative justice. When religion as resentment gets a hold of justice, the aim of justice becomes punishment. That is weak religion according to Nietzsche.

Nietzsche considered Christianity to be the victory of the weak, and the consequence of the victory was the inevitable slide of Christianity onto the resting place of resentment. Still, Nietzsche did understand that Christianity as a whole had little to do with the Jesus of history, whom he admired. He came to understand "the Jesus of history" through the work of David Friedrich Strauss, though Nietzsche was quite a bit more conservative in opinion than Strauss. In place of Paul's term "the strong," Nietzsche used the word "noble," and we can see in the following quotation how his analysis is similar to Paul but with a markedly different direction and fundamentally different conclusion.

> To be incapable of taking one's enemies, one's accidents, even one's misdeeds seriously for very long—that is the sign of the strong.... Here alone genuine 'love of one's enemies' is possible.... In contrast to this, picture 'the enemy' as the man of *ressentiment* conceives of him—and here precisely is his [the one of *ressentiment*] deed, his creation: he has conceived 'the evil enemy,' *'the Evil One,'* and this in fact is his basic concept, from which he then evolves, as an afterthought and pendant, a 'good one'—himself![16]

Nietzsche thought that the act of the weak was not to overcome enmity but instead to create an enemy, an evil one, against which an individual can pose as the good. This act of creating an enemy in order to be the good is the basic act of resentment, and to Nietzsche this is also the basic act of Christianity.

If we use Nietzsche's analysis, but change his and Paul's words back from weak and strong to closed and open, there is a chance, going forward, to raise several critical questions about the meaning and value of religion in the Western tradition. In the first place we can again say that religion is a psychology, meaning an art-form, that concerns how one thinks about life, about being in the world.

Then, we can say further that, so considered, religion has two natures or even two psychologies that co-exist, the so-called weak, controlling, and closed form and the so-called strong, letting-go, and open form. As we think further about these two forms, I will suggest that the first can be understood as apocalyptic theology and the second as non-apocalyptic theology. In going forward, though, it remains important to see how theology in the Western tradition developed with two operating models and how each model holds both a closed and open form.

3

Enlightenment Theology

Unlike religion in a general sense, theology is a subject directly concerned about the philosophy of a religion. While a particular religion expresses the practice of its philosophy through a psychological system of interrelated parts, theology is reasoning about why the parts go together. In Christianity, the psychological part is "salvation," the experience of solace related to the death of Jesus; the theological part is the "Doctrine of Salvation" or the reasoning about why the death of Jesus has salvific value. Even more easily stated, religion is about the heart where the experience of the symbolic system is held, and theology is about the mind where the reflection on the symbolic system occurs. We can say, then, that theology is the philosophical face of religion.

The word "theology" was born in the Western tradition from philosophy and used to describe the study of the gods, as we can see in Plato's *Republic*.[1] In Plato's case, theology is a work of the state. It is what lies behind the surface of epic stories about the state, such as the myths of its founding, to address the patterns of speech that a politician should use to highlight the meaning of statehood.[2] The Bible is not terribly different from Plato in this respect. God in the Bible has a lot to do with how a society is governed and who should lead it. With the rise of monotheistic religion in the West, theology as a subject found its home and advanced its major developments through Judaism, Christianity, and Islam. Yet, the very relationship theology has traditionally held specifically with Western

monotheism made the word problematic by the mid-twentieth
century, and today universities commonly have departments of
Religious Studies rather than departments of Theology. Many other
universities mix the study of religion into other departments such
as Anthropology, Sociology, or Philosophy. Indeed, it might be said
that there is a crisis for the study of critical theology as an independent subject in the university today.

Against such a crisis it is important to assert that theology is still
significant as an independent subject. It concerns how a religion
thinks out its problems and poses solutions or sometimes a lack of
solutions. Theology is also that place where a tradition pushes itself
to the limits of its own thought. Theology is or can be about raising questions at the edge of a religious tradition and holding in this
provocative act the stewardship of the tradition's "atheism" or non-
belief. What is meant here is that theology is not just the philosophy
of a tradition but also the question of the value of the tradition. It
questions the value by moving to the outside or, at least, to the edge
of the tradition's "confession" in order to re-evaluate the tradition
itself. Christianity confesses that Jesus is the Christ, the Son of the
living God; Christian theology questions, or can question, from a
"virtual atheist" point of view why and if such a claim makes sense.
Theology is at liberty to conclude that the confession no longer
makes sense, and thus good theologians, when placed in the right
positions of power, can enact things like Vatican II. Such acts unfortunately are rare, for "good theologians" are generally regarded as
dangerous in the eyes of ecclesiastical authorities. But if we accept
that a good theologian is one who pushes a religion to the edges
its own confessions, and by this push seeks to escort it meaningfully
into the contemporary world, if we accept that a good theologian
holds this strategic form of "atheism" or radical questioning in relation to the tradition, then the "dangerous" acts of the theologian
are in fact the faithful acts of working out the tradition and theology
is the hope of this work.

Theology, as the philosophical face of religion, looks upon the cosmos and articulates the quandary of being in it. The quandary of life begins with the question why; theology ventures inside this question to explore its depths and discover whether there is a meaningful answer. Theology is about thinking out a code by which one should get on in life. Theology is the great meme[3] of life embedded in a culture as its religious reasoning and sense of mission. Inside the practices of a religion one can experience meaning, but if one is to articulate the reason for the practices, then what is sought is the theological *raison d'etre* or mission of the religion and of, by extension, the worldview of the culture that values the religion. We can talk about "the American way" and mean something semi-religious even if we do not intend to. Underneath the expression lies the American myth of the individual who conquers a new land and fends off enemies. It is a myth founded upon the figure of Abraham as the great individual and on the Exodus story of conquering and settling a "wild" land. The story is told from the point of view of those who did the so-called conquering and not from the point of view of those already in the land, like the Canaanite nations in the Bible and the indigenous nations in North America. It is hard for those who tell the story to admit that the Canaanites and the indigenous peoples were here (or there) first and consequently have priority rights. It is hard for the dominant story tellers to admit there is equally valid religion and theology on the other side. Today, we also experience how hard but also how important it is for the dominant story tellers to apologize for their historic presumptions. Why is it so hard to make such an admission? The reasons are religion and theology. Religion is the psychology of so-called conquerors, the way the conquerors feel about their culture, and theology is the *raison-d'être* or purpose of conquerors, the way they imagine the righteousness of their actions.

Culture on its own expresses only collective habits and indulgences. One needs religion to express a mission and a purpose. This is what makes theology a most interesting subject. When theology is understood as a critical subject, it has a significant job to do. Theology is the place where the question about the orientation a cultural tradition holds can be taken up. Why does a certain cultural tradition reason the way it does? Why does it figure things out according to a particular line of thought or what can be called an orientation toward the world? And then, with such a question raised, the more difficult questions about where a tradition is headed and whether or not it should consider new directions or serious reform can be addressed. Far from being an abstract academic exercise, theology is the heartbeat of a cultural system. It is utterly discouraging that such a significant study is often exiled from the university curriculum or else confined to "Religious Studies" or another safe discipline.

If we accept that the word theology means *the study of god(s)* (*theos-logos*) then theology is a study of cultural ideology and the way that ideology, as the thinking of a culture, impresses its authority—its gods, whatever shape they may take—upon the scene as the *aim* and *purpose* of a people or a nation. It is hard to break the power of the gods, and for those who try the consequence is often a personal sense of guilt or angst. When the gods die an age of anxiety is born. It is the fate of a theologian to carry this burden forward to a new day.

The task I undertake here is to make a distinction between two orientations in Western theology and to label them Enlightenment and Covenant theology. Before engaging this task, it seems important to address the issue of typology, which is the concern about reducing complex questions to simple formulas. If I were to critique myself, this would be the question I would raise.

Typology basically means typecasting: it derives from the Latin word *typus*, which means emblem. The Latin parallels the Greek *tupos*, which has the sense of striking (branding) something with a mark. Typology is a way of gathering several concepts and experiences together under one brand. It is easy to think of a corporation and how all the products of a corporation, however diverse, can be labeled under the same brand name.

Early Christians, as an example, used the word pagan as a brand name or type to identify all the non-Christian varieties of cultural and religious practices in the Roman Empire. To Christians, pagan was the right word to use to amass all "others," all non-Christians and non-Jews, under one name. Even though the word pagan previously held a different meaning, Christians found here a convenient way to typecast non-Christian Greeks and Romans. The origin of the word *paganus* is not clearly known. It is usually linked to *pagus*, a word used by the Emperor Diocletian (244–311 CE) for a small administrative district. It is expressed in the English word "peg," that is, a boundary marker, and it is also present in the French word *payee*, which means country. But to Christians the word could be used to identify country folk who generally did not know about or had not been directly affected by the empire's acceptance of the new faith. Christians, thus, used the word in a new typological way to classify all non-Christians under one category. The problem with this act is obvious. It ignored the differences and uniquenesses among the people placed under a single term. It created, in this reductive act, the basic and historic prejudice of Christianity against people placed under the blanket term paganism.

Typology is particularly problematic in scholarship for at least two reasons. One is that it takes scattered events, often varied and subtle, and stamps them with one word or description. In Christian scholarship, the word gnosticism is problematic for this very reason. Gnosticism was a word created to collect under one "brand" all the varieties of non-orthodox Christianity in antiquity.[4] The attitude was that if it was not orthodox, then it was gnostic. This analysis substituted two types of Christianity for the great variety earliest Christianity held. Then, with the division in place, gnosticism was judged from the point of view of orthodoxy. Gnosticism effectively became something divergent from and inferior to orthodoxy. This collecting of all forms of Christianity into two basic camps became the operating assumption in the study of the history of Christianity. Such uncritical judgments are still problematic today.[5] So, the use of a typology introduces this troubling double act: it reduces a complex picture to a set of catch words and it implies there is an original or pure form of a movement from which a divergent group arose. The powerful typology of "gnostic" and "orthodox" Christianity ignores how difference and variety has been part of Christianity from the very start. Not all "Gnostics" were gnostic and not all "Orthodox" were orthodox. These two typologies arose later. Gnosticism as such never existed but was branded into existence by a corporation called Orthodox Christianity.

Typology, then, is problematic on these two fronts: it is hides complexities under one name and it assumes there is an original or pure form of a religion or other cultural phenomenon. Despite the troubles, however, typologies cannot be avoided. Human beings employ language to communicate, and when we get right down to it every word is a "type" or an expressive stamp that represents a multiple number of experiences. The word justice holds a complex of meanings that is determined circumstantially, but despite this complexity we necessarily use justice as one direct word. If we did not do this, then by the time we all explained our individual intended meaning the important moment to use the word would have passed. If not for typology, both the efficiency and effectiveness of language would be impossible. Human beings do not even have to share a language but only a simple nod of the head to share a typological understanding of an event.

In philosophy, it would be impossible to engage a subject like "Platonic thought" if there was no way to collect the material appropriate to this subject under a heading. So, even though typologies are troubling because they reduce and hide problems, at the same time they make thinking possible. Christianity itself is a "type," and this makes it identifiable in relation to Judaism and Islam, which are also types. Typology makes identity possible, and identity allows for the discussion of the problems a subject holds.

Inasmuch as academics like to criticize typologies as simplistic, it is impossible not to use them. Even to critique "typology" is to use a typology about typology. Typology is ineluctable.

A better option than dismissing typology is to overcome its negative aspects with awareness. It is irresponsible to take typologies literally. Typologies only serve to gather common things together under one heading like Christianity, but they do not limit what can be gathered under the heading nor do they make a value statement about what is so gathered. If I were to use the word "heresy" to identify Christian movements that were persecuted, it would be best if I knowingly admitted that I am using a typology manufactured by "orthodoxy" designed to exclude various groups and experiences from Christianity. That does not mean that I think the heretics are heretics; it only means that I am using a typological expression to help me identify groups or ideas that orthodox theologians interpret as threatening.

When we return to the question of two orientations in Western theology called Enlightenment and Covenant theology, some caution must be expressed. Employing these names does not mean that only these two names are useful. Neither does it imply that they exclude each other. There can, of course, be lots of others names depending on the analysis one seeks to achieve. In addition, in making a distinction between two forms I do not mean that one is a pure or original form. There is no suggestion on my part that one is better or worse than the other. Still, I use two forms of theology to identify certain features of a cultural heritage that have influenced the shape and *raison d'être* of theology in the Western experience. This identification makes a discussion possible; it allows for the pursuit and debate of a question, provided the division does not also hide from view complexities and exceptions.

The first type proposed, what I have called Enlightenment theology, can also be called wisdom theology. I mean here to identify a form of theology that sees the basic human problem as ignorance and the basic solution as enlightenment. In the Christian and Jewish

Bibles, the book of Ecclesiastes is a full and forceful display of the quest for enlightenment as both the gift and problem of being human. The book of Ecclesiastes is the Greek translation of the Hebrew Qoheleth, which means "(the) Preacher" or the speaker before a congregation. The writer of Ecclesiastes sees ignorance as both the problem of being human and the reason we "cannot find out" the meaning and purpose of it all.[6] The emphasis on wisdom is a form of Enlightenment theology because it is a theology in which truth dwells in the human experience, in the secular or worldly experience, that comes to light with self-examination. A wisdom teacher is someone who can lead another in the act of self-examination and encourage decisions about self-becoming, that is, about how to be in the world. But a wisdom teacher is powerless to enlighten another; enlightenment is the task of each individual.

By way of comparison, the principles of Enlightenment theology can be seen in Hinduism, which holds a deeply historical relationship to Western thought and which has the interesting idea of an avatar. The word avatar means "passing down" and, in a sense, "passing across."[7] The avatar incarnates or makes present in the secular world the divine principles of knowledge and order. An avatar appears in the life of common human beings to reveal the true qualities of our human frame that lie in divine origins. An example from Hinduism is how the supreme god Vishnu moves from the realm of the sublime into (or across to) the human form of Prince Rama.[8] As the Prince, he exemplifies virtue, he masters self-control, and he overcomes many challenging obstacles that might otherwise corrupt his being. In other words, as an avatar, Prince Rama shows us how it is done. He shows what life is like when a human being realizes the divine reality within. The idea of the Christian incarnation is essentially the idea of the avatar. Though arguably not exactly the same, it is certainly easy to see Jesus Christ as the Christian version of an avatar. Jesus holds a heroic status as the exemplar of a human being who perfectly realizes the divine. Indeed, were Western history predominantly an avatar tradition like Hinduism, we might expect that Moses and Socrates would form with Jesus a sacred heroic trinity of virtuous leaders.

In his great novel, *Lord of the Flies*, we can see how William Golding expresses culturally the trope of Enlightenment theology as that emphasis on waking up the human conscience to its proper virtue. The story is about children who survive a shipwreck and manage alone, without adults, on an island. The children prove unable to sustain a social order. In effect, the novel involves witnessing the steady collapse of order into anarchy. At the end a rescue ship appears, and in the midst of utter chaos in which a murder is about to unfold, an adult from the ship stands amidst the children shockingly to remind them of the world of order from which they had been in temporary exile. Effectively, though not always explicitly, this is what an avatar does. An avatar comes into the world and, sometimes shockingly, enlightens us with knowledge of the universal order from which our ignorance and temporality have left us in exile. Enlightenment theology is all about waking up the avatar within.

In a more general sense, enlightenment is about the cosmic order and how every individual, indeed every form of life, participates in and is the product of the order. In Hinduism, the true human self is aligned with the Dharma; in Greek thought the true human self is aligned with the Logos; in Christian thought, the true human self is aligned with the Christ. Each of these images expresses Enlightenment theology. In the Gospel of John, Jesus is the Logos, the Word made flesh.[9] Jesus comes into the world to bring light to the darkness, which is the strongest theme of this gospel. Theology conceived within the boundaries of enlightenment does not primarily emphasize sin. The trouble is not the sin of pride that separates human beings from the will of God, but the darkness of ignorance that hides the divine order from the true self. The problem lies particularly in sense perception. When what we perceive remains isolated from the knowledge of the Logos then our perceptions lead to deceptions. Enlightenment theology, then, is not really about god stories in which divinities cross over to human form. Such stories

only illustrate the point of enlightenment. Enlightenment theology
is about that hidden element of light at the heart of every individual,
which is a universal light everyone holds and can realize in the act
of self-becoming. Enlightenment theology is the emphasis on this
act through the basic message that the divine is here in our midst.
We do not lack anything for enlightenment except a trustworthy
guide, whether that be a teacher, a strange story about a god, or
wisdom itself.

Three qualities or elements of Enlightenment theology can be
found in Judaism, Christianity, and Islam. The first is the way humans beings can be co-creative with God, the second is in the idea
of universal salvation, and the third is the understanding that the
divine nature is perfect stillness. A look at each of these elements
will show how Enlightenment theology, often underappreciated, is
a significant part of the heritage of the Western tradition.

The co-creative element is seen in many biblical stories and expressively stated in the six days account of creation. In this story,
human beings are to be fruitful and multiply, to be caretakers of
the earth, and to work the soil for food. These three directives arise
from the hand of the Elohist (E) writer, whose version of creation
is found in Genesis 1:1 to 2:4a. The writings in the Bible identified
as E likely arose from the ancient Northern nation of Israel.[10] The
story, with human beings created in the image of God, expresses
a reliance on the human ability to tap into the world order. For
example, E is partial to dreams as a means to realize in human visions the divine intention. E also names Abraham a prophet, a status
which is unique to that writer, and which makes Abraham a relay
of divine messages. That human beings are made in the "likeness"
of gods (1:26–27) means that human experience is itself similar to
divine experience. How human beings perceive the world, because
of their likeness, must be similar to how the divine being(s) perceive
it. What, then, is the connection between the human and divine in
terms of "perceiving the world" in and through our experience?
The answer is something like reason or even wisdom. As the cre-

ation story relays, it is because human beings are in the image of God, both male and female, that they know the order of things, which entitles them to be responsible as caretakers of the earth.

The Hebrew words used here to describe the human responsibility for creation are royal words. They are relayed with the images of ruling over subjects. The creation narrative relays, "fill the earth and subdue (*kabash*) it; and have dominion over (*radah*) the fish of the sea and over the birds of the air and over every living thing that moves on the earth" (1:28). These words are related to imperial power. The first word translated as "subdue" is a word for slavery when one nation subdues another nation and its people; the second word "dominion" is related to the royal dominion or hold of lands. These words do not sound very promising as enlightenment words except when they are given an appropriate context. One nation only seeks to subdue another nation when the other nation is hostile and intends harm. The E writer is indicating that nature, while necessary for life, does not always cooperate with life. Human beings have to work with it using labor and knowledge to gain sustenance from it. But this knowledge is there because human beings as the image of God have the power to figure things out on their own. They have dominion over nature, as a royal figure has dominion over a state, because they can (a least theoretically) rule justly. Although the E writer did not write the later books of the prophets, we can see in prophetic writing elements of E and the emphasis on human responsibility. Prophets like Amos or Ezekiel express frustration with royals who rule unjustly. In a particular tirade against aristocrats, Ezekiel states, "The weak you have not strengthened, the sick you have not healed, the crippled you have not bound up, the strayed you have not brought back, the lost you have not sought, and with force and harshness you have ruled them" (34:4). To the E writer the order of what is just is already part of human judgment, and prophetic voices like those of Ezekiel exemplify the conviction that it is within human power to be just. Governing figures or regimes cannot be castigated as unjust and ignorant if it is not within their power to be just and knowledgeable. Though the language is couched in ancient ideas of the state, the E writer in fact says that subduing and having dominion over the earth are acts of human creativity that ought to be undertaken as those who are in the image of God. It is as enlightened beings that humans are on the earth or, at least, are supposed to be according to the perspective of the writer called E and to later prophets like Ezekiel.

The second element in Enlightenment theology is its universalism. Since the world operates on the principle of order (the Logos), the cosmos, despite its disorder, naturally moves toward order and balance. When the world falls out of balance there comes a need for someone to show up to name the needed corrective. It is not just anyone, though, who qualifies but a divine emissary like a prophet. In this sense a prophet can be understood as enlightened, for a prophet speaks the word, that is, the order or wisdom of God in an effort to correct the perceived chaos. The aim of prophetic speech is not to judge the chaos evil but to return the chaos to order. So, the prophetic voice at its best is very much a universal voice. It encompasses the whole order of life, which we can see quite sharply in the book of Isaiah. There the writer understands that the important thing about the Torah or Word of God is that it shines like a beacon across the whole world to call all the nations to peace, justice, and love. Sometimes such words sound naive, even hypocritical, but the writer of Isaiah is quite serious. If Israel follows the Torah faithfully, the benefit spills out not just for Israel but the whole world. The whole world is brought back to the intended "order" of things, at least the writer so interprets, and every nation on earth turns back from war to peace. It is an astounding, overflowing, and universal image that has been repeated in all ages and is still for us a great vision that nations "shall beat their swords into ploughshares and their spears into pruning hooks" and "neither shall they learn war anymore" (Isaiah 2:4). As the writer of Isaiah sees it, this time of peace is a consequence of the light of God being realized on earth in the acts of nations. It reflects an understanding that the Torah is not "law" in a harsh sense but "enlightenment" or order for the whole world. When the Torah is seen as enlightenment everybody is Jewish.

In the Christian tradition the idea that the whole world will one day return to God, that is, to the originating or intended order, was expressed as early as the theologian Origen (182–254 CE) in his idea of *apokatastasis*.[11] Origen's term, from Stoic philosophy, is based on the supposed and eternal cycle of the destruction and restoration of the universe. For Origen, the vision of this cosmic cycle means that all forms of life will be restored in the end in God. Perhaps some people will have an easier go of things since their lives have been good, but to Origen even evil folks and fallen angels will ultimately return to God—though their path is a bit longer and their suffering a bit harsher. This is expressively the heart of Christianity for Origen because all life is formed through the intellect of God. All forms of life are therefore Christ-forms or elements of the Christ-nature scattered into the created order. If we imagine a large pane of glass shattered into a million pieces, that is essentially how Origen saw the act of creation. The pieces belong together and are of the same material, though they are presently separated from and alien to one another. One day, though, they will be gathered together to form the whole they are destined to be. This imaginative way of thinking makes enlightenment, the realization of one's innate Christ-nature or true self, the centerpiece of Christianity—at least for Origen. It also makes Christianity as a religion universalist in nature. It is this element of universalism that expresses Enlightenment theology because of its founding not on sin and the exclusive clubs of the saved but on ignorance and the universal potential of awakening.

The third element of Enlightenment theology is the stillness of God. This does not mean that "God" does not move around on various excursions but that the very idea of God is calmness or, as philosophers say, Absolute. There is an important reason why this is the case. Philosophically speaking, God is Absolute Reality, which means that God is without qualities or specific characteristics. The real God is not really God, so to speak, but Being. God as Absolute means God is the Being or the foundation of reality but not anything specific in reality. Unlike individual things, Absolute Being cannot have peculiarities. Only things in time can have qualities that make them peculiar like a location, a shape, a color, or some other feature. Accordingly a religion will speak of its god in relative terms with various qualities like goodness or justice, but God as ultimate reality itself is not an object or thing in reality. Ultimate or Absolute Reality in itself is not really something human beings can talk about over coffee; only the imagined qualities of such a concept can be put into language. When the notion of Absolute Reality "in itself" is grasped, there is stillness and silence.

Great expressions of stillness characterize Enlightenment theology. Some of them are found in Plato and Aristotle, and subsequently Neo-Platonism and Medieval Christian and Jewish mysticism. In Plato's thought everything that we experience in the world, that moves around and is available to our senses, is an imperfect image of a more perfect world. Before we were born, according to Plato, we must have known perfect images because, now that we are in the flesh, we can recognize in imperfect things the trace of a lost perfection.[12] We can recognize the trace because, even if dimly, we know it. The knowledge of the trace comes from the same place we come from. There are great varieties of plants, for example, but we can tell the difference between a rose and a tulip with barely a thought. We know they are both plants. Plato asked how do we know? To Plato within the appearance of things lies a hidden or common perfection of things. We can see variations in roses but know they are all roses because we grasp perfection in the idea of a rose. The idea of perfection is innate. Grasping the innate idea is the basic act of Enlightenment.

The philosopher Aristotle was Plato's student, and like a good student he disagreed with his master. So, Aristotle devised that the idea or form of a thing and the material in which it resides are inseparable. All material objects are "something" in space and time and must, as such, have a form. If something does not have a form, then it is does not have matter either. Matter necessitates having a form. So Aristotle turned Plato's abstract idea about pre-existing forms into forms understood as a type of energy in matter. Forms for Aristotle account for the movement of things through change from lesser to greater expressions of perfection. The acorn already holds the form of the Oak Tree in potential, which means the acorn holds a perfection in its present state. A form in this way is the inherent purpose of a thing and the energy that moves it toward its goal. When a thing realizes its goal it no longer seeks to change. If we were to ask Aristotle what happens when a thing reaches its goal, the strange and wise answer would be nothing. To arrive at perfection is to reach the state of stillness. God for Aristotle is unmoved and absolutely still. To Aristotle, God is perfection and so by definition is stillness. Absolute reality cannot engage the process of change, for that which changes is not perfection but rather the movement toward perfection. A perfect thing is beyond movement, and to Aristotle this can only be God.

In both Plato and Aristotle, and in philosophies that emerged after them, there arose strong affections for mysticism. For both philosophers, God is a metaphor for ultimate reality, and for both philosophers God is not "something" or "somebody" but a final point of stillness. With these philosophers and in forms of mysticism that followed, the experience of God is like the shattering of personal identity and the breaking apart of peculiarities in the face of silencing awe. Stillness is a trace of the divine in the flux and energy of being alive. Every human being can realize the trace of the stillness in their activities of life. This means that every location of life is also a location of enlightenment.

There are instances in the Bible where traces of Enlightenment theology express stillness as the fundamental principle of the divine reality. The most obvious is the Elijah narrative in which God is not present in any mighty act of nature but only in the stillness that follows such acts. In the Elijah narrative (1 Kings 19:12) the hero prophet is running for his life because he has just caused the deaths of the prophets of Ba'al (18:40). He finds refuge in a cave where Yahweh tells Elijah to stand upon a mount before his God. Here a great wind passes by, an earthquake occurs, and a fire arises, but God is never present in these natural expressions of power. God is present only afterward in the "still small voice." Of course from here the adventures of Elijah continue, but it is enough to notice that even an ancient writer like the Deuteronomist, the author of this narrative, who loves God as power and as judgment, can still understand that eventually God is beyond the chaos as stillness. For this writer, it is the stillness and not the power that speaks to Elijah.

Inasmuch as I have extolled Enlightenment theology above for its wisdom-based virtues of co-creativity, universal salvation, and stillness, this does not mean it lacks problems. There are, as I stated earlier, open and closed forms of religion, and Enlightenment theology can contain elements of both. The constant worry of theologians is that among those who embrace enlightenment as the central feature of theology will be found also those who suffer from *hubris* or pride.[13] After all, to think that ultimately God becomes actual through human enlightenment holds the potential for creating self-deception. If Enlightenment theology sees in the secular the realization of the divine, then the danger will be that the divine ends up being equated with one's culture. Taken to the next level, Enlightenment theology could support uncritical forms of patriotism. Human history is well acquainted with the problem of theology supporting a political regime as if the regime was the realization of the principles of truth or the will of God on earth. Christianity's historic justification of the divine right of kings and its priestly overseeing of fidelity vows issued from impoverished servants, two acts that justified both political and ecclesiastical hierarchies of power, are unfortunately also an expression of Enlightenment theology. We can call this the closed expression of enlightenment, the kind of expression that limits choices and sets agendas. It is in this type of theology that Enlightenment is a code word for the privilege of power that seeks to silence the critique of prophets.

But if there is a closed side to Enlightenment theology, this does not cancel its very open and often very brilliant offerings. The Logos of enlightenment expresses the inner order of the cosmos, but this is only an initial insight. The grander insight still is that since every living creature is of the cosmos, the innermost reality of every single thing is beauty. Every human being is an avatar, every life form is the handiwork of the cosmos, every kind of energy is a moment of incarnation. The true human self is not a chaotic bundle of nerves but an ordered and calm spirit. The true human self holds a profound understanding that what is perceived on the surface is not always what is true in the depths. The true human spirit is capable of bringing the insight of peace to any situation of anger or violence. To cut through deception and into depth is to liberate knowledge from misshaped ignorance. Every human being is an avatar, an enlightenment waiting to happen. It is not a question of intelligence. It is a question of willingness to participate in the world.

The enlightenment tradition then, loosely stated, is one that juxtaposes ignorance and insight. It seeks the manifestation of the divine in the life of human beings. It is overtly, when at its best, about a vision of reality that can be entered "over there," that is, over where the divine crosses human boundaries to find its home in the now. This converting of history into the now of the divine or, perhaps better stated, convergence of history with the divine presence in the now, delivers to the examiner several noted characteristics that can be collectively called Enlightenment theology.

4

Covenant Theology

A second major influence on the Western tradition of theology comes from the peoples of the Ancient Near East, specifically the cultural influence of closely related Canaanite populations and the political manipulation of dominating empires like Akkad, Assyria, and Babylon.[1] Out of the settling of ancient Canaanite lands and city-states arose the Jewish people and the historic twin nations of northern Israel and southern Judah. The Canaanite writing system was a cuneiform (wedge-shaped) script, historically adapted through Akkad from the unrelated Sumerian people of southern Mesopotamia. Hebrew was a southern Canaanite dialect and Ugarit a northern one. In the Ancient Near East powerful storm gods were often the witnesses of covenants formed between nations. If one of the nations was a dominant empire, like Assyria, a conquered nation was virtually forced to confess the truth of the dominating gods within the imperial territories. As a result, smaller, subdued states had always to deal with foreign gods, which represented the integrity and power of the larger state. Since the making of a covenant between both nations and families was widely practiced in the Ancient Near East and so central to the Biblical tradition, it is reasonable to call this second major influence on the Western religious imagination Covenant theology.[2]

In the Bible the word translated as covenant is *berith*, which occurs some 280 times in Hebrew. It is often found in the phrase *karat berith*, that is, "make a covenant." When Abraham had a dispute with Abimelech over the use of a well, Abimelech indicated that he was unaware that Abraham had no access to the well and that, to recognize Abraham's right to water, a covenant between the two was necessary. As the Bible records, "Abraham took sheep and oxen and gave them to Abimelech, and the two cut a covenant" (Genesis 21:27). Various translations of the Bible will use another word here in place of "cut" (usually "made"), and likewise another word is sometimes used in place of "covenant" (such as "agreement"). In fact the word *karat* really is "cut" because, in the story above, the animals Abraham gave to Abimelech would have been slaughtered and cut into halves.[3] Then, the two men (and their servants) would have walked between the pieces to seal the agreement. Should one party break the covenant, the fate of that party was basically displayed spread out on the ground as cut up pieces of flesh. A covenant was a serious deal, usually between a dominant and a subordinate party, and it was the subordinate party that would be sacrificed like the animals should the inferior party dare entertain defiant thoughts.[4]

To translate the word "covenant" as an agreement or a pact does not really do justice to the intensity of the word. To break a covenant was deeply insulting both to the dominant party and to its gods; it was also, of course, extremely dangerous. A weaker nation in covenant with a stronger one took a calculated risk if it chose to revolt. There needed to be an accurate judgment of the superior nation's decline, and the gods too needed to be consulted to ensure the judgment was true. Prophets of a royal court were like government advisors, perhaps even like cabinet ministers today. But sometimes the signs of the weakness of a mighty nation were deceiving. A subordinate nation could misjudge the situation. If so, only trouble would follow. Ancient Israel and Judah on many occasions misjudged the situation of ancient empires and paid dire consequences. Israel, to the north, fell to Assyria in 722 BCE due to misjudging the apparent weakness of the great empire. It turned out the empire was only experiencing a respite from its otherwise mighty character. Israel fatally misjudged Assyria's momentary stumble for a fall. Again in 650 BCE the southern nation of Judah misjudged the imperial power of Babylon and suffered the consequences of exile. In 167 BCE Judea, the land of Judah so named in Greek and Roman times,[5] correctly judged the weakening power of the Greek Seleucid empire and won both an astounding victory and independence for the nation. In the first century of the Common Era the people of Galilee misjudged the power of Rome and incited a revolution against the occupiers. This divided the Jewish people, with many against the revolt due to their knowledge of Rome, but the revolutionary parties, as Josephus explained, held the upper hand, defeated the opposition, and then faced Rome. The consequence was the destruction of the Jerusalem Temple in 70 CE. Judging one's place among mighty nations was a precarious matter involving events of seemingly miraculous victory but more often utterly despairing defeats.

Agreements in antiquity were not like agreements in modernity. We can change our minds, take things back if we are not satisfied, and usually rely on guarantees. To cut a covenant in the ancient world was not to reach an agreement. It was more like reaching a settlement between two often unequal sides, and the stronger side set the terms. A covenant, then, is best translated as a binding or a bond. In the Ancient Near East the symbolism was the dramatic walk between sliced up pieces of flesh that served to remind the weaker party how the bond was literally written in blood.[6]

Gods were involved in covenants, which adds another dimension to the tradition. The gods observed the covenant-making ceremonies, with the god of the weaker nation being humiliated before the power of the stronger one. A now famous Akkadian-Hittite covenant from the thirteenth century BCE records the bond between King Mursilis, who was King of the Hatti people, and King Duppi-Tessub of Amurru. Mursilis was the overlord, and the covenant begins by reminding Duppi-Tessub of this fact. Duppi-Tessub is to be loyal, as his father was loyal, to the Hatti nation and their gods. The mighty gods of Mursilis, specifically sun and storm gods, oversee the cutting of this covenant. Both parties walk between the cuts to seal the bond, but the walk reminded Duppi-Tessub and the gods of his people of their inferior relationship to the observing gods of the overlord or Suzerain power. A revolt on the part of Duppi-Tessub would be against the gods of Mursilis who, through the symbols of Mursilis and his court, are the whole royal regime. Breaking a covenant is an insult to the royal identity played out in the identities of the gods: an insult against the laws, the way of life, and the collective dignity of the overlord people. A British monarch can say (or used to say in the age of Queen Victoria), "we are not amused," and the meaning rested on the Royal-Divine identity. The "we" are the gods of royal identity and the non-amusement refers to undermining the dignity of the British people as a whole. Royal identity is a collective, not singular, one.

The covenant recorded between Mursilis and Duppi-Tessub was a covenant between gods. The superior nation, in this case the Hatti people, are the Suzerains of the subordinate nation. Accordingly, this covenant is called a Suzerain Covenant. The agreement is enacted in rituals involving gods but the real humiliation for the subordinate people is the demand that the agreement made with a foreign god be proclaimed in the temples of their god in their land.[7] The remarkable nature of this act can be imagined if we think about ancient Israel being made subordinate to Assyria during the reigns of Jehu (841–815 BCE) and Shalmaneser III (858–824). Jehu is the King of Israel best known in the Bible for his bloody seizure of power from Jehoram and his mother Jezebel. He participated in coalition forces against Assyria's Shalmaneser III but eventually lost the battle. In the end Jehu had to pay tribute to Shalmaneser, and the still existing "Black Obelisk of Shalmaneser" (now in the British Museum) depicts Jehu, among others, in a supreme act of abeyance kissing the ground before his master Shalmaneser's feet. We do not know but can imagine that a Suzerain Covenant was enacted, that Jehu and his court walked between cut pieces of flesh before the god Ashur, the god of Assyria, and that the covenant proclaiming the superiority of Ashur was publicly read in the North Israel capital of Samaria (presumably with the god Yahweh either approving or being humiliated or both). Now, we can think about how some of the ancient prophets of Israel, like Amos and Hosea, spoke in this northern context of abeyance against the acknowledgement of Ashur and other foreign gods (that the Bible collectively calls Ba'al), but such prophetic speech was not conducted in a modern atmosphere of freedom of religion. To call the local royal court to the strict worship of Yahweh in spite of Assyria was a call for the breaking of the covenant with Assyria. The ancient prophets in this sense were utterly courageous but, if you were the King of Israel, equally troubling. For what King, with the sure knowledge of defeat, would risk breaking a covenant with a mighty power and bringing certain destruction upon the land and the people? Inasmuch as a king or other governing officials might contemplate the possibility, timing was everything. Only if and when an empire was poised to fall could a smaller nation contemplate a break for independence, but this, as we have noted, was by no means an easy decision to make.

In similar fashion, but not with the same kind of language, recognizing the spirit of Augustus Caesar through sacrifice (libation) in the Roman culture was the normal way to express respect for the imperial dignity. Augustus was a "son of god" because he was adopted by the divine Julius Caesar. In contrast, the cultures of the Ancient Near East did not understand their leaders to be gods but God's anointed representative (whoever the god happened to be) and an envoy on earth.[8] The role of the king was to represent the will of the god, and in this way we can understand how the prophet can stand as an "envoy" or messenger of God against a presumptuous royal court that is judged to be a false representation of the will of God. The prophetic spirit, which is identified here, arises with that critical engagement of society on the basis that society, in a fundamental way, is in covenant with the wrong God.

It might be that in addition to covenants between nations, a nation also had a covenant with its god. As far as we know, however, ancient Israel and Judah are the only nations that understood their relationship to God on the basis of a covenant. This unique feature holds a deep and lasting effect on Judaism, Christianity, and Islam. All three modern religions identify profoundly with the covenant between God and Israel, through Abraham and Moses in particular. The Abrahamic Covenant is the one in which God chooses Abraham to be the father of many nations and seals the covenant, in place of cutting animals, with circumcision. The Mosaic Covenant involves the giving of the Torah to Israel, which essentially is the founding act of "ethical monotheism," that is, the recognition of one God as the principle of justice in social relationships. In these acts of covenant, God is not just God. God through Abraham is universal in appeal as the deity of many nations, and through Moses, God is the dignity of relationship held among members of a society. To insult God by chasing after other gods, for example, by means of corrupt social relationships, is to the prophetic eye an act of insubordination demanding repentance.

When highly insightful people, like the writer of Isaiah, arrive on the scene, the strength of Covenant theology can find its boldest, and most universal, expression. We can call this its open aspect. Isaiah realized that God is not just a national icon but, in philosophical terms, ultimate reality itself. God is beyond any nation and addresses all nations. Out of a universal understanding of God but on the strength of a covenant with God, Isaiah understands God to be bound with *hesed* or the quality of faithfulness to international peace.[9] The point of the divine covenant is that nations will cease to learn war and that the conveyor of this covenant hope is Israel, the light to the nations. In this sense the writers of Isaiah can be honored as the founding school of prophets who promoted God the covenant maker as God the vision bearer, and God's vision opens the covenant to the nations.

The first great strength and distinguishing feature of Covenant theology, then, is the prophetic voice: that courageous voice that calls for justice on an international scale. It is a heritage that cannot be quickly dismissed or belittled.

If we call the imperative for justice the open aspect of Covenant theology, then the problem with this theology—its closed aspect— arrives when the covenant is presented as an authoritative book frozen in time. In this case the words of the book become the "Word" and the book itself starts to become heavy like a millstone that fails to notice the weight of its intolerance as it rolls over human rights. In the Bible the figure of God is sadly allowed to suffer, in the hands of writers, a reduction to such small-minded intolerance. The book of Ezra was written in the political atmosphere that followed the Babylonian Exile. Judah had become the province of Jehud and allowed to rebuild its temple and city under the leadership of returning priests and court officials. Ezra was one such priestly leader who confused ethnic identity with the righteousness of God and in the process rejected the legitimate marriages between Jewish men and gentile women. Ezra demanded that Jewish men put away their gentile wives and children (Ezra 10:3) as if the divine covenant was made on the basis of genetics and preferred interpretations of scripture. Whatever this writer imagines the covenant is about, the imperative in Exodus about loving the stranger and alien is lost. Ezra forcibly demands gentile women with their children to be divorced from their husbands and left destitute. We do not know for certain but can well imagine that many, if not most, Jewish husbands rejected the ultra-orthodoxy of Ezra. We can see this rejection in the story of Ruth where a gentile woman marries Boaz, a Jewish man, and becomes the grandmother of David, the once and future King of Israel. Ruth is written about the same time as Ezra and is the protest against Ezra's unethical policies.[10] What book in the Bible, we might then ask, Ruth or Ezra, expresses the covenant truly? The answer will lie in what one believes is loyalty to God. For some writers of the Bible loyalty to God in covenant means reducing the interpretation of the book to the interests of the group. For other writers it is rather the very nature of the covenant to shatter group thinking with the imperatives of justice.

A second distinguishing feature of Covenant theology follows from above, which is precisely that a covenant is a recorded document. With a covenant comes a book. The three Abrahamic religions of Judaism, Christianity, and Islam, are all major covenant religions and all have sacred books considered to be revelation. The particular book for each is the witness to the covenant with the divine that contains both the words of promise and of warning. Theoretically, the literal words in the books are not the covenant. The words, symbolically, are a witness to the true covenant, which is the spiritual "Word" of the covenant. To make a book and its words or sounds into the ultimate Word would be idolatry in the covenant understanding. It would be an act that substitutes specific and culturally bound words for the Holy Mystery that is God. In traditional understanding, Judaism, Christianity, and Islam all express that the words in their books witness to the fact of revelation but are not identical to revelation, which is beyond words. The Torah, the Bible, and the Qur'an, in this sense, all witness to the revelation of God, but each tradition is, in theory, careful not to reduce God to a literal set of words found in their respective sacred writings.

Sometimes practitioners of the covenant-based religions focus wholly on the words in one of their sacred books such that the words morph from words into being the Word itself. This is why we need to remember that the Bible is not really a book. The criticism of Holy Writ is an important reminder that nothing comes into human experience without passing through human experience. Everything human beings have or think about follows from the experience of the thing and its impression upon us. The Bible, likewise, is a product of cultural history and experience, and biblical criticism, with its emphasis on sources, redaction, and theologies, is the reminder that "sacred books" are not really sacred. They are symbolically sacred due to their history among people and their status in a culture. Biblical criticism and similar disciplines remind us that the experience of the "sacred" is a human experience within cultural history and not something that comes from outside cultural history. Biblical criticism tempers the human imagination so that it remains realistic in relation to religious traditions that so often and so quickly claim supernatural, and this means false, authority.

It could be said that biblical criticism is an example of the open aspect of the covenant as a written document. Such criticism opens the document to its own humanity and lets us see ourselves and our values in the covenant, that is, in its deep history and deep cultural value. The focus of the open aspect rests on the critical task of understanding a tradition in context and, with this insight, understanding that a tradition is at liberty to change over time with changing contexts.

Sometimes, though, this open aspect associated with a text is closed down by a literal reading of the text and a loss of its context. Fundamentalism, which is the popular name for literalism, is predominantly the loss of context. It is an amazing and absolute rejection of the integrity of the text even though it poses as an act of absolute honor for the text. This irony needs to be carefully understood because it is the irony that defines the modern struggle with the ancient "texts" involved in the expressions of Covenant theology.

James Barr, an original and formidable critic of Christian fundamentalism, held that the two main features of this theology consist of regarding a sacred book as inerrant and as infallible.[11] Inerrant means that the text contains no errors in its transmission from antiquity to the present, and infallible means that whatever the text says is certainly and absolutely correct. Biblical criticism indicates that these two principles are not only wrong but willfully held fallacies. It is the case that over the course of transmission from antiquity, the Torah, the Bible, and the Qur'an do have variant readings, and in some cases these variants have been repressed.[12] It is also the case that these texts originate in the context of antiquity where assumptions about how the world works differ from those commonly held today. Fundamentalism is about ignoring these basic observations that do not need to be proven since they are axiomatic knowledge, that is, knowledge too obvious to be debated. Still, fundamentalism puts these axioms up for debate, often in ludicrous ways, as if the integrity of the text was at stake. But when a text is made "context-less" through a strict insistence on inerrancy and infallibility, the text loses its connection to history. When something is taken out of the context of its historical setting it becomes subject to being interpreted only in the way the present context allows. When the biblical writings are taken out of antiquity and interpreted as if they were twenty-first century documents, the writing is transformed from itself into a twenty-first century fabrication. The writing loses its integrity because its historical context is ignored. This is the ironic way in which fundamentalism is highly disrespectful of the texts it so adamantly reveres.

One antidote to Covenant theology fundamentalism is Enlightenment theology mysticism. We can recall that Enlightenment theology is that form of theology in which the goal is to realize union between the self and the divine reality. Though the subject of mysticism is complex, we can see its basic intention of union with the divine in Jewish mysticism where the aim is a true relationship with "the Infinite" (*Ein Sof*). Mysticism is an antidote for fundamentalism because in mysticism the vision is entirely expanded beyond the limits of literal interpretation. Indeed, in mysticism a literal interpretation of a text gets in the way of understanding the text. The Torah taken literally misses the point of the Torah. The Bible taken literally misses what the Bible is about. If mysticism is about expanding the horizons of the self through union with the infinite, then literalism is the reverse of this intention: literalism is the collapsing of the text into personal and limited definitions. Similar to Jewish mysticism, Christian mysticism emphasizes union with the divine through being in Christ as the cosmic reality. A literalistic reading of the gospels misses the basic point of being in Christ, which is not something written but something experienced. Islam also has complex mystical traditions, but here, too, in the Sufi practices the aim is union with the divine. The Qur'an and its sounds serve as a metaphorical vehicle along the journey of union, but to take it all literally severely misses the point. In each of these monotheistic traditions there lie forms of Enlightenment theology that act as correctives to the fundamentalist temptations of Covenant theology. From the mystical point of view, sometimes observing the covenant becomes a case of not seeing the forest for the trees.

Christianity as a major Western religion has struggled historically with the internal tension between Covenant and Enlightenment theology. Sometimes there is an interesting balance struck between the two forms. Justin Martyr (100–165 CE) might be just such an example of balance. Martyr was able to join the covenant in the Bible with the philosophy of Plato. As a consequence he created an interesting, though not always laudable, new theology. It is difficult now to support his conclusions, but if we keep him in context we can see what he was trying to do.[13] Justin managed to see the covenant, the Word, in the universal aspects of the Logos. This meant that non-Christian witnesses to the Logos, regardless of their beliefs or backgrounds, were effectively witnesses to the Word in Christ. Socrates was such a Logos-filled witness, and in this way he was a Christian, whether he knew it or not. Abraham was also a Christian in this sense for Justin, because Abraham, by his righteousness before God, was a witness to the Logos.[14] To Justin there was an absolute tie between the covenant God made with Israel and the Logos that was the order of the universe. In other words, the covenant was effectively the cosmic order, and anyone who was a witness to the order of the universe was also a witness to the covenant. The *Dialogue with Trypho* is an example of Justin's cosmic theology, though the thoughts are set in what is now for us a strange understanding of the cosmos. In the *Dialogue* Justin thinks that the Antichrist is about to break in on the world and indeed is already "at the doors" to initiate the tribulations of the end of time and the return of Christ (using Daniel 7, Thessalonians 2:3, and a

dose of Jeremiah 4:22, among other conflated biblical allusions).[15]
The Antichrist, of course, is an anti-covenant figure who insults
God, and this is why the second coming of the Christ is at hand, for
Christ will restore the true worship of God. In the midst of these
visions Justin finds enough generosity to be relatively inclusive.
Though he is strict about ensuring infidels who insult God will suffer, he seems to favor the idea that ultimately every soul will finally
be reunited with God through the Logos. In this respect, he bal-
ances his temptation to understand the covenant as something for
a closed group of people with a mysticism that forces him to open
up the covenant to all. Justin in fact is not very clear on this point,
but we can see in him the struggle of these two aspects of Covenant
theology: its open and closed aspects.

A third feature of Covenant theology can be found in the struggles of the Apostle Paul. If the first two features were the emphasis
on social relationships and the central place of a book, the third can
be called the ongoing struggle to interpret the covenant in a new,
contemporary setting. Paul is impossible to understand without the
covenant God made with Abraham and the loyalty this covenant implies. Paul is also impossible to understand without recognizing his
sincere effort, successful or not, to translate this covenant into the
setting of Judaism in relation to the nations of the Roman Empire.

Paul at times mocks the wisdom of philosophy and looks down
upon the Greeks and their remarkable culture. He is in this way
very distant from Philo, a contemporary Jewish philosopher of
exceptional learning. In his letter to the Corinthians he asks rhe-
torically if God has not made foolish the wisdom of this world (1
Corinthians 1:20). The answer to Paul is yes. The wisdom of this
world is foolishness to God, and this fact is displayed for Paul in the
crucifixion of Jesus. A crucifixion publicly displays the powerlessness of the victim; to shame through displaying powerlessness is the
worldly wisdom of the cross, the reasoning of it. In the eyes of the
world the power of God is certainly not here. Paul, though, in place
of weakness alone sees in the cross the transformation of weakness

to strength. In the Letter to the Romans (4:19), Abraham is an example of this. Though Abraham was old, weak, and without an heir, God made both he and Sarah strong enough to copulate and bear a child of promise. Paul understands the crucifixion of Jesus in a similar fashion. The death of Jesus puts weakness on display, but God raised up Jesus in strength as a sign of the coming restitution of creation. The crucifixion as a sign of weakness is the wisdom of the world, but the act of God raising up Jesus is the strength of God that turns the wisdom into foolishness. God's folly is wiser than human wisdom.

Against this background Paul sees the covenant of God with Israel. Like a prophet, he understands himself called to bear witness to the faithfulness of God to the covenant. Like Jeremiah, he claimed his call was "from the womb" and that his call concerned "the nations" (compare Jeremiah 1:5 to Galatians 1:15–16). Paul becomes convinced that in Christ the nations are welcomed into the covenant with God. This solves for him the problem of Jews and gentiles: the problem of Israel knowing the true God while the nations of the Roman Empire do not. This was a fundamental change for Paul who formerly either had no solution to the problem or else held a different one. The change in Paul was not necessarily dramatic. In Galatians he suggests that in fact it took him fourteen years or more to figure it out (Galatians 1:18–2:1). We can guess that the change did not occur on the road to Damascus[16] but in a study room where Paul had a copy of Isaiah on his lap and read 49:6, "It is too light a thing that you should be my servant to raise up the tribes of Jacob and to restore the preserved of Israel; I will give you as a light to the nations, that my salvation may reach to the end of the earth" (NRSV). In Paul's context, as Brandon Scott significantly points out,[17] the "nations" and "the ends of the earth" are to Paul all the people living under the domination of Roman imperial authority. In Paul's mind his news about God's Anointed, the Christ, is aimed at this audience: the Greeks of the eastern provinces to be sure but also, as the letter to the Romans indicates, the people of Gaul (modern Spain) and beyond. In the Letter to the Romans, Paul indicates that he has finished saying what he wants to say to the Greeks and desires to go to Rome where the people may sponsor him to go on to Spain. Paul probably did not make it to Rome—we do not know for sure—and almost certainly did not make it to Spain, but he did live long enough to leave letters behind from his work among Greek communities.[18]

The covenant of God includes the nations of the world, and for Paul the problem is that the nations do not know this. Paul is very clear about what such ignorance means. It means that the nations operate under a different law and suffer from moral depravities like idolatry, sorcery, enmity, strife, jealousy, anger, and several other less than flattering qualities (see Galatians 5:20). This list of vices can be understood as a prejudiced view Paul holds of gentile life in the first-century Roman world. To Paul these questionable gentile habits typify the problem the nations have, which is "bondage to beings that are by nature no gods" (Galatians 4:8). The solution is liberation, which is the "world transforming news" (the good news) concerning the nations. The act of liberation consists of recognizing one's slavery to the powers that seem to be dominant, such as elemental spirits (Galatians 4:3) if not the Roman imperial government itself, and seeing the real power of the real God in the transformation of the cross from weakness to new life. Paul labors among "weak communities" who know the new strength. This is evident in the Philippians correspondence where Paul speaks to those who know weakness but who see in the humiliation of the cross the exaltation of Christ and the dawning of a new age (Phil 2:8). For Paul, then, the problem of the alienation of the nations from the covenant of God with Israel is solved in the crucifixion of the faithful Jesus in which the nations cross over from being strangers to God to being children of God, from being slaves to a different promise to being heirs of the true promise (Galatians 4:7).

What is noteworthy in Paul is that his theology is not widely shared. The disagreement with Cephas in Antioch concerns the right of gentiles to equal status with Jews that should be expressed through dining at the same table. Cephas does not agree (Galatians 2:11–16). There are certainly intricacies to understanding the confrontation at Antioch, but the point here is simply to indicate a clear disagreement existed.[19] Beyond this, when Paul appears to quote in his letters confessions from the Church in Jerusalem, it becomes evident that the theology of the Jerusalem Church and Paul's theology differ. Lloyd Gaston wrote a significant essay outlining the substance of the differences, which will not be reviewed here.[20] It can be noted, however, that whereas the Jerusalem Church sees the cross of Jesus as a sacrificial act, Paul does not share this view. The cross to Paul is a transformational act in which the nations are brought into the covenant with God. In the Jerusalem Church, Christ died for the sin of Israel; for Paul, Christ became a sin for the sake of the nations. Becoming a "sin" for the nations and then transforming that sin through the resurrection is how Paul sees the nations transformed from sinners, alien to Israel, to righteous partners with Israel. Paul re-interprets the understanding of the covenant; he awakens it in a new setting and finds within it a new expression of its meaning and a new extension of its justice imperative. Though Covenant theology can be tempted to freeze the covenant into a past time, Paul is an example of a third feature of Covenant theology, which is the ability to hold the covenant before the constant challenge of renewal in a new time. Paul is an example of how the covenant must be constantly interpreted in the setting of a new age.

In reviewing Covenant theology we can see that three important features define this way of thinking, and each feature has an open and closed aspect. The features identified were the prophetic voice of the covenant, the fact that the covenant in the monotheistic traditions is a book, and the fact that the book needs to be interpreted. The prophetic voice is open when it is focused on the justice imperative, but, as with Ezra, closed when that justice imperative collapses from international perspective to questionable ethnocentric concerns. Then, the fact that the covenant tradition for Judaism, Christianity, and Islam involves a book can be equally troubling and promising. Critical historical study opens the book because it shows that the "book" is not really a book but a collection of writings, textual variations, and genres. The criticism of the book gives to the book its context and allows the reader a chance to struggle respectfully with the contents. The lack of critical thinking, though, can close the book, freeze it in place, such that it can neither speak to the present nor be respected as a document from the past. Finally, because the covenant comes with a book, it needs to be interpreted. In this third feature the Apostle Paul was an example of someone fervently interpreting the covenant in an entirely different context from that in which the words were recorded. No writer of the Torah had an idea that one day the Jewish people would be in the Roman Empire. That was Paul's new context, and he struggled to determine how the Torah, the covenant of Israel, related to the nations of the world. The act of interpretation, though, can be denied or suppressed by refusing the value of critical thinking or denying the fluid nature of history and culture. The covenant becomes closed when, with such brutal acts of ignorance, its vibrancy is stilled, its relevancy is lost, and its words forced into oblivion.

5

Jesus the Teacher
of Nothingness

When one stands in front of an artist's great work, the natural question to ask is, what does it mean? I have gazed many times at Vincent van Gogh's *Starry Night*. I see vibrations. I wonder, what did the artist see? Did he see a divine eternity? Or was his vision set on the splendor of nature's energy? Was he theistic or atheistic: inspired by the fullness of it all or the emptiness of it all? Maybe both, maybe neither.

The nature of art is interpretation. The craft of the fine artist is not formula but vision, and every vision, to be effective, must engage others, an individual or community, in the question of meaning. It is pointless to ask if van Gogh's *Starry Night* really exists: of course it does, and it does not. It is a vision, and as such it exits, yet as a vision it truly exists only insofar as it is imagined by those who behold it.

A poet is someone who places artistic vision into words that play out the same imaginative game of existence and nonexistence, of fullness and emptiness, of being and nothingness. The poem is never really about the poem. It is mostly about the experience of the poem. It is about bringing to life the images and feelings the poem invokes. And yet the poem is not truly "there" as an object: its truth is in the experience of those who read or hear it. Its real existence is not out there in the world as an obvious thing to encounter or touch. The poem exists in a very important way: in a way that is lost in literalism but brought to life in imagination. The poem is, finally, the awakened imagination, which is something to be lived rather than touched as an object.

The trouble with the historical Jesus is that he was a poet. The form of his poetry was the artful and invocative parable, a product of his imagination. The parables of Jesus are set in the everyday world that was his life experience long ago. There is nothing in their content that is particularly extraordinary. The events depicted in parable were common. Lots of ancient peasants stood outside city gates at the crack of dawn waiting and hoping to be hired as a day laborer. Many went home empty handed. Some only managed a few hours' work. It was hardly unusual for a woman to bake bread. Children, then and now, run away from home, often holding tensile relationships with their parents. I tried the "running away from home" routine several times with my parents. Some children enjoy the fortune of a good inheritance, and it is not beyond the pale that some spend it all away. We all have enemies and depict them in distorted and unflattering images. It is difficult to accept that our enemy has dignity let alone also something to teach us. These images of everyday life were played out in the first-century Roman Empire as much as they play out today in our own cultures and societies. Kids will be kids, and people will be people. Common as these images are, they are the subjects of the parables of Jesus. At first it seems like there is nothing unusual going on in a Jesus parable. Or is there?[1]

Jesus was a poet, and his vehicle of expression was the parable. Just as a poem is not really about the poem, the parables of Jesus are not about the parables. The Prodigal Son is not really about a spoiled kid running away from home; the story of a woman searching for a lost coin is not really about the woman or the coin; the story of the Samaritan who cares for the one who fell among bandits is severely bland if it's only about how to be nice. To interpret the parables of Jesus as a set of exemplary illustrations is a disservice to the vision these stories invoke. The point of a parable is not to display good behavior or warn about reward and punishment. To take the parables in this way is to turn them into moralistic tales. Taken at face value, the parables are at best good, if airy, advice on what God would like us to do. To the contrary, parables, like good poems, are the way Jesus cast human life out on the horizon to behold, to wonder about, and to re-image. What does life mean? What liberties have human beings to think and act differently? In what ways do we get caught up in life and its struggles such that we forget it's free? These and questions like these, not moral advice, are what the parables invoke. And just like good poems, the vision the parables cast against the horizon speaks even to their creator. In the end even Jesus wondered about the meaning of the parables. It is not unusual for any artist to respond to the question of what he or she really means with the answer, "I don't know."

When we ask what Jesus meant in a given parable, we are led astray by the gospel writers who recorded it. Like us, the gospel writers had to interpret the parables, seeking, as they often did, for a deeper meaning or a secret, if colorful, explanation. The tendency of the gospel writers was to affirm first the special nature of Jesus and beliefs about him before figuring out what a parable was about. Consequently, the gospel writers see parables as coded messages from God to which Jesus, in some peculiar way, had the interpretive inside track. In taking a "hidden message" approach to the parables, the gospel writers mistakenly assumed the parables were allegories. Every character in a parable or every named item stood for something else, was secretly about something hidden and divine. In the parable of the Sower, one of the best examples of this, the writer of the Gospel of Mark assumed the seeds are the "word" sown into the world and among the hearers; in the parable of the Lost Sheep the gospel writer of Luke assumed that the sheep is the sinner whom God searches out; in the parable of the Dinner Party, the gospel writer of Matthew assumed the parable is about an end-time apocalypse with only the righteous being chosen to participate. In these and other ways the writers of the Christian gospels turn parables into coded allegories with secret, hidden messages for believers. For

Luke they are to inspire us to care for the poor; for Matthew they are to inspire us to enter the building, but Matthew would also like us to close the door behind us.[2]

The mistake of interpreting parables as allegories is characteristic of Christian gospel writers who want divinity out of Jesus and authority in his stories. It was not until 1870 that the German biblical scholar Adolf Jülicher (1857–1938) was able to recognize and name this misleading habit.[3] From the late first century and all through the Middle Ages, Christian writers had interpreted parables as allegories. They interpreted the parables as stories that held embedded signs about the divine or supernatural world. A central image in a parable was thought about like a signal, a flare from heaven, tossed into the dark human world. If we can just locate the origin of the flare, we can surely locate the dwelling place of God. When Dominic Crossan succinctly noted that "Jesus proclaimed God in parables, but the primitive Church proclaimed Jesus as the Parable of God,"[4] he was effectively defining how the parables of Jesus were turned into allegories. Parables in earliest Christianity became stories about Jesus himself, about his gospel, and his insider information about God. Each event within a parable told the reader or hearer something about the secret. When taken as an allegory, for allegory means "another or different language,"[5] a parable is assumed to be a way of expressing truth in symbolic forms. As Crossan pointed out above, the parables of Jesus effectively became symbols for the identity of Jesus and his divine instructions.

We can easily see the importance of Jülicher's scholarship when we examine the historic error of misreading parables as allegories. The error is evident whenever we delete a gospel writer's interpretation of a parable and see the parable standing on its own. When examining the resurrection of Jesus, Brandon Scott pointed out drawing the analogy from Frank McCourt,[6] how the children's rhyme about Humpty Dumpty serves as an excellent and humorous demonstration. The origins of the rhyme are unknown, but virtually everybody associates Humpty Dumpty with an egg. It is likely that the images of a "great fall" off a wall and how Humpty Dumpty can't be put back together create the association with an egg. The popular comedian Ricky Gervais[7] once claimed that the only moral he could draw from this rhyme was not to sit on a wall if you are an egg. But who said Humpty Dumpty was an egg? Though the rhyme might remind us of one, in fact there is no egg in the rhyme and no reason to assume the rhyme, in its origin, concerned an egg. Our imagination places the egg there, and in so doing we add to the story a type of allegory or extra layer about an egg. The non-existent "egg" becomes "other-speech" for a cryptic moral about carelessness.

That is how an allegory works: it places into a story a subject from the outside, and then it interprets the story symbolically as an illustration of this new outside subject. In the Humpty Dumpty rhyme, the egg is a strange but additional subject that appears for unknown reasons. In the parables of Jesus, God is the additional subject. God never actually appears in a Jesus parable but is always assumed (that is, always the allegory or the added subject). God comes into the parables because Jesus is "supposed" to be holy and is supposed to talk about God. Later Christian assumptions about the divine Jesus created, in the Christian imagination, the new allegorical subject of the parables, which must be something about God or God's reality or God's glory, otherwise why would Jesus have said it? Christian allegory (Christian "other-speech") brings into the parables of Jesus the new subject of God.

Yet, in the parables, Jesus never actually speaks about God. God is never the subject of a parable, God never appears as a character in a parable, and God is never even referred to in a parable. Even to say, as Crossan did, that Jesus "proclaimed God in parables" might betray a touch of allegory resting on the interpretation of parable. Care is needed not to assume that a parable holds its source in divine inspiration and intends, to some degree, to be a "proclamation" about God. Brandon Scott exercises such care when he indicates that a parable is about a vision and about imagination but not

necessarily about a specific meaning or idea or even reality.[8] Robert
Funk thought about the parables of Jesus as fragments of a vision
but not worked-out plans or schematics about the kingdom of God.
The persistent question in relation to the parables of Jesus is what
are the parables a vision of? The answer has always been the Empire
of God (or Kingdom of God).[9] But a second problem emerges immediately, which is how does one envision the "Empire of God"?
The speech about the empire is not direct; perhaps it is not even
implied. The parables are introduced with the phrase, "the Empire
of God is like," but that is not the same as saying, "the Empire of
God is." God cannot become Humpty Dumpty; that is, God cannot be the assumed subject of a parable when God is only at best
implied—and even then, not God but a realm of God. God cannot
be assumed to be hanging around in the background wearing the
traditional garments of an omnipotent divine being. Indeed, should
God, in any form, be added to the parables at all?

The writer of the Gospel of Mark gives us a good example of
what not to do. To return to the parable of the Sower, Mark demonstrates exactly how an allegory works. The parable is found at
Mark 4:3–8.

> Listen to this! This sower went out to sow. While he was
> sowing, some seed fell along the path, and the birds came
> and ate it up. Other seed fell on rocky ground where there
> wasn't much soil, and it came up right away because the soil
> had no depth. But when the sun came up it was scorched,
> and because it had no root it withered. Still other seed fell
> among thorns, and the thorns came up and choked it, so that
> it produced no fruit. Finally, some seed fell on good earth
> and started producing fruit. The seed sprouted and grew:
> one part had a yield of thirty, another part sixty, and a third
> part one hundred.[10]

Mark's elaborate explanation of the parable follows in verses 13
to 20 of the same chapter. Here the writer brilliantly displays each
element in the parable as a symbol of the gospel and the faithful-

ness of the hearer to the gospel. Mark effectively adds the would-be followers of Jesus to the parable as its primary and real "other" subject. The sower is presumably Jesus or an early Christian preacher, the seeds thrown are the "word," and the ground on which the seeds fall is the character of Mark's audience, the early Christians who were not yet even called Christians. Some, like seeds sown on rocky ground, hear the word but it immediately withers away; the word does not take hold in their system. Some Christians are like a tangle of thorns where the word sprouts up but then is choked off by the seductive cares of life. Finally, some seeds fall on good soil. Of course, a Christian is supposed to be like good soil, someone who allows the word to root deeply in the heart such that it bears the fruit of the gospel despite the worldly temptations and the sufferings of life. In the parable of the Sower, the gospel writer called Mark continually sows new subject after new subject into each image the parable holds. Nothing is taken to be what it is in the original story. To Mark everything in the parable is a parable (4:11). To make a parable out of a parable is the classic act of allegory.

The historical Jesus, of course, lived before Christianity had started. He told no stories about the emerging Church or the fledgling movement soon to be called Christianity. So far as we can tell, Jesus never even used the word "Christ," unless perhaps he ever referred to Cyrus the Great.[11] Jesus was not teaching anything about a new religion; it is doubtful he would have understood what he had to say was "religious" at all. We have seen, after all, that the word religion as we use it today only arose in the fifteenth century. In place of a religion Jesus offers a poetics of life construed within the Roman Empire and reflecting both his peasant status and experience. As poetry, the parables escape exact meanings because they are works of art. But Mark misses this. Like the other gospel writers Mark too is busy seeing God in Jesus and focusing on what God's Christ is really up to. Since Jesus is God's Christ, God's Anointed, he must have a mission (otherwise, why call him the Anointed), and that mission must be evident in the one thing about Jesus the gospel writers knew with confidence: that he told parables. So it is that Mark can quickly convert the parable of the Sower into the allegory of the Sower where the real subjects are the hidden ones: the preachers, the word, and the hearers of the word.

To hear a Jesus parable as a parable, which means to hear a parable as a poetic work of art, it is necessary to use some basic tools of the historical-critical method. This method allows us to recognize that the commentary Mark adds to the parable in verses 13–20 do not belong to the parable at all. These interpretive comments are the compositions of Mark; they are Mark's theology. They are Mark's way of looking at a work of art and interpreting its meaning. Additionally, when comparing Mark's version of the parable to the version found in the Gospel of Thomas 9:1–5, it is possible to construct an earlier, closer to oral form of the parable—something near the original story. These basic critical moves allow us to see the parable as it stood before Christian theology was developed and laid upon it. Then, taking the parable out of the hands of the early Church requires us to place it back into the context of peasant life in the first century. This must also be done with critical sensitivity.

With these two acts accomplished, that of identifying an earlier tradition of the parable and that of placing it in context, I will take a shortcut from here into the parable to read it as a poetic presentation. First, a proposed earlier form of the presentation:

> Now a sower went out, took a handful of seeds, and scattered them. Some fell upon the path and the birds came and devoured them. Some fell on rock, did not take root in soil, and they did not produce. Other seeds fell among thorns and the thorns grew up and choked them. And other seeds fell into good soil and brought forth fruit coming up and growing and bearing one thirtyfold, and one sixtyfold, and one a hundredfold.[12]

There are so many minor elements in this story that cause us to wonder about what sort of vision is expressed here. The enigmas are the same ones we encounter with great painters, great playwrights, great novelists, and great tellers of parables. First, as Hal Taussig pointed out, we have to ask the honest question. Who taught this guy how to sow?[13] If the hearers of the parable included peasant farmers, the opening descriptions are hilarious. What is the sower doing, planting a crop or feeding the birds? Yet despite this we are led on by our hope for a happy ending, and this is where the Jesus parable haunts the interpreter. It seems to be building up to an intense bliss. Despite the "screw-up," as Taussig put it, a great crop comes in.[14] But are we being misled here? Is it really a great crop? This raises the second major question for the parable. What is a great crop for a peasant in the Roman Empire? What did the landlords want out of the land, and how much yield was considered superb? Brandon Scott indicates convincingly that we should really expect something like one hundred, two hundred, and four hundred fold. Such a progression starts out modestly, then doubles, and doubles again. It ends with a remarkably good yield, something defining a great harvest in the ancient world. One hundred by itself would be disappointing, four hundred, six hundred, and eight hundred are the numbers that move from excellent to miraculous. This parable has none of those numbers. It ends with the modest one hundred. In addition, the parable is flat in the way that it ends. Its numbers are thirty, sixty, and one hundred. The progression is first double, from thirty to sixty, and then less than double, from sixty to one hundred. The numbers move up the scale but not in the manner expected, thirty, sixty, and 120. It is like the words are set up to resemble an orchestra crescendoing to a grand climax. The conclusion names a yield that is doubled and then doubled again—suggesting a build-up that might be considered a marvel. Then, at a crucial point the orchestra's crescendo fizzles into a note that sounds slightly flat. A double measure crests at a lower than expected and certainly average yield. We anticipate the miracle but we get the average. We hear no climax but instead a sad trombone sound. In one of the most significant books on the parables of Jesus, Scott concludes that the outcome of the harvest disappoints.[15] This peasant worker receives no miracle. If this parable reflects a vision of God, it is not the almighty God. But God, of course, is not in the parable. What is in the parable is human *pathos*, the heart wrenching tragedy of life in poverty where there lies some comedy in the midst of debt. The vision here is relayed through a type of set-up. It plays with our wish for triumph, our hope for the underdog, and our instinct for resolution. But what it delivers to us is life in both its brutality and honesty. We are, in the end, brought down to earth and must feel deep sorrow for the figure who fails as a sower and as a family provider.

Failure, it seems strange to say, is the nature of wisdom. It seems strange because the common mantra in life is about success. Especially when it comes to God, is it not all about gaining favor and enjoying success? How can failure pose as wisdom? Yet, a saying or a story or a painting is wise, or can be, when it withholds something from us, when it remains elusive, when its success holds the shadow of failure. If wisdom was simply about giving the right answer to a question, oddly, we would never learn anything. The greatest teachers withhold something and make the student struggle. The greatest teachers have students who are lost and who, therefore, will not settle for the easy answer. When Socrates claimed that his wisdom consisted of his ignorance, he was withholding. No one can know how wise Socrates was because he became the search for, and not the finding of, wisdom. To understand Socrates is to lose him as a human being and to gain him as the search for our humanity. It is something like this with a parable of the historical Jesus. The parables withhold something, they draw back, and take with them a final resolution. Sometimes they deliver elements of comedy, sometimes elements of tragedy, and sometimes elements of reconciliation, but they always withhold. There is a "not this or that" element in a Jesus parable, an emptiness within the parable, that defies a final conclusion. It is in this way that the parables invite us into their vision. It is the emptiness of the parable that converts the story from being just a story into being a way to be in story. When the parable hits its mark the hearer is no longer just hearing a story; the hearer is now in the story or part of it, for the story becomes life and how one lives it. The tragedy is to say that it is only a story, and even a stupid story at that, for who would sow precious seeds in such a ridiculous manner? The tragedy is to seek advice from the parable and realize, in this regard, that it is empty. But a hearer becomes a student when filled by this emptiness, filled by the invasion of nothingness into all that is, and overwhelmed by the gratuitousness of it all. The "good student" becomes the parable, the student of life, who awakens in the emptiness of the parable to the fullness of being alive. In the end, though, maybe it is only a story, and Jesus did not know what it meant any better than we do. It really depends on how the story is heard and whether life is awakened by means of it. The parable really depends on whoever has ears to hear.

Jesus as a teacher whose lessons hold emptiness with a content of failure is not necessarily appealing. Someone who teaches things about nothing is not usually someone of mass appeal. Nothingness, for example, makes a poor political platform and does not get very far in the settings of a mega-church. Nevertheless, as we know, nature no less than the Church abhors a vacuum, which is how a teacher of nothingness can become a substantive thing like Christianity. Christianity emerged from all that was crammed into the silence of Jesus. Where Jesus emptied, the church filled. And where parables dug into the *pathos* of being human, the church planted signposts of something bigger and better, the Kingdom of God. When the poetic discourses of Jesus were taken from a context of pedestrian wisdom into the ornamental power of God, the parables became secondary to the nature of Christ. Few today, when describing Christianity and what Christians believe, start with parables. Rather the Apostles' Creed is the usual reference point and the location from which a parable is interpreted. Hence a return to Dominic Crossan's fine statement, "Jesus proclaimed God in parables, but the primitive Church proclaimed Jesus as the Parable of God."

If Christianity should one day become about what Jesus said and not about who Jesus was, then emptiness will come into play as that unavoidable silence covering human experience. Emptiness can have no theology since it is not about what is spoken but what remains after the words are said. A parable as a poetic construction is a form of saying that un-says what it presents, and thus invokes the quandary and the question of its meaning. A shepherd goes out to find a lost sheep and returns to celebrate the find with a great feast that includes several sheep in the meal. A woman searches and finds a lost coin, and then spends more than the value of the coin to celebrate finding it. A man finds a hidden treasure in a field, but he does not own the field. So, he deceptively remains silent in order to buy the field and steal the treasure. The idea of having treasure leads him to fraud where his moral self is lost. These three parables, the Lost Sheep, the Lost Coin, and the Hidden Treasure, are rarely seen as sleight of hand moves that open the undoing of the action that is done. They are so rarely seen this way because the Christ and God and the mightiness of God get in the way. Jesus Christ is the great treasure of Christianity who has displaced the teaching of Jesus with the historically questionable morality of the Church.

To talk about emptiness and nothingness as themes of the historical Jesus sets thinkers and hearers alike on an uncharted course. It brings Jesus in line with the great Qoheleth, the writer of Ecclesiastes, the supreme teacher of wisdom who wore the clothing of Solomon to voice the struggle for meaning. Human beings do not have meaning automatically given to them in life; it is something that must be shaped as if a sculpture out of the raw material we receive at birth. The material is the setting we are born into, the genetic disposition we inherit, the wealth our families hold, the reasoning our community assumes, the moral code our tradition bears, and the forms of national patriotism that seek to forge our identities and win our loyalties. To face and overcome all of these things, to be someone who cannot be reduced to the ideologies of any one of them is, as Jesus would have said, to gain the self by losing the self and, as the philosopher Michel Foucault said, "to become someone else that you were not at the beginning."[16] A theology of emptiness is not in the Christian deck of cards to deal out but rather in the hearer to whom, upon such exposure, is delivered the questions rather than the answers of life. And how else can such subjects be raised except in poetic acts? The dogmatic act of working out an answer is an explanation that belongs briefly to its time but soon evaporates. But a poetic expression, an image, a vision, a parable, takes the context of life and opens to it the emptiness of being, which is the eternal question. The question that escapes an answer is always the question that returns. It is always the question now. It is always the present that opens but never the answer that closes.

In the history of Christianity Jesus is usually the answer; he is usually the door that, having been opened briefly, closes permanently. Like the Gospel of Matthew, the Gospel of John has the sense that the Christian door should be closed once a believer has entered. Jesus explicitly is the door in John (10:7–9) as well as the way, the truth, and the life (14:6). Yet, Jesus is so only to lead people across a threshold. Having entered the room, the act that Matthew liked emerges with John, too. The door is closed on the outside world, which is also the condemned world. The Jesus of history taught love your enemies, which is an ironic aphorism that cancels barriers of hatred between people, but the gospel writer of John teaches "love one another," which is love among people inside a club behind a barrier and with an entry fee. Where Jesus had shattered the very possibility of enmity, which after all relies on a small mind, the Gospel of John does all it can to rebuild a wall as a rampart against the world and to shut out the enemy. The great temptation of any religious system is seen in the writer of the Gospel of John. The temptation is to avoid the emptiness of life and its perpetual question by satisfying the desire for security, closure, and insular reasoning. The temptation is to define religion with a small mind.

The Jesus of history, though, is the one known to us as the teller of parables. He is not the history of Christianity, though he is its subject. He is, rather, Christianity's own built-in anti-Christ, the one who delivers the unwinding of its dogma. He does so in the face of positive claims about him with the elusive vision of the parables. Whereas a dogmatist will want to make that vision a statement about truth, the historical Jesus spurns such temptations by making truth the thing the parable is prepared to void.

The truth about God should be a mighty and certain truth that is on our side of history, but parables like the Good Samaritan show that the reality of God is in and with our enemy. Parables like the Mustard Seed display the reality of God humbly in relation to a weed-like plant that is anything but mighty, and a parable like the Hidden Leaven relates the presence of the divine to the utterly non-divine sign of leavened bread. A Jesus who takes away what is given is a Jesus who plays with fullness and emptiness or perhaps one who fools us with fullness only to slip in emptiness. Let there be no mistake, however. Emptiness is not a letdown; it has nothing to do with disappointment. It is awakening. It is part of recognizing the "now-ness" of time, the way time is not set on a predetermined course but is open to new possibilities. The energy of a parable is its vision carved into story in order to awaken the immediate gift of awareness, the recognition of the possible, and the realization that the "now" is both all we have and all the universe has to offer. The crime is to forfeit the fullness of this emptiness for the deceptive fullness of dogmatic securities.

It is natural, of course, for human beings to be conservative since the most basic and instinctive act is to preserve our lives. The parables of Jesus attempt to replace the instinct to preserve with a foreign instinct to give away. It is an almost impossible task, but it is a move that reveals his poetry as if it were a voice from the outside.

To the historical Jesus the covenant is that which comes from the outside and breaks in upon the people and guides their way of being. What is strange about Jesus is that the covenant is oral and poetic. It is lived as an alternative vision realized in performance. The covenant does not hold itself as its own subject any more than Jesus is the subject of the parables of Jesus. The covenant is not about the covenant; understood in parable the covenant is about life. The covenant is about opening life to alternative ways to be in life. It is about pouring out or emptying the covenant into life. We might say that for the historical Jesus, if we attempted to catch the spirit of his theology and the way in which enlightenment and covenant thinking defined it, the covenant is the presence of God insofar as it is the experience of the eternal now. It is hard to know whether the historical Jesus knew anything about the great Rabbi Hillel or things that he reportedly said, but we can hear in Jesus something of the question of Hillel, which is "if not now, when?"[17] When the covenant becomes as the reality of God conceived as the eternal now, that is the only reasonable question left. If not now, when?

Is the historical Jesus, then, primarily an enlightenment or covenant theologian? Unlike Paul with whom the covenant works out its meaning in relation to the nations, Jesus leaves us nothing written but only a memory of oral presentations in parable. The question about the theology of Jesus in this way makes less sense. Parables express his poetry, and his poetry is closer to Qoheleth than to Paul. Even further, poetry when defined is not defined, for the poetic expression is elusive and interpretive. To define a poem is to kill it. Jesus was a child of the covenant but worked out its meaning through the elusive form of the parable, through stories composed from the threads of daily life that rarely hold explicit conclusions. The promise of a great yield in the parable of the Sower never materializes; the runaway boy in the Prodigal Son returns home but never gets back the inheritance he had wasted. Our expectations in the parables expand as a balloon and then Jesus takes out a needle to puncture them. He collapses the story into the absolute nature of real life, its drudgery and disappointments as much as its false hopes and deceiving beliefs. In this, he is able to raise that Zen-like question about getting into life as it is and not betraying oneself with deceiving schemes and self-serving ideologies. The parables of Jesus empty life back into life and, in this way, fulfill it. They do not call us to the distances of an apocalyptic end time. They ask for a turn to the now and for a vision of the now as the possible.

The parables are open, then, and in their openness are elusive. They open up the now as a certain platform of authentic experience, and in this way the parables express God's reality not as a location but as a form of being, not as a future time but as an eternal now. The parables bring us into life, but they express in life the fundamental nature of the covenant as the revision of life. In relation to Jesus the Christian religion had to come to grips with an elusive teacher, and in some ways it had an example in Paul who gave to Christianity its basic metaphor of the body of Christ. Paul, to his credit, was inventing a way that the covenant could be expressed to the nations as "world transforming" news. His voice was that of creative rhetoric. The Church, in its later times, took Paul too seriously and created from his rhetoric a new subject called dogmatics—the study and explanation of doctrines. In so doing, the Church also created Jesus Christ as its supreme avatar and its covenant. Still, what type of theology did the historical Jesus hold? The parables of Jesus leave little option but to relate his vision to the enlightenment struggles found in Qoheleth. For Jesus enlightenment comes through the covenant whenever the covenant becomes the energy of transforming vision given in parable. The question is how did the Christian church manage to mistake such an open, elusive, and transforming vision for closed, certain, and dogmatic claims? One answer is found in the deliberations of the Council of Nicaea in the year 325 CE.

6

Creating God
in 325

Life defined biologically is energy used to maintain a semi-permeable membrane. In the process of using energy this way, an organism has a metabolism, responds to stimuli, reproduces, grows, and over generations adapts to the changing physical environment.

In the year 325 CE, biology as a scientific study did not exist. Life, consequently, was defined on an entirely different plane. First, there was the basic division between matter and the spirit. Secondly, things of the spirit were either pure or impure. And finally, the desire not to reproduce (and thus to maintain purity) was the sign of a good life.

Even further, true life, when philosophically considered in the Roman Empire of 325, was centered on reason and not the misleading fluctuations of emotion.[1] The mastery of life, the great ideal of the ruling aristocracy, demanded that reason dominate emotion. This understanding of life conceived of human beings as a puzzle to be decoded. The spiritual element of the human makeup belonged to the world spirit or *logos*. It expressed itself as the principle of order through reason. It was fundamental to *enkrateia* or mastery of the self. When reason was sufficiently actualized in self-mastery, one was more or less fully alive because one was "in order," so to speak. Puzzle solved. Lacking such mastery, human beings were driven downward with the weight of their flesh to be chaotically directed by their passions. If fallen to such as state, a human being was effectively in exile from the genuine element (the spirit) of life where the real nature of life was located. This ancient way to think about life expresses itself most practically in the way people thought about disease. Inasmuch as today we look for the causes of disease in the natural functions of the body, that is in "matter," in 325 of the Common Era disease was first about the spirit. For the average physician of that era, the "obvious" cause of epilepsy was too much phlegm on the brain resulting in the imbalance of humors. The cure was related to purification practices that sought to re-balance the spirit through restrictions in diet, taking medicines, visiting the temple of a healing deity, and sometimes suffering harsh and utterly deadly treatments.[2] To be a superior human being, an ideal figure, was to have one's internal spirit participate in or even resonate with the world spirit where changes in temper did not exist. Such a person was a master of life, was fully alive, and was pure in mind. That, in 325, was about as healthy as one could get.

In Constantine's world, then, real life was about stability, and the *logos* was the permanent content of that stability. Flesh undirected by reason was susceptible to instability, which consisted of the deceptions of emotion. Unlike postmodern times in which reason too is caught in the fluctuations and diverse contexts of life, human nature in 325 consisted of the clarity of reason buried in the fluctuations of the passions. In the world of philosophy, the Roman Emperor and noted Stoic philosopher Marcus Aurelius (121–180 CE) talked about the inner spirit as the "sole guide" to a life "unviolated and unharmed" where one is a "master of pleasure and pain."[3] In the same general fashion, the philosophy of Neoplatonism, which dominated the time of Constantine, held to the dichotomy of spirit (intellect) and matter (flesh). Plotinus (204–270), the founding figure of Neoplatonism, when discussing the question of life stated that "the soul is intellectual and intellectual activity is its higher life."[4] Iamblichus, a popular Neoplatonist who died in the year of the Nicene Council (245–325), held that the first principle of the cosmos is the intellect.[5] In 325 popular imagination conceived of the world soul as a hidden element in the flesh of human beings that is realized if the passions are mastered.

When Christian bishops gathered at Nicaea to face the problem of the nature of Jesus Christ as the divine logos who appeared in human flesh, this was their cultural context. Their concern was not just an abstract theological question as it may impress us today. The question involved culture and politics. It involved the need to align Christianity with the normal view of life then in place. And it involved Constantine's great desire for political stability that would justify his entitlement to the imperial crown.

The Council of Nicaea gathered to address the identity of Jesus Christ as the logos of God. In what way was Jesus Christ the world spirit? That is how we would likely put the question in today's language. In the era of Constantine, the question concerned whether or not Christ was an eternal spirit or a created spirit. Was Christ uncreated with God in the beginning or was Christ the first creation of God at the beginning? This mattered to human life, for it concerned answering how the human spirit, the living part of us, gets into the right program of life. How does the human spirit correctly align itself with the spirit of God? How does it achieve its health, that is, salvation? Though we can repeat these questions today we cannot easily identify their significance. The difference is that we start with the matter of our bodies rather than the abstract principle of our spirit; and we answer the question about health on the premise that the body and mind are integrated, if not even co-determinate. To understand Constantine and the Council of Nicaea is to accept the task of "goin' back" to a different way or reasoning "in a foreign land," as the popular lyricist Neil Young sang.[6]

The story of Nicaea begins in politics and in the messy state of affairs Constantine inherited after the reign of the Emperor Diocletian, a shrewd and patient Emperor who is best known for persecuting Christians. Diocletian sought to bring consistency to government through a massive reorganization of state bureaucracy.

He created more and smaller provinces, dramatically increased
the civil service, officially shifted Rome from a Republic to an
Autocracy,[7] established what we might call a "cabinet" (*consilium*),
and ensured that his government had "departments" overseeing
specific functions. In this momentous overhaul, Diocletian also gave
Christianity much of its official language. He called a provincial unit
a "diocese" and the governor of each diocese was a vicar (*vicarius*),
two words Christianity loved. But all of this was built to address a
few big issues. One was the succession of Emperors. The Roman
Empire had been suffering for generations from generals rising up
to take the imperial crown and defending it against the next general
of high ambition. This led to constant turnover with only a few great
generals occasionally providing stable government. Diocletian knew
he had to solve the problem of succession. Another issue was gov-
ernance. Diocletian lived when several years of so-called "barbarian"
invasions and several generations of quickly changing leadership had
brought various levels of chaos to the functions of government.
He was determined to restore order, and with his great reforms he
expressed his vision of both peace and order. The Christians of that
era were persecuted because they disrupted the imperial designs by
adding a stubborn and insubordinate "other" to Diocletian's desire
for consistency. So, he suppressed the Christian movement while
at the same time he created a systematic way to handle transitions
of power. Diocletian made himself Augustus, which was the top
job, and co-reigned with a second Augustus (who was Maximian
250–310 CE) as his brother in power. Each of the two Augusti had
a second in command, a "Caesar," appointed under them who were
like Augusti in waiting. This arrangement of two senior and two
junior Emperors was established to solve the problem of succession
with a reasonable way to handle transitions of power. Constantine,
who will become our subject, was only a child at this time, but his
father, Constantius, was the Caesar under Diocletian.

The appointment of four simultaneous Emperors, more or less,
with two moving from a junior to a senior position, was supposed

to solve the problem of rival powers and chaotic government. Instead, and no doubt predictably, it brought to the fore the problem of a divided empire through even greater rivalries for power. In Diocletian's system, despite his intentions, tension between the Caesars was the norm. Everybody wanted to rule over a united empire as the sole Augustus. In effect, everybody wanted to be like the great Octavius Caesar of old (63 BCE–14 CE). No one accepted Diocletian's notion of shared power. In his administrative revisions, Diocletian had divided the empire into Eastern and Western realms. He had Caesars-in-waiting in both realms; one was Galerius and the other Constantine's father, Constantius. Having finished this work, in 305 Diocletian made the unparalleled decision to retire. Who retires as the Emperor of Rome? Maximian, who was the second Augustus, followed the lead of Diocletian and the two Caesars, Galerius and Constantius, were elevated to the status of Augustus. It seemed like the new system worked perfectly, but human nature is never so predictable. Galerius quickly appointed two Caesars under him, Maxentius and Severus. Galerius knew that Constantine, the son of Constantius, would be a rival and promoted as a potential Caesar under his father. Our young hero, accordingly, took refuge with his father in Gaul. Unexpectedly before he appointed a Caesar, Constantius took ill and died. This enabled Constantine to bypass the title Caesar and he claimed his father's title Augustus directly for himself. So, the political picture was suddenly very complex: there were now several Augusti or would-be Augusti simultaneously. Maxentius was present and seeking power; his father, Maximian, returned from retirement to support his son and also regain power; Galerius was present and in the mix, and his new appointment Severus was also on the scene; and our Constantine was seeking his rightful place. Thus the inevitable wars for securing power ensured. One would think in the midst of such chaos Diocletian, who was still alive, would have returned to set his creation back in order. He did not. Diocletian in retirement remained a serene and detached gardener. Meanwhile, Maxentius rebelled against Galerius, who had imposed a tax on Rome. Then, in a brief vacuum of power, Severus decided to claim the imperial title, but Maxentius defeated and killed Severus to put an end to this ambition. Maxentius held the support of his father Maximian, and the two forces combined with the intention to wrest from Galerius the control of the empire. Galerius recognized that he would not be able to defeat the forces of Maxentius and Maximian. At Carnuntum, an old Roman fort, in 308, he reached an agreement with the father and son team that allowed yet another claimant, Licinius, a chance to be Augustus of the Western Empire. The heretofore unknown Licinius joined forces with Constantine, and Constantine now entered into the fray of rivalries to defeat Maxentius and share the status of Augustus with Licinius. So, at the end of these many transitions, two claimants remained: Licinius and Constantine. Unable to share power, they too faced one another for the office of sole Emperor of Rome. Constantine was the victor.

In retrospect, Diocletian created more problems than he solved, but along the way he inadvertently made Christianity, the very religion he had persecuted, a most valuable tool for imperial unity. When Constantine defeated Licinius to stand as the sole Emperor, he did so (according to Eusebius his biographer) as if he were a combination of Alexander the Great and Moses.[8] Like Alexander, his conquering acts brought a new unity to the nations of the empire, and like Moses, his mission was divinely inspired. Constantine, somewhat uniquely, restored the dignity of a united Rome while establishing the culture of a Christian society. Even though Constantine only made Christianity legal and did not outlaw pagan and Jewish practices, he clearly saw Christianity as the ascendant vehicle of unity. The gift of the Church, for Constantine, was its built-in hierarchy of power through bishops and its consequent efficiency at dispersing information among the general population. As Eusebius so relays, Constantine understood himself to be the bishop of "external affairs" for the Church, which made the Church like his personal media giant.[9]

The sincerity of Constantine's Christian piety has always been questioned, though there is no specific reason to doubt it. What does invite general doubt about his religiosity is the way he used the Church for political advantage. He found two great ways to use Christianity as support for his projects. One was to employ Christianity as a type of nationalism. His troops in battle could rally around a cause that was posed as a just one, divinely guided. Constantine might mark, maybe even certainly marks, the first time that Christianity was converted into patriotism. Then, beyond inspiring his troops, Constantine also faced the task of consolidating a divided empire with its many ethnic identities, languages, and histories. How could the many be one? Christianity was not the sole answer to this question, but it was a major one. It was not until 380 that the Emperor Theodosius and his eastern counterpart Gratian, made Christianity the only official religion of the empire. Constantine's situation was comparatively modest and practical. He had bishops organized according to Diocletian's "diocese" model, and he had in the office of the bishop a means of popular communication. What he needed from the bishops, just as he had sought in the empire itself, was peace, cooperation, and imperial representation. He needed a deal, even a covenant, among the bishops and in the churches, set on goodwill and a common confession. He needed an ecumenical council to accomplish these basic tasks that involved inventing an official Christianity and an ultimate claim to imperial authority in the name of Jesus Christ, the universal God.

Christianity, in various ways, had been "inventing" Jesus as God before Constantine arrived on the scene, and in various ways Christianity continues to do so. With Constantine, though, the matter rose to a new and critical level. Jesus now had imperial backing. The location of the remaking of Jesus this time was not Jerusalem but Nicaea, where he would receive not condemnation but exaltation under Constantine, a new kind of Pontius Pilate. When Constantine opened the proceedings of the Council of Nicaea, unlike the original Pilate, he aimed no threat at Jesus. As the ancient historian Socrates Scholasticus (380–439 CE) recorded,[10] if any threat existed it was directed at dissenting bishops. Constantine began the proceedings by burning letters of contention written to him from various bishops in discord with one another. If this act is historical, it had the effect of the "cutting" of a covenant: Constantine could burn the letters but he also had the power to burn a bishop if an agreement was not reached. One imagines that the symbolism did not escape the audience.

Imagine what it was like to be a bishop at the Nicene Council. Think about arriving at your seat inside the chambers the council would occupy. We know what is at stake: the unity of the empire through the peace of the Church. We also know how wealthy Constantine is because of the displays set out before our eyes when entering the council. And now there he sits, in front of us, the Emperor who just burned our letters of concern. This guy means business, and he has all the power in the world to put words into action. So, we know that we better get the words right. Our task? Our task is to define the true meaning of life by way of a statement of universal and timeless validity. After all, true life, as we all know in 325, is consistency. Being fully alive is being unchanging and eternal.

From the point of view of Christianity at this time, the problem of life could be solved in three main ways. One was to emphasize that the spirit of true human identity was embedded in human flesh as its content. In other words, a type of Enlightenment theology was possible in that a human being could realize the self as a true and worthy creation of God. Coming into contact with and realizing this identity in life was to realize the stable and proper wisdom, the logos, in the midst of life's changing circumstances.

A second option was to see Christianity as a type of purity club where, once one crossed over into Christianity through baptism, there was no going back. Those who did go back only proved that they never really crossed over in the first place. They were, accordingly, "traitors" to the community. Christianity in this way was about the pure soul facing and bearing physical threats and bodily harm against the sin of bailing out.

The third option was to interpret God and Christ as Diocletian and Maximian: that is, two Augusti or principal leaders sharing one identity. In the case of Jesus and God, however, both identities are timeless, unbegotten, and unrivaled. There is no retirement option and no appointment of Caesars. God and Jesus as a single identity also means that human being can never really be pure as long as they are in the flesh. Being human is like being in a holding pattern where the body is as a station in life. It is a stop for the soul while on its way to destiny. What happens is that at this station you can get your ticket punched provided you know the right answer to the right question. Christianity, in this third way, is the set of rituals involved in answering the question and living out its implications.

The three options have names: the Arians, Meletians, and Orthodox.[11] Each was present at the Council of Nicaea, with the main players being the Arians and the Orthodox whom historians represent mainly through the Presbyter Arius (250–336) and the Deacon (later Bishop) Athanasius (296–373).[12]

The Meletians were the followers of Meletius, Bishop of Lycopolis in Egypt (his dates being uncertain). Like the Donatists in North Africa who followed Bishop Donatus,[13] the Meletians formed an independent "Church of the Martyrs" that excommunicated clergy who had denied their faith during the persecutions of Diocletian. These latter were called the "lapsed" (*lapsi*). The Meletian bishops prevented clergy who had lapsed from entering penance and reconciliation. They held that rituals like baptism and the Eucharist counted for nothing if conducted by lapsed clergy, for it was the character of the clergy that gave integrity to the ritual. The Council of Nicaea did not see it this way and issued a letter to the Egyptian churches addressing the Meletian controversy. In the letter, Meletius was allowed to continue as bishop of Lycopolis but with limited authority and no right to ordain clergy to office. The intention of the council was to isolate Meletius and prevent the growth of his movement, but of course that did not work. The movement continued into the fifth century.

At the heart of the matter for Meletius were clerics and laypeople who, under the pressure of torture, made a sacrifice to state gods. To Meletius this transgressive act revealed a false or corrupted spirit within the individual. The stance taken by Meletius, then, does not simply draw a line between the faithful and the lapsed but also puts up a wall to block forgiveness and restoration. Those in Christ stand in the purity of light, and those outside Christ stand in the darkness of error. To the Meletians, there is no transitional point set between these two states, and in the case of Christian leaders, there is no return from the dark side. This expresses a theological understanding in which the quality or health of the spirit is focused inwardly on the character of an individual and not outwardly on the rites of ordination. To the Meletians lapsed clergy were lapsed in nature. Their ordination held no dignity because their souls were corrupt. For the Nicaean Council, though, there was a recognition that while an individual needed to face penance, the rite of ordination was an independent dignity apart from the personality involved. The legitimacy of the rite rested on the transcendental Being of God acting through the ritual and not on the character of the individual enacting the ritual.

Christianity, in its historical expression, has often struggled with the question of an individual's character and the dignity of an office or rite. It remains an ecclesiastical nightmare on those occasions when a church official can use the office of the ordained to evade or avoid justice issues related to clergy simply by moving them from one church to another. The Meletians, and like them the Donatists, brought this theological dilemma forward. In the process, they inspired the orthodox Church to affirm that ordination is a dignity related to an office independent of a person's character.[14] Without the Meletians in 325 one might ask if there could have been the rationale in place, in 1870, for defining the dogma of *ex cathedra* at the First Vatican Council.[15] This is the dogma that defends pa-

pal infallibility when a Pope speaks out of the office of supreme authority of the Church. *Ex cathedra* is troubling because we must ask, what if the Pope is wrong? Should the office of Pope, in these instances, protect the Church from its own human nature? In 325 the Orthodox answered such a question with a yes.

The Meletians were a minor concern at the Council of Nicaea compared to the controversy over Arius. The followers of Arius had another idea when it came to Christianity and the problem of life. The thinking of Arius is not easy to reconstruct. The anathemas (curses) recorded following the Council of Nicaea let us know how Arius was perceived and how he was condemned, but they do not let us know what Arius had to say for himself. According to the Letter to the Egyptians, written in the name of the Council following its conclusion, it was unanimously agreed that "anathemas should be pronounced against his [Arius'] impious opinion and blasphemous terms and expressions which he has blasphemously applied to the Son of God." The letter indicates that Arius held "before he [Christ] was begotten, he was not," "there once was a time he was not," and "he is a creature and a work."[16] In these expressions, the Arian position is blatantly condemned as one that places Christ in second position to God. To Arius God is One and uncreated, but the Son follows from the Father as the first creation. So, "there was a time when Christ was not" expresses not only a belief about how things began but also a theological statement about a monotheistic conviction—that there is only one God. To the Orthodox, if Christ once did not exist but came into existence as the first creation of God, then Christ is only a typical, albeit the first typical, god-human hybrid. What's the difference between Christ's ability to offer salvation and that of Hercules, for example, or another divine-human hybrid already at hand in the lore of the ancient world? The condemnation of the council reflects the conviction that Christ must be co-eternal with God rather than a consequence of the divine act of creation. If not co-eternal, Christ cannot fully be the divine logos in the flesh, and lacking this status Christ cannot assure salvation any better than a Hercules or a Dionysus or what have you. The Nicene anathemas relay the common theological opinion, as Paul Tillich put it, that "this solution of Arius is in line with the hero cults of the ancient world"[17] and therefore would not work to place Christianity at the pinnacle of truth in the year 325.

Arius, though, is not always given a fair hearing, and it may be that his Christology (his way of thinking about Christ) makes more sense to most people today. At the beginning of the controversy, Arius wrote a letter to his bishop, Alexander, in Alexandria. Alexander died approximately 328 CE, and one imagines Arius was the bane of his existence during his final three years. Prior to the Council of Nicaea Arius wrote that Christ was the "fountain of all things" and that "all things are delivered" unto Christ, whose primal origin is in God. Arius also claimed that Christ "came forth from the Father."[18] These confessions express a Christology in which the sole reality of God (there is no God but God) is affirmed but equally where Christ is the sole imprint of God in all created things. To Arius everything that exists has a Christ nature or a Christ form. If we briefly recall Plato, what Arius has done is replace the idea of the good, which exists in all things, with Christ. Jesus Christ is the aim or proper purpose of all things and the only genuine form of salvation for human beings. In order for a human being to reach the absolute highest form of life, the logos of Christ must be realized in life, for Christ is our true human nature. For Arius, of course, we can never be exactly like Christ because we are not the firstborn of creation. We are effectively too far away from the primal reality, and our distance causes alienation from God. Nevertheless, we arise from the primal reality and are fulfilled when we return to it. The Church exists to direct our lives from the distance of our sin to the blessedness of reunification with God.

The orthodox position issued its critique of Arius based on the reasoning that God cannot save us in Christ if we do not encounter here the "Light of Light, very God of very God," as the Nicene Creed puts it.[19] But Arius did not need Jesus to be eternal with

God; he just needed Jesus to be the perfect creation of God who expressed the logos or World Spirit. Salvation for Arius is the realization of Christ within and trust that at death this inner peace leads to reunification with God. The question to debate is why did the theology Arius proposed not work for Christianity? Why isn't it good enough for Jesus to be Christ as the first creation of God?

Above I suggested that the theology of Arius was a type of Enlightenment theology where an individual can realize the Christ nature of the self. This being the case, an individual may not have needed the Church, or may even have found the Church a hindrance to the fulfillment of this promise. The Church is a guiding community, but not necessarily the authority. Perhaps it was this very ecclesiology rather than the theology that undermined the position taken by Arius. To say that "there was a time when the Son was not" implies that there is also a time when the Church is unnecessary. It implies that the vehicle of enlightenment is found in trusting the natural order of the cosmos and not necessarily the order of the Church. The mistake of Arius was twofold. He underestimated the power the Church sought to grasp with Constantine's blessing; he overestimated the ability of theology to be a creative rather than dogmatic enterprise.

This brings us down to the Orthodox position at Nicaea and the majority tradition of Christianity. There is much to say positively about the Orthodox view even though, as it emerged, it slowly outlawed the forms of pluralism Christianity had previously known. On the positive side, the Orthodox insisted that Jesus Christ was fully human in the flesh and not a demigod with a more fully developed logos-spirit than most human beings. The Orthodox position was completely comfortable affirming the full humanity of Jesus. The theology of Arius made Jesus an ideal beyond the reach of common human experience. For the Orthodox, Jesus as Christ experienced pain, hunger, oppression, and even misunderstanding like we all do. The Orthodox position, then, placed overwhelming emphasis on the incarnation of God in the flesh of Jesus Christ who, when in a good mood, forgives the whole of our humanity, embraces the temptations of our flesh, and stands in solidarity with the impoverished who suffer under our economies. Through the incarnation, the Orthodox position at its best aligns God with the despised and rejected. Potentially, the central chord of Orthodox Christianity is liberation theology in which the will of God for the earth is justice and equality and in which God is willing to suffer to reach these ends. God in Jesus Christ has taken on human weakness for our sake, becoming one with the world. This sounds excellent except that such solidarity with the poor was not the main voice of Christianity as it emerged after the Council of Nicaea.

What was really important for the council was the question of salvation, that is, the question of Jesus Christ "working" to satisfy questions about a full life. When we recall that full life means an eternal and unchanging spiritual reality, Jesus cannot be effective in this way if in Jesus the eternal and unchanging God is not encountered. Everything centered on the full identity of Jesus with God and the according necessity of his eternal divinity. This takes us back to the ancient idea of perfect health (soundness, wholeness, *soteria*, and *salve*) being understood as the state of having been "rescued" or secured from corruption. Jesus Christ is necessarily the absolutely unchanging and eternal Spirit of God fundamentally ingrained in the changing and unstable world. Jesus is so and must be so in order to save us. Jesus Christ cannot save us if he is only a being of this world, even its first creation. A being of this world is subject to time and to change, making such a being the same as any other human being. A creation of God, such as Arius proposed, is not the absolute spirit of God that necessarily breaks into the world from outside in order to save that which is corrupted by the world. Jesus Christ, in this orthodox sense, must be of one substance with the Father, co-eternal and uncreated, *in order to be* the savior who brings to earth from outside or above the full and final intention of God.

The council needed a way to place Jesus Christ fully into the supernatural Godhead and it also needed to preserve the Christian confession of the monotheistic God. When young people today, and older ones too, think that the Christian Trinity is complicated if not incomprehensible, it is because it tries simultaneously to do these two things: ensure the full presence of salvation in Jesus Christ on earth and preserve the monotheism of God in heaven. As the Bishop Gregory of Nazianzus (c. 329–389) famously said, "For that which he [God] has not assumed he has not healed."[20] If the absolutely divine Jesus did not assume absolutely human flesh, then Jesus cannot "heal" humans but merely represents them in a special way. The Nicene formula with its emphasis on the divine Jesus remains both the supreme ecumenical statement about the nature of Jesus Christ as the same essence or being (*homo-ousia*) of God and the supreme confessional statement about Jesus suffering for the sins of the world. With the conclusion of this council, Constantine had his theological settlement. There was now a God for the empire, and there was also a Church to defend the divine right of kings, or emperors as the case may be.

The rise of the Orthodox position in Christianity is an incredible story of creative, religious engineering. It managed a seemingly impossible task. It took the ancient understanding of a necessary and unchanging God and combined it with the changing conditions of human beings. It became a dynamic statement about how God truly embraces both human and divine elements.

Yet, this marvelous and imaginative solution, despite itself, manages to hold some striking drawbacks. The Orthodox position holds that Jesus is "fully human," but this betrays a fictional understanding of reality. No human being, even the fully human kind, is also at the same time perfectly, eternally, and absolutely divine. Jesus cannot really be human in the Orthodox statements precisely because he is not human. No human anywhere also just happens to be God. At least with Arius there was hope that human beings could realize their potential. In the Orthodox expression, this hope is significantly crushed. No one can be like Jesus. We can only depend on Jesus (and the Church) for salvation. The second very difficult aspect of Christian Orthodoxy is the hopeless way it treats human nature. By default, a human being is permanently separated from divine potential. Only Jesus Christ bridges this gap, but he can do so only through our negative confession of helplessness. Human beings must confess the helplessness of their flesh before the purity of Jesus Christ. This dictum of confession gave the Church, historically, tremendous power over the souls (the psychologies) of individuals. Even though the Orthodox statement from antiquity intended to solve the question of health (salvation), it effectively created a Christianity where a damaging and guilt-ridden psychological dichotomy between the spirit and the flesh became the norm.

What might be the egregious error in the Orthodox expression of Christianity is the way it betrays the humanity of Jesus, making him significant not because he lived but because he died. The Nicene confession claims that "he was born of the virgin Mary, suffered under Pontius Pilate, was crucified, dead, and buried." As is often indicated, the appearance of the historical Jesus in this confession is reduced to the comma between his mother Mary and his suffering under Pontius Pilate.[21] In the Orthodox tradition, despite the confession of his full humanity, the Jesus of history does not really matter. What does matter significantly is that he is the eternal and unchanging Word of God not spoken but crucified for our sins. The great thing about his death is his resurrection, and the great thing about his resurrection is that he is returning to judge the world, and the great thing about his return is that it never happens, leaving the Church in charge. In the Orthodox tradition of Christianity, it became extremely important that the historical Jesus who relayed his vision in the poetry of parables be reduced to silence before the Church and its rituals of salvation.

The Christian church evolved from its early pluralism into the more efficient and authoritative form of Orthodoxy. The attractive advantages of this development were not lost on Constantine and his desire for unity in the empire. Constantine was a political genius who well knew that an emperor needed a religion on which to rest his power. After being the persecuted child, the Church was all too eager to gain Constantine's trust by helping his cause along. The cause, though, ends up pushing Christian alternatives like the Meletians and Arians to the side. Constantine in this way was both the birth and death of Christianity. Empires do strange things to religions, and one thing they certainly do is advocate intolerance. When the imperial desires of Constantine coupled nicely with the advantages of a universal church, a perfect storm arose to define new doctrinal norms for Christianity and to set in place powerful social identities for empires yet to come.

When Jesus, a teacher of nothingness who told parables, is lost to the Church that seeks to cooperate with power, the important questions about Jesus become questions about his identity with God, his authority over society, and his ability to provide for salvation. With the loss of Jesus the teacher and with the gain of the backing of Constantine, the Church conceived of itself as the house of salvation. It was and is a house that no longer translates directly into a house of character development or a house of spiritual maturity. It sadly, to my mind, very rarely translates into a house of education. The Church, at least from the perspective of history, has a hard time asking itself, "What does it profit to gain the whole world but lose your soul" (Mark 8:36)?

We might ask, as this chapter concludes, what then is the expressed theology in the rise of the Orthodox form of Christianity? It is a theology creatively constructed from both Greek and Hebrew sources. The value of philosophy is evident in the understanding of God as eternal and unchanging and in the idea of truth related to the purity and stability of the logos. But it remains necessary for the

Church to house in ritual the doorway to these divine benefits. The Church has a covenant in this sense with the people. It is certainly one influenced by the Hebrew Bible, though it is not necessarily one that demands ethical behavior and the love of one's enemies. What it does demand is the recognition of the Church as the keeper of salvation with a basic agreement in place: confess sins to office holders and receive blessings. This new form of covenant with the Church rests on the power and truth of the incarnation. It rests on understanding Jesus not as a supreme teacher but as a supreme avatar.

7

Meet the New Jesus, a Christian Avatar

What did Jesus mean or not mean when he told the parable about the Samaritan? We need to use the art of biblical criticism to identify the story; once such criticism has done its job, we can stand before the parable, letting go of the critical act, to behold its beauty. The Samaritan parable is not a theological doctrine. It is an artistic achievement.

The main metaphor of the historical Jesus was the Empire of God. It is a place "away from here," as Kafka's deft parable so put it,[1] accessed only by "meta-phor," which means to carry across. What is unexpected is that when Jesus talks about the Empire of God he never mentions the Empire of God. His metaphors are playfully indirect. In place of straight talk, his vision comes alive in the ambiguities of everyday life that hold no metaphysical propositions. A setting in life demands the appreciation of context, which is why one employs historical critical methods, but a setting in life also expresses something trans-historical, which is basic human behavior. Parables do one of two things. They bore us or they change us. Much depends on the teller of the tale and whether the time is right for us to hear it.

The history of the Jews and the Samaritans from the birth of Israel to the time of the Roman Empire is a very difficult one to tell. Many pieces of the puzzle are missing, and the story definitely has two points of view. The Samaritan people descend from the northern nation of Israel and are those who remained after the Assyrian conquest of 722 BCE. The Jewish people descend from the southern nation of Judah and are those who were forced into exile after the Babylonian conquest about 600 BCE and returned to Judah about one hundred years later. From the Samaritan point of view, the Jews of Judah changed the religion of Yahweh while in exile and only the Samaritans remained the true Israel. In their eyes they were and remain today the true heirs of the ancient tradition. They have the right Torah, the right Mountain, the right Priesthood, and the right location for the Temple. They are exactly the same as the Jews of Judah, except they are the opposite. Both traditions have ancestors like Abraham and Sarah, a common Exodus story that features Moses, and a Torah given to Moses by God on a mountain. It is not unusual for heated enmity to exist between people who share common histories and who remain difficult for outsiders to distinguish. Catholics and Protestants, Sunnis and Shias, Vaishnavites and Shaivites all share history, basic beliefs, and common doctrines, and yet in history all these groups have had their turn at persecuting each other. So it is that, to the ancient Jewish audience, a heroic Samaritan sounded like an oxymoron. Can there be a Samaritan who not only knows the Torah but does it better than the three Jewish identities the parable presents: a priest, a Levite, and our expected common hero?

We all know stories involving the rule of three. A priest, a minister, and a rabbi walked into a bar. We know immediately to expect humor. Two characters will do something relatively typical, and the third character, whether the priest, minister, or rabbi will provide the unexpected humor. The Good Samaritan parable is like that. It presents three characters, of whom the first two perform typical acts. The first character is a priest, and the second a Levite. Both are revered in public but easily represent the hypocrisies of religious experts. The priest and the Levite fail to observe the most basic imperative of the Torah: when someone is in trouble, help. The third person should provide the punchline. A commoner, perhaps even the town fool, should come along to provide the irony. A nobody who does not really know anything will innocently fulfill a *mitzvah* or work of the Torah without a second thought. The educated professionals only know how to talk the talk, but walking the walk is left to others. Our hero is supposed to be one of us who shows, as Paul would have said, the foolishness that shames the wise and the weakness that shames the strong (1 Corinthians 1:27). But the parable ends with shock rather than humor. In place of nodding our heads, we are outraged. It is our enemy, the one who has the wrong Torah, the wrong mountain, and the wrong temple, who yet does the Torah as it should be done and does it better than we could have imagined. There is no way a Samaritan should have been anywhere near the scene. The victim, if he was able, would have commanded the Samaritan not to touch him. In his helpless state, however, the victim cannot resist the Samaritan. How embarrassing! Imagine having to go home after such treatment by your sworn enemy, telling your family this unexpected tale, and then asking them to guess who you have invited home for dinner. Imagine the original audience being asked to accept a Samaritan as a figure of righteousness and even as an example to be followed. Are we, as Jews, asked to be Samaritan in this parable; as Protestants, asked to be Catholic; as Sunnis, asked to be Shia? In its context this is both a beautiful and disgraceful story.

In Christian history there is a great distance between the first-century Jewish setting of Jesus and the orthodox beliefs defined in the Nicene Council and beyond. To the average Christian today, the Samaritan no longer stands as the outrageous suggestion that our Torah or Gospel might be a little off in some places. Rather, the Samaritan represents an exemplary citizen of high morals. The parable that once upon a time provoked became, with the distance of time, the moral that instructs. This basic difference between Jesus set in first-century Judaism and Jesus of later Christian interpretation also marks the separation between the historical Jesus and the Church. The historical Jesus tells a story that has no direct interest in God. The Empire of God, already an indirect expression, is not mentioned in the Good Samaritan parable. What is present is a picture of an alternative way to experience life. The historical Jesus consistently presents alternatives through common experiences. The Samaritan story is not about God but about an experience of the "Empire" of God; an experience in daily life not given over to a direct correlation with God. Jesus Christ, on the other hand, who developed over time and whose being became the subject of the Council of Nicaea, is in direct correlation with God. Jesus Christ is not a parable but a metaphysical construct. The word metaphysical refers to something "after the physical," that is, something abstract and supernatural (beyond the physical senses), and as I use it in relation to Christianity the word denotes how Jesus, after his death, became about matters "after" or beyond physical life. The Nicene Council, as we saw, did not care about the Jesus who lived but only about the "after" Jesus who died to become a set of doctrines. No one, of course, is directly at fault for the transformation of Jesus from a physical human being who told stories about common experiences to a metaphysical God who offers salvation through doctrines. Over time Christianity created Jesus in this way and, in the process, turned everything about Jesus and his parables into everything about God and salvation.

A quick return to the parable of the Samaritan and a look at the famous theologian Augustine (354–430 CE) offers a case in point. Augustine is often used as an example of how not to read a parable, and it is frightfully easy to see why. Augustine was a supreme crafter of Western philosophy and psychology, but one thing he was not was a good biblical critic. To Augustine the Samaritan parable dances with metaphysical meaning. Jerusalem represents the peace of heaven. Jericho represents our mortality. The beating of the traveler on the road to Jericho represents the brutal persuasions of sin. The priest and the Levite are, respectively, the law and the prophets. The Samaritan is Christ, the Inn is the Church,[2] and the innkeeper is the Apostle Paul. Augustine even adds more: the binding of the wounds is the sign of the containment of sins and the Samaritan's pack animal is the Body of Christ.[3] It is not that

Augustine is foolish, for even today the best of us do not really know what Jesus might have been up to in this story, but we see in Augustine the glaring fact that he lives after the Council of Nicaea and with the assumption that Jesus Christ is fully divine and of one substance with the Father. Whatever Jesus is doing in his parables, for Augustine, he is no artist talking about life. Since Jesus is God, his words are signals of the divine drama of the creation, the fall into sin, and the salvation of humankind. Augustine mistook an assumption about metaphysics for the vision of Jesus. The Christian Church today largely carries on in the same way, although with not as much flare as Augustine. Most leaders in Christianity will take the parable about the Samaritan as a moral story about being a decent person. We take the story as moral instruction because we hold the metaphysical assumption that Jesus "came to earth" from beyond to teach us something about God's proprieties. Certainly, we ought to do what is good and help those in need. That's a fine reading of the story, so far as it goes. But more than this the story is telling us that perhaps our form of Christianity leaves a bit to be desired and that perhaps to be a real Christian it is necessary to be more than just a Christian. We cannot truly be human in the limitations of any one religion, for every religion in theory teaches us to move beyond the borders of our egos. To be a Jew or Samaritan or Muslim or Buddhist it is not enough just to be these identities: we become human in religion when we learn about ourselves from those places outside ourselves.

Christianity did not develop with a human Jesus. It did not become popular on the basis of his stories about life in the first-century setting of his world. It did not develop in a way that would shatter human egos and cultural assumptions and open its adherents to other teachings and traditions. By not seeing the righteous "Samaritan," that is, the beauty and integrity of another religious or secular tradition, and by not having the grace to admit that perhaps Christianity falls short here and there, the Church instead developed a self-righteousness that distanced itself from Judaism and that by the fourth century of the Common Era proclaimed Jesus as the only way to God. The historical Jesus enlivened Moses and the Torah in parable; in history, the Church replaced Moses and the Torah with doctrinal beliefs involving the crucifixion and resurrection.

Following the Council of Nicaea and after the Jesus of Christianity moved from being human to being of one substance with God, Jesus was no longer a member of the covenant community but now the God who gives another covenant from on high. He is the new Jerusalem, divine in nature, and the bridegroom of the church. With the meaning of the symbols now passing back and forth between the Church and Jesus, where one refers to the other and where earthly matters are heavenly matters, all parables became revelations of heaven and all teachings took on the authoritative status of divine metaphysics. It must be said that this shift in status for Jesus from storyteller to divine revelation was part of the process of Jesus becoming the *logos* of philosophy. Jesus was given to the world, if we put it this way, out of the Jewish tradition, but the world that received him was that of Greek philosophy. In Jewish philosophy the idea of the covenant is central, but in Greek philosophy the idea of stability is central. This brings us back to two types of theology, Covenant and Enlightenment, but this time we will look inside the Christian imagination as it developed in the Middle Ages.

It is often repeated that in Christianity Jesus became Plato for the masses. This curious remark, originating with Friedrich Nietzsche,[4] indicates how in Jesus God employs imperfect human flesh to signify eternal, unchanging truth. In the same way that for Plato an imperfect physical object reflects a hidden and perfect form, so Jesus reflects in a concrete human form the heavenly perfection of the God he (also) is. The difference, though, is authority. In Plato, the heavenly world holds all the perfect forms, we might even say spirits, that give order to worldly phenomena. As reviewed earlier, we can see things and distinguish between them because our intellect grasps the principle of things, or the order of things, hidden in variable appearances. A physical object like a cup, to use Diogenes

Laërtius's example, has "cupness" that makes it identifiable within its family despite all the variations of cups in the world. "Cupness" is the hidden principle of cups, the spirit of cups, which we grasp because our intellect holds *logos* or the world spirit of order. Plato rarely refers explicitly to his Theory of Forms but rather holds this theory as his *modus operandi*, and he explores this idea through dialogues that unfold its meaning.[5] Also, it is worth noting, the highest form for Plato is the Good, which is the form we ought to love. The structure of this basic theory, which I have called Enlightenment theology, falls into Christianity from Greek philosophy as if into a royal court. Because the orthodox form of Christianity emerged with the companionship of the imperial state, its theology could not help but don the regal clothing. What I mean here is that the operating assumption of Christian theology fast became, in the Middle Ages, the principles of order and authority. Jesus became the substance of these two elements as well as the great Christian avatar who expresses them. The state, for its part, took on Plato's idea of the Good, for it was that through which the social will of Christ was to be manifest on earth.

The Jewish covenant with God is both the social expression of the will of God and the problematic situation in which God's will is combined with royal figures and government policies. When restricted in meaning to the Torah and Mount Sinai, the covenant is sometimes poorly represented as stringent decrees. The author of Deuteronomy might have something to do with this impression. Deuteronomy prefers an authoritative God who gives the Torah as a path to be followed with quite serious consequences for failure. Still, even in Deuteronomy the people are free to ignore the Torah if that is their sincere choice (Deuteronomy 30:19).[6] When the Torah is given to the people in the Exodus narrative, God is very upset at the people for deciding a golden calf is more attractive. However, in contrast to the absoluteness in Deuteronomy, Moses is able to negotiate with God in the Exodus narrative, and God consequently allows the people another chance (Exodus 33:12–23).

In the Genesis narratives, Abraham and God engage in negotiation over the destruction of Sodom, and Abraham draws concessions from God.[7] The covenant in Judaism is certainly serious, but for the writers of Genesis to Numbers it is not uncompromising. To use terms from Western legal history, the covenant is more like common law than legislative law. It is more like law that arises from the history of people interacting with it and determining its meaning in circumstantial settings than like uncompromising dictates that are incredibly hard to change.

The idea of covenant arrived in Christianity with Jesus as its foundation. It was received from Judaism with the philosophical proclivities of Platonism, and we must admit that as a result some strange consequences followed. One was that in Christianity Jesus became the assumption behind the covenant. He was and is the one who makes it true and who, as its *logos* content, is necessarily immovable and immutable. In other words, Greek philosophy made a human Jesus into something like legislative law: dictates that are incredibly hard to change. In ancient Greek philosophy, with the noted exception of Heraclitus,[8] if something can change, then the very fact that it can change proves it is not true. So Jesus Christ is the permanent and transcendental truth distinct from the historical Jesus who once appeared in the flesh but is not known this way anymore.[9] Prominent theologians of the recent past such as Martin Kähler, Karl Barth, and Rudolf Bultmann all made the point that a Jesus of history, though an interesting question, is not the subject of theology.[10] The problem, as Luke Timothy Johnson sees it, is that a Jesus of history is subject to the frailty of historical research, which must change its conclusions with new or revised judgments of evidence. That is how common law works. But how can a faith tradition be subject to the changing predilections of historical research? To Johnson the subject of theology is outside the question of history, so he can conclude that "The 'real Jesus' for Christian faith is the resurrected Jesus."[11] Acknowledging Johnson's reliance on Platonic thought for such a statement, we can say that traditional

Christian thinking about Jesus Christ relies on the historic Western philosophical assumption that human existence is a variable and passing truth in which is hidden an eternal and metaphysical principle. When Jesus is received from his historical setting into this tradition, the reasoning is that he cannot be an "avatar" (incarnation) of salvation if he is not simultaneously eternal and unchanging. As J. Kameron Carter put it, "the historical Jesus is overcome by the universal Christ" in the tradition of Christian theology.[12] Overcoming the particular with the universal is not just theology but also social practice, for that is how legislative law works.

The second element of the divine Jesus that comes over from the Jewish setting into his new avatar-like identity in Greek philosophy is the order of the cosmos. In the Jewish biblical tradition, wisdom is the order of the cosmos conceived as the principle of creation. At Proverbs 8:30 wisdom speaks as the one who was beside God at the beginning "like a master worker."[13] This is similar to the Platonic worldview where the logos plays the same role. When applied to Jesus, the historical person quickly shifts from being a wisdom teacher to being transcendentally the wisdom principle of all that is. The writer of Colossians, who is called the Deutero-Pauline writer,[14] links the identity of Jesus to the creation of the cosmos. The writer states that in Christ "all things in heaven and on earth were created, things visible and the invisible, whether thrones or dominions or rulers or powers" (NRSV, Colossians 1:16). These lively comments express the understanding that Christ is not only the principle of things but also the righteousness of things, that is, the order of the cosmos as it is "supposed" to be. Christ is the aim of the order or its perfection. When Colossians was written, the Council of Nicaea was still on the distant horizon, but we can see constructed here a platform that would support the marriage of Christianity and Platonism under the auspices of the imperial state. The state, after all, has its order too, and following Constantine it easily welcomed the forms of Christianity that valued state sovereigns above common people as the expression of the will of God. Christianity did not start out with

the intention of religiously defining Platonism in order to support
state governments, but through the Middle Ages it cultivated and
ultimately defined these very aspects of Western history.

What enabled the parables of the historical Jesus to fall silent
before the structures of metaphysical philosophy and the powers of
the state? The answer, in part if not in full, was the shift of focus that
philosophy brought from frail humanity to permanent identities.
The Jesus question at the Council of Nicaea was an identity question, not a historical question. Christian theologians subsequently
put in centuries of tremendously committed work to the question of
the identity of Christ as the cosmic order. From our contemporary
viewpoint we might regard all that mighty work with regret. We
might do so especially if we take the human Jesus seriously as the
best way forward for Christianity today. Still, we cannot belittle the
work of ancient theologians. Their task was both sincere and difficult. They sought to define the cultural acceptability of Christianity,
and they sought to proclaim the relevance of the Christian gospel
in a culture without losing the integrity of the faith to the culture.
Theologians like Origen (185–254 CE) admirably tried to strike this
balance. He saw in Christ the cosmic reality, and he understood
this reality to be about universal peace because it and not the state
was what Plato called the Good. Origen suffered for his vision and
deserves respect in this way. Still, his is a Jesus Christ far removed
from the teller of parables. Thomas Aquinas (1225–1274) can be
highlighted as another great example. Living during the full cultural
expression of Christianity in the Middle Ages, Aquinas was able to
articulate Christian theology as the apex or highest expression of
culture with new insights from Aristotle's philosophy. The Christ of
Thomas Aquinas is the fundamental purpose of the cosmos, but this
Christ too easily shifted to the purposes of the state. In both cases,
here is another Jesus far removed from history.

After the Council of Nicaea, the Church's new role is to justify
and complement the power of reigning governments. Christ is the
head of the church, but this image now duplicates the emperor as

the head of the state, and both are divinely instituted to sustain the proper order of society. The order is hierarchical and patriarchal because it is based on the control of chaos, elements like gender, sex, political activism, heresy, treason, et cetera. In the Middle Ages—in as much as today, one might suggest—we encounter in the new Jesus the malevolent side of Enlightenment theology. An order, even a heavenly one, cannot be sustained without threats. But if a religion is to be of value to a state, the threats cannot merely be metaphysical; they must also play out on the earth. In its history Christianity was able to oblige. The Church offered the state all the justification it needed to use violence to preserve order. First, Christ was placed at the top of the order. Then, when history unfolded in ways that God did not want, the Church blessed and handed over a military sword for use by the state. In this the Church remained one step removed from direct violence, but it kept this distance in order to justify violence. That was the legacy of Nicaea in the Middle Ages. It played out in the divine right of Kings and in many horrible stories from the crusades. Lest any Protestant, like myself, might wish to distance our history from these severe times, we can remember too how Martin Luther's words added fuel to the fire of the princes who unmercifully slaughtered peasants in the revolt of 1525.[15] Jesus conceived in his new status as the principle of truth and order came to define the Western tradition's way of thinking about God. It is a tradition that employs royal imagery and the authority of the Bible to celebrate Jesus with the costly idea that God's covenant is about keeping order.

A little more than a century after the Council of Nicaea, Pope Leo I (c. 400–461), whose famous letter was read at the council of Chalcedon, displayed how the new Jesus of authority and order would work. Pope Leo I is the first Pope to be called "the Great," and, somewhat like the Apostle Paul, is known mostly for letters, but in Leo's case it's about a particular letter. In his time, the Church continued its debate on the nature of Christ. One option, which is called Eutychianism, held that Christ had two natures before the incarnation (one human and one divine) but only one nature in the incarnation, both human and divine. Leo's letter condemned Eutyches of Constantinople (c. 380–456), expressing what would be the orthodox position on the incarnation. Jesus held two natures, divine and human, that are consubstantial. The two natures exist together in what (at the Council of Chalcedon in 451) was called the hypostatic union.

Pope Leo I is remembered mostly for promoting the orthodox position that Jesus Christ is two natures and one person. However, in the course of making this clarifying argument, Leo's letter held two other significant, even daring, assumptions. First, Leo assumed—and was perhaps the first Pope to do so—that as the Bishop of Rome holding the authority of Saint Peter, he speaks out of the primacy of Rome. In the course of the controversy over the nature of Christ, which continued after Nicaea in 325 until Chalcedon in 451, Flavian, the Archbishop of Constantinople, had attended what is called the Second Council at Ephesus (499 CE). At this meeting his opponents condemned and physically attacked him. He died of his injuries, and thus this Second Council of Ephesus became known as the Robber Council. Before this Council took place Flavian had been condemned by his colleagues but Leo had exonerated him. Leo daringly based his exoneration on the power of Rome over that of Constantinople. His reasoning was that Rome as the See of Peter was primary and above Constantinople in authority. Then, even more amazingly, Leo overruled the Eastern Emperor's choice for the new Patriarch of Constantinople.[16] Leo accordingly is cited as the first Pope to exert the primacy of the Bishop of Rome over all others and the first to exercise this authority with overt political aim. When Leo sent his letter to the Council of Chalcedon, he did so with the insistence that the content of his letter be read and dealt with. No matter what the other bishops may have been thinking when they gathered at Chalcedon, Leo assumed that his concerns were the agenda. Leo did not even attend the council; he simply dictated to it. This is now an entirely different "Church." It is a Church where there is only one primary position on earth, and from this point of origin the order of things follow. Leo's directives reached through the Church's people, bishops, and council to—so he thought—the office of the emperor. The level of such authority was unimaginable even a generation earlier. It could not and did not last. Still, we see a basic assumption now well established. Jesus Christ is about power, and more specifically in the West, the power that must necessarily be reckoned with in the political order.

Such authority has a cost because order must be justified, and in Christianity the justification was the reinterpretation of Covenant and Enlightenment theology. In the Samaritan parable the covenant becomes alive in the interaction of people. It is about circumstances and new judgments, about attitudes and the revision of attitudes, based on experience in the world. It is what I compared to the common law tradition: judgments considered circumstantially with the precedent of past cases. Expressing the covenant through parable enables the parable to portray ordinary scenes as extraordinary events. When describing the difference between the generally illiterate and oral culture in which the historical Jesus participated and the highly literate and abstract culture in which people today participate—and we might add in which the bishops of the Nicene Council participated—Brandon Scott observed that "the greatest difference between oral folks and us literates is that they think concretely, we think abstractly. Concrete thinking is not a substitute for abstract thought; it is a different way of thinking."[17] The Church's historic move from Jesus of Nazareth to Jesus Christ of the Creeds is a shift from concrete to abstract thinking; it is thinking in which the covenant is no longer about how to live one's life in the world or even how to poetically conceive life in the world. It is no longer about the art of life. Christ is about the identity of God and the righteousness of the Church. After Nicaea, the Church focused on the purity of correct beliefs, labeling outsiders who would not conform as heretics. Christ is the covenant that defines the created order, justifies its hierarchical arrangement, claims its unchanging nature, and, somewhat shockingly, supports powerful states into whose hand the Church had given the sword. After Nicaea there is certainly struggle in the Church and with it; there always has been. Now, however, the struggle is not to enliven its gospel in the world as art. This would be too much like Jesus. The struggle now is with the Church itself, its very claim on eternal truth, and its utter unwillingness to suffer change.

Enlightenment, as the second type of theology, equally undergoes transition following the deliberations of Nicaea. The emphasis of Enlightenment theology is not on the interactions of the community but the quality of the individual. Enlightenment focuses on the heart of the individual where the divine nature and potentially its expression can surface in the contexts and challenges of history. Enlightenment is the dynamic of becoming human rather than a static if not pedantic truth about being human. The element of enlightenment is found in the parables of Jesus, and Lloyd Geering was right to relate Jesus in this way to Qoheleth, the author of Ecclesiastes. In Ecclesiastes we read the writer's struggle and eventual resignation before the question of life and its meaning. The author recognizes the paradoxes that come into play when considering the experience of life and finds no easy road to follow. Righteous people die in their youth, and wicked people prolong their days (Ecclesiastes 7:15). This is not welcomed news to the writer but upsetting news, and it causes Qoheleth to consider the very personal question of what is really of value. In the Samaritan story, eventually the judgment falls on the hearer; eventually the point is also personal. Can I remain, after encountering the Samaritan parable, an individual who is happy with the assumed contrast of friends and enemies? Can I remain closed to the possibility that my enemy has a point and perhaps even something to teach me? If I am open to this then I am also open to truth understood as a change of attitude and a vitality of life. I am open to truth as the process of being alive and the very challenge of meaning.

These life-centered words that seek enlightenment are not the ones issued from the Nicene Council. At the Council the words were "we believe," not "we seek" and certainly not "we question." The Christianity that followed from the Council had a different way of thinking. Enlightenment in Christianity moved from the historical life of Jesus into the transcendental reality of Jesus Christ. Enlightenment became about heaven and afterlife and an inflexible, eternal, and confessed reality. Commonly Christian enlightenment became about coming into belief. It occurred with the conversion of "barbaric" nations. It was lived in the confession of creeds and the acceptance of the Church's authority. It was about life insofar as life was about being included in the chosen who follow Christ and who, therefore, can only regard the Samaritan as an enemy, someone outside of Christ or at least outside the right way to believe in Christ. This heritage from the Middle Ages slowly made it difficult for Christians to be Christians, for who can keep confessing what became, with the advent of science, impermeable, unchanging doctrines genuinely impossible to believe? Christianity had worked hard to preserve itself as the apex of enlightenment. Yet, this very effort increasingly restricted the faith to the corner of incredulity. Truth understood in Christ as eternal and unchanging only meant that when truth in fact did change, the old Christ started to seem like a relic frozen in a past age. When such happens, as Nietzsche so poignantly asked, what then is the Church if not the sepulcher of God?[18]

When we entered the age of science and the birth of technical philosophy, the centuries-old habit of restricting the covenant to morality and deferring enlightenment to heaven had taken its toll. God, who once so finely ordered the cosmos and who handily picked our governments, stopped working. In effect God died, and it is the essence of religious struggle today to discover whether or not the concept of God has life after death.

8

When God
Stopped Working

As Western history unfolded after the Nicene Council and through the Middle Ages, God continued to be extremely effective at explaining the workings of the world. God explained the age of the earth, the origin of life, the origin of language, the nature of nature, and the purpose of human beings. Along with these insights, God also provided the human mind with a copy of the logos, the world spirit, that allowed mathematics and logic to be like mirrors that reflected in reason the intentions of the divine mind.

On this foundation the power of reason as a reflection of God became somewhat overwhelming in the Middle Ages. As long as an idea made logical or perfect sense, then the idea could be understood as a primary and necessary being. This meant that as long as a proof could be accepted as irrefutable, then the proof itself reflected a necessary and actual reality. Insofar as God made perfect logical sense, God was a necessary, primary being. In fact, even more than a primary being, God was the ultimate or absolute Being. God was the pure act (*actus purus*) of Being, was the fullness of Being itself. All other beings, what we would call *qualities* today, that made perfect sense were, accordingly, expressive qualities of God—great in themselves but still dependently related to the Absolute Being of God. In the Middle Ages, the world was admirably arranged, and God, as Absolute Being, explained the existence and meaning of everything.

When we ask how did God explain things specifically, we fall into the great logical proofs for the necessity of God. Moving forward from the time of the Roman Empire and the emphasis on the order of things, theology in the Middle Ages accepted the hierarchical arrangements of feudal Europe and assumed the social order was justified in the Christian God who resided at the top. God then descended through the order of the world by means of perfections or, again, qualities that diminished in value as we move down the ladder from great beings like kings and great subjects like theology to lesser beings like peasants and lesser subjects like the natural sciences. The idea of perfect and therefore logically necessary primary beings, though abstract in appearance, explained why this hierarchical order necessarily existed. It explained why, in effect, the order made sense.

Consider a simple illustration. I used to have an old, beat up baseball glove when I was a child. It was handed down to me from the time of my father's childhood. I loved it. I knew, though, that logic dictates what is old was once new. I used to imagine how the glove looked when it was newly purchased and given to my dad. I imagined how he might have used it. I did not need to experience the glove as new to know that it once was. Logic told me that it had a primary quality, a primary being, that was lost in its present appearance. The old, beat up, and somewhat dysfunctional baseball glove indicated to me that there was a primary, new, and perfectly functional baseball glove implied in its present state of reality. By way of this analogy, it was once common to think that everything in existence, even when old, dysfunctional, and subject to passing away, signified a more perfect quality that persisted in God and that was God's word at creation. Primary being is what God spoke at creation.

This was the basic Platonic understanding of the world during the Middle Ages. It was a type of social-Platonism in that what had been for Plato the principle of things, such as "cupness" being the principle of cups, became the qualities of being that arranged the social hierarchy. High, abstract proofs for the existence of God demonstrated necessary qualities in existing things and the place those qualities occupied in society. The hierarchy, as such, was conceived as the system of the qualities of God that maintained the social order. Accordingly, in a social position like a king there is a "divine right" in which royalty is supposed to hold the ruling qualities that express the will of God. The common person holds a much humbler but still similar station in life: expressing even in menial acts a basic quality or identity within the hierarchy of beings. What is important to note in this social expression of Plato's philosophy is the centrality of two classical ideas: substance and endurance.

Every existing thing obviously consists of something. This is its substance, like wood or metal. Every substance consists of qualities that identify it. These qualities are sometimes called the "quorum" of qualities or features. A philosopher might turn to an apple and say that the quorum of apple qualities consists of the core, the fruit, and the skin. Of these three, we can debate about whether an apple is still an apple if one of the quorum elements is eliminated. But probably we all agree that if one of the quorum is missing, the apple is no longer whole. Still, every apple is distinctive. One has more spots than another, and different kinds of apples have different flavors and colors. Here, then, is the philosophical question: what of the apple's substance endures and what changes? This question is important because it is a question about identifying the enduring quality of a being that sets its social position. In the modern world we ask this question as an identity question: "Who are you?" In the Middle Ages, it's a quality question: "What is the correct place or position of a person or thing in the matrix of the social body?"

In the Middle Ages, philosophy answered the question above by saying that while *primary beings* endure, *secondary appearances* change. A primary being is not an observable thing but rather the idea of the thing, and it is the idea of the thing, its quality, that fixes its position in the cosmic order. We need physical characteristics (skin, fruit, and core) to identify a whole apple, but these characteristics can deteriorate and change. An apple can simply rot away. However, the idea of an apple as a whole fruit continues or endures despite whatever befalls a particular apple. The quorum of qualities necessary for the idea of a whole apple signify what endures even when a particular apple disintegrates. The whole apple idea is the enduring truth of every apple despite the variable appearances of particular apples. The qualities of the whole apple are its primary being and place every apple in the order of fruits regardless of the particular or secondary states an apple can hold.

To this way of thinking it seems, then, that there must be unseen enduring qualities that preserve ideas no matter what happens to particulars. And these unseen or ideal qualities are the permanent qualities of primary beings. To get the sense of traditional philosophy even more acutely, we need to think that the ideal quorum of qualities of a whole apple is in fact "really" the real apple. The apple that appears to us physically, because it can change, be eaten, or rot away, is not that in which the ideal qualities can endure. The endurance of the apple happens only through its primary being. The endurance of the qualities of an apple must be assumed in order for there to be physical apples. Just like that old and tattered baseball glove signified the unseen but necessarily new qualities it once had, so do all physical objects remind us of primary qualities that endure despite how things look on the surface. A primary being in this way is a necessary being. A primary being is "necessary" because without the ideal of a primary being there can be no recognition of things and no endurance of things, which effectively means there could only be chaos and disruption both in nature and in society. Primary beings, then, are "real" things; the real apple comprises the primary, enduring qualities that make a particular apple possible.

When such forms of thought are related to God, it is easy to see why it was once believed that without God nothing was possible. God was not just a primary being, but the absolute or first primary being. God was the source and final destination of all primary beings. No other forms of primary being could exist, have purpose, or hold endurance without the work of God as the creator and sustainer of all. God was a logical necessity—an idea that must be—before any other primary beings could be, and without whom no physical appearances, like an apple, could be seen, identified, and put to use. God was the ultimate being who was the power of endurance for all things seen. Up until the late Middle Ages, the act of setting down logical proofs for the existence of God was enough to indicate that God had to exist. With the conviction of God's existence held as a given, God "worked" to explain the world. God explained how the world originated in the enduring qualities of God; God explained how things in the world served a purpose in the hierarchy of enduring qualities; and God explained how things held their proper place in the enduring hierarchy of the social order. To transgress the hierarchy was effectively to transgress the will of God.

These three claims about the origin, purpose, and place of things in the world were expressed in philosophical arguments for the existence of God. The point was not, like today, just to prove the possible existence of God; the point was social as much as philosophical, for God's existence was simultaneously the justification of the world order. Purely on the basis of logic, we can agree or disagree with the arguments, but that's not really the point. The point is to understand the social significance of the arguments. The arguments apologetically defend the order of life by defending the necessity of the Christian God at the top of a hierarchy of qualities. In the late Middle Ages and early Enlightenment era when these arguments fail, we witness not only the critique of earlier thinking but also a change in society. God stops being necessary to the social order, and this is a radical, if somewhat terrifying, event in human history. Arguments for God's existence lose both their vibrancy and importance. Chaos as well as the wrath of God seemed the inevitable consequence, and yet the attractiveness of thinking that God was no longer necessary for the construction of knowledge and society would continue to rise to the top.

Before we can understand the radical nature of a new age when God stopped working, we need to clearly understand the demonstrations for the existence of God as necessary for the origin, purpose, and place of things. These demonstrations are called the cosmological, teleological, and ontological arguments for the existence of God. Today, we know them only as logical proofs; we no longer share the social experience that gave the arguments a vital nature. Still, they must be reviewed because in their failure lies a significant cultural change that is at the heart of modern questions about God, religion, and the human future.

The cosmological argument in its classical form might also be called a causal argument. At its heart it argues that everything must have a cause. When we look at the universe, it cannot have started on its own but must have a cause. Thomas Aquinas (1225–1274), the foremost theologian of the Middle Ages, explained that "it is necessary to arrive at a first mover, put in motion by no other; and this everyone understands to be God" (*Summa Theologica* 1. 2. 3.). In the cosmological argument, God is the Prime Mover, the foundation on which all things have their originating motion. To Aquinas this was not enough to conclude that God created the cosmos, for that knowledge is derived from revelation found in the Bible. The Bible tells us in Genesis that God created the world. For Aquinas, the nature of the cosmos as motion is sufficient natural knowledge to lead to the acceptance of revelation. The cosmological argument was sufficient evidence for the necessary origin of things in God.

The next two arguments, the teleological and ontological arguments, can be considered as ways to fine tune the basic cosmological argument. While the cosmos gives evidence of a Prime Mover, the teleological argument gives evidence that every moving thing has a purpose. The word *telos* in Greek can be translated as purpose. The teleological argument holds that everything is designed for a purpose. Sometimes this argument is call the argument from design. The most famous expression of this argument is William Paley's (1743–1805) example of the watch. Paley suggests that if we discovered a watch in a natural setting, we would rightly infer from the complex workings of the watch that someone designed it. Likewise, the complexities of the natural world indicate the reasonable inference that there is a designer. Thomas Aquinas was somewhat subtler than Paley because Aquinas did not focus on the design of things but on their purpose. For Aquinas a certain thing holds its place in the created order based on its purpose, which contributes to the overall design and function of the cosmos. Every material object is designed for a purpose, and this purpose is its excellence. The excellence of a baseball bat, for example, is to hit a home run. Aquinas employs no such modern example, but he does call the excellence of a thing its "blessedness." When a baseball player hits a home run, the player might well refer to the "blessed bat" and thus inadvertently acknowledge Thomas Aquinas. The aim of all things, the highest aim according to Aquinas, is in the will of God. Everything moves toward the fulfillment of the creator's will, and everything yearns for unification through that will with its perfect form. This state of unification is blessedness. Aquinas succinctly states the argument with the concluding words, "some intelligent being exists by whom all natural things are directed to their end; and this being we call God" (*Summa Theologica* 1. 2. 3.).

In the ontological argument God is presented as a perfect being who is logically necessary for there to be degrees of quality. While the preceding two arguments indicate the necessity of a creator and a designer, the ontological argument puts created things in their place among the order of beings. It all begins with the inherent idea of perfection found in things. The apple I am eating is too soft, and this desk at which I work has a scratch in it. With these observations, I am unwittingly comparing "too soft" to the idea of a "perfect apple," which I think is not soft. I am assuming a perfect desk that has no scratches in contrast to the one I sit at that has this scratch. In such comparisons I assume degrees of perfection. I understand what is better and what is worse, what is greater and what is lesser, what is good and what is bad. But in order to have this sense of degrees I must first understand perfection, for only with the encompassing idea of perfection can I know of degrees less than perfect. The ontological argument states that I must assume the existence of God as the Absolute Perfect Being in order to recognize degrees of perfection in being. There must be an understanding in my observations about what is closer to perfection. If I follow this understanding to the furthest end, there must be a most perfect Being before all other things. God's Being or existence is proven by the logical necessity of a most perfect Being. When Aquinas stated this argument, he said, "Now the maximum in any genus is the cause of all in that genus; as fire, which is the maximum heat, is the cause of all hot things. Therefore there must also be something which is to all beings the cause of their being, goodness, and every other perfection; and this we call God" (*Summa Theologica* 1. 2. 3.). The very idea of perfection, to Aquinas, necessitates not only the idea but also the existence of God. To this, we must also add that the qualities of perfection found in various things account for the place of things in the order of the world. This is why theology was a higher subject, at this time, than the natural sciences, for theology deals with universal ideas which are prior to and necessary for the order of particular things. The Absolute Perfection of God that makes each other perfection possible also places each perfection into its location along the chain of being.

Up until a certain day, this was the understanding about how the universe worked and why God was necessary for it to work. God spoke and the universe came into being. With the Word of God came the motion of all things, the aim of all things, and the degrees of perfection in all things. The world in its operation was the witness to the Word of God. God as the Prime Mover, the End Cause, and the Perfect Being was a logically necessary foundation for an intelligible universe.

Then one day it seemed as if humanity woke up to a new morning when God was no longer an explanation. Abstruse logic stopped being self-evident proof for the existence of God and the order of society. A day came when we thought about the very idea of God in exactly the opposite way to former times: unnecessary rather than necessary. Of course, it did not happen suddenly on the rainy day of March 25, 1811.[1] It is not that God unexpectedly had to be proven rather than assumed by the general intelligence of human beings. But it is the case that gradually through the era of the Enlightenment, roughly the seventeenth to nineteenth centuries, God and other religious ideas became subject to critical thinking based on evidence. The existence of God, or anything else, must be proven not by logic but by demonstration, and without sufficient evidence to the contrary the default position was that God's necessary being fell out of existence. What is necessary in logic is not automatically necessary in reality. I can imagine a perfect island in the sea, as Gaunilo once responded to Anselm,[2] and I can even demonstrate its logical necessity as the most perfect island, but that does not mean the island actually exists. When this new day arrived, God became belief, not logic, and believing in God concerned faith in the supernatural, not the necessary Being behind nature. What happened?

The reversal of God's status from the assumption of truth to that which must be proven arrived by way of attrition. Eventually the authority of science replaced the authority of religion, and with this change God became a questionable idea that lacked evidence. With this shift theology, which is the study of God, stopped being the queen of the sciences,[3] as it was known it the Middle Ages, and swiftly descended down the academic ladder. The ground shifted from understanding reality as that founded on a logically necessary Being to a new reality founded on human experience. Any number of philosophers might be named to highlight this shift, but I will recall three philosophers in particular who can be briefly reviewed: René Descartes (1596–1650), Baruch Spinoza (1632–1677), and David Hume (1711–1776). To be sure, philosophy at times can be technical and pedantic, but it is also the case that certain philosophical ideas can become the new operating assumptions of culture experience. In the case of the West, these three philosophers express arising new assumptions.

Descartes very much wanted God to exist and valiantly tried to prove God was still necessary. He remained tied to the Middle Ages despite himself, but his attempt proved somewhat naive, which allowed human reason to overrule his faith. Descartes was the great skeptic who doubted the existence of everything except himself. He famously imagined that he was deceived into thinking every object that he perceived out there in the world was real. He decided his best option for being safe from such deception was to doubt the existence of everything. This systematic approach is famously called Descartes' method of doubt. Could anything be free of doubt? He concluded that only the knowledge about his own existence was free of doubt. Though Descartes could doubt anything at all, in the act of doubting he had to assume that something or someone caused him to doubt. He must be receiving sensations from outside himself first in order to doubt the validity of the sensations he receives. If so, his own thinking self must already exist prior to the causes of his doubts. He concludes that his one unshakable certainty is the fact that he is a thinking being first in order for anyone else or any other thing to cause his doubts. From this humble but irrefutable platform Descartes considers how everything he experiences, from physical things to ideas, could have their origin in himself as the thinker. After all, everything he could think of shared, to some degree, something similar to himself. He sees a physical object, and he is a physical object, so the idea of a physical thing could have emerged strictly from the experience of himself. Therefore, the existence of physical objects can be doubted. Or, he imagines something unseen like an angel. Is it real or imaginary? Descartes concludes that it is possible the idea of an angel emerges strictly from his imagination because the form of an angel, aside from wings, is a human form like his own. Therefore the existence of angels can be doubted. Everything potentially arises from the mind, Descartes concludes with further examination, and therefore everything can be subject to doubt. As long as there is reason to doubt something we remain insecure in our knowledge about it. Outside of the certainty of his own existence, Descartes wondered if there was something else he could possibly claim was certain. A positive response did not seem forthcoming, but then God stepped in as the answer. There is one idea Descartes can say that has not arisen from himself: God. God is so radically other than his own doubting humanity that God cannot be his own creation. Descartes gives to God all the usual qualities: perfection, power, eternal being, independence, supreme intelligence, etc. None of these supreme qualities that express the universal Perfect Being could have their origin in Descartes who is by no means perfect at all. It must be, Descartes reasoned, that such an innate idea is not his own creation. Therefore God exists.

Descartes' proof is recalled here not because it is convincing but because it indicates a turn in the nature of such proofs. We need to note immediately that Descartes' proof rests not on the austere principles of metaphysical logic but on innate human reason. Though he wants to say that God is Perfect Being, just as the tradition upholds, he reaches this conclusion based on the authority of his own, internal, thought process. The authority of Descartes' argument rests on the authority of his autonomy, his own "self-rule." He, that is, his human nature, is the authority (foundation) for God's existence. This is entirely different from the Middle Ages and the logical necessity of God's existence for the creation and the social order. In the Middle Ages, the starting point was outside the self in the necessities of order, but for Descartes the starting point is inside himself in the power to reason. He uses his power of reason to prove there is anything at all.

In addition to the authority of human autonomy, there was another, more troubling side to Descartes' proof. The trouble was that God was no longer necessary for the universe to exist and make sense. This might initially sound like liberty, but the immediate consequence was not necessarily great. God was no longer necessary for the world to make sense; God was only necessary for Descartes' inner reason—his own perception—to make sense. God was in the service of Descartes' autonomy, Descartes's own ego, though Descartes did not see this. Remember, Descartes wanted

God to exist and wanted to defend the integrity of Christian faith. But the bowstring, as it were, slipped too early from his hands and he actually hit another target. God did not remain an independent reality but rather answered the question about whether or not Descartes could trust his senses. Descartes concluded that he could trust his senses because God would not deceive him. That was great for Descartes but not necessarily for God. To support his achievement, Descartes turned God into the principle of autonomous human sensation. If not for God, Descartes could not trust his senses and therefore could not be autonomous. But God made this new autonomy possible. Once God verified that Descartes could trust his senses, effectively Descartes had no further need for the Perfect Being. In a remarkable way, God had become the principal reason why there is no need of God. Descartes could move forward on the basis of natural reason alone. With historic irony, Descartes created on the basis of God the condition of God's obsolescence.

Another step is taken in the rising autonomy of human reason and God's subservience to reason in the naturalist philosophy of Baruch Spinoza, a follower of Descartes. For Spinoza, as with Descartes, human reason can discover the laws of the natural order and, due to God, can trust reason to hold these laws as knowledge. For Spinoza God is like the energy or animation of nature, something that is in all things. Nature is consistent and dependable because of the consistency and predictability of this underlying energy. It is as if every element contains a type of directive by which it fulfills its natural purpose. So, in this sense, while God transcends all, God is in all, and all things in this sense contain God. With this thought in mind, it is a simple move from theism (the belief in God) to Deism (the belief in a primary cause of things). God might be needed to set the universe in motion and to give it a kind of direction, but once this initial act is completed only human reason is needed from thereon in. Descartes established the power of reason over God, and Spinoza brought God out of the heavens and into the nature of things. With such subtle changes in the climate of knowledge, the doorway was opened to a new universe without God at all, which was the passageway David Hume chose to walk through with "empiricism."

Hume's idea is that, basically, human reason is all we have to work with when it comes to understanding both our own experiences and the world around us. But human reason is a complicated matter because reason is particularly good at making stuff up. Human beings always have to check their reasoning, monitor it, to ensure it does not slip into fantasies that are allowed to stand as knowledge. Many times fantasies do stand as knowledge, so Hume must ask, how could reason so betray itself? How can human beings, for example, believe in God—and not only God but also a God of extremes in jealousy, violence, and revenge—when reason on its own cannot be certain that God exists? Hume answers such questions like this with his main thesis about the sources of human understanding. For Hume there are only two sources for human understanding, impressions and ideas, so one great quality of Hume is his simplicity. Impressions are "when we hear, or see, or feel, or love, or hate, or desire, or will."[4] Impressions are common physical (what we touch out there) and emotional (what we feel inside) sensations. Meanwhile, ideas arise from the contemplation of the impressions I have. Someone bumps into me and it hurts; my immediate impressions are physical pain and emotional anger. However, whatever I construct from these impressions is my idea. I might make an enemy out of the person who bumped me, but I might regard the person with sympathy. Suppose I realize that the other person is from a distinctly disadvantaged social background and, sadly, has learned to use abrupt actions to gain the space of identity. The incident could change my ideas about society and life. I begin to work for social change. Or perhaps another reaction is possible: I begin to think that certain people are evil and that there is a mysterious evil force in the world hidden from common view.

My impression of anger moves into ideas about a fantastic, hidden world. Both reactions are possible, and both arise from an initial impression being absorbed into the creativity of ideas.

Ideas arise from the reflection on received impressions. Ideas can combine and recombine to become very complex, major creations of our own imagination. Suppose my response to the incident of being aggressively bumped by another is to conclude that there is an evil force in the world and that this other person is possessed by the devil. And now, just as I am in the midst of entertaining this thought and believing how this person needs the intervention of an exorcist, suddenly the other one says to me, "Oh, sorry. I didn't see you." Ideas, Hume understands, can escape natural impressions and can run away into fantasy unless checked against the world out there. This is how human beings can be as complicated and incomprehensible as we are. We use our reason to construct ideas from impressions, but unless we have a way of checking whether or not our ideas are helpful, they can become delusional and self-destructive. How then do we check out our ideas to ensure they are helpful rather than self-destructive? There is only one way to do this, and that is to use evidence-based reason. In other words, it is necessary to use critical thinking to judge ideas and check them out against the impressions of the external world. This is exactly the foundation of modern science, which must check out impressions like falling objects against ideas like gravity to see if the idea can adequately explain the impression.

Hume missed one dynamic in his thinking that is important, but nevertheless his thinking is still summarily how modern people—even the most abstract, postmodern philosophers—continue to think. Philosophy is basically a natural consequence of impressions. However, what Hume missed is the question of culture. Different cultural settings will operate with different ideas based on the culture's history of impressions. So, a culture that has been historically colonized by another nation or people will have a set of impressions unique to that experience that will feed ideas about liberty or justice or (perhaps) vengeance and that may seem, to another, irrational. Equally, in another historical period, such as the Roman Empire, people thought differently about the world because the impressions of the time were not received with the same set of ideas common today. We cannot ask ancient people to be like modern people because ancient impressions were not received with the ideas that modern people hold. An obvious example is health. Ancient people simply thought differently about the human body and the cause of disease. Ancient ideas about health and cures seem to us now truly peculiar and sometime simply ridiculous.

The *pièce de résistance* of Hume's thinking, at least concerning religion, is the absolutely clear implication that God is a human creation. God is a construct of ideas emerging not from an independent metaphysical reality but from the way common and natural impressions play out in the relationship of ideas. The real question in religion, from this point of view, is just what natural impressions have created the idea of God in human experience? The difficulty is that the question has no explicit answer. God is a complex idea. God emerges from the combination of innumerable variables involving culture, language, and history and the way in which all three over millennia have combined and recombined impressions. Yet, we can ask with Hume, what is more likely, that there is an intelligent being in the universe who is unverifiable or that the idea of an intelligent and unverifiable being arises from the impressions of nature upon the human mind? The answer can always be debated, but it is a stronger stance to agree with Hume than to disagree. Why? Because even to disagree with Hume is to engage impressions and ideas. We know by our own experience that we create fantasy all the time. Human beings are very good at talking about things that do not exist or creating ideas that correspond to nothing in particular. There are any number of examples of this from UFOs to angels to unicorns. One look at the demon world in the art of Hieronymus Bosch (1450–1516) should be enough to convince us about the human ability to imagine and portray the unimaginable.

To Hume, ideas like God emerge from the experience of natural impressions that I will here call repetition but Hume might call habit.[5] By repetition I am referring to natural laws, like gravity, which are both dependable and necessary for life. Repetition in nature is the reason why there is oxygen to breath, water to drink, and complex life forms on the earth. Because the natural world repeats life-sustaining acts in its constant movements of evolution, in its structural replications of DNA, in its natural cycle of life and death, and in its ability to sustain a climate, human beings (who are a product of such repetition) can expect the world to be as it is. We experience the world as an order because repeated experiences (like the sun rising every morning) become the expectation or habit of life.

The human experience of repetition is perhaps the most fundamental impression. Everything based on predictability is based on the impression of repetition. Due to this impression mathematics is possible. Mathematics can predict things because of the expectation of repetition. We could not have a theory about something if we had no experience of repetition in relation to it. Now, what if a scientist explains to an audience that tides are the result of the position of the moon in relation to the earth? The scientist tells us that because the orbit of the moon around the earth is a dependable repetition, not only can we depend upon regular tides but, based on the consistency, we can also predict them. Then, what if I amazingly stand up, interrupt our scientist in the midst of conveying this scientific information, and claim that tides are due to my dog's name being Chesser! I make the unbelievable claim that this name in itself holds a specific quality that influences the moon and that from time immemorial God so ordained my dog should hold this name. The power and the forethought of God is held in the sound of this name destined to be my dog's name, and that since the beginning of earthly time God's tidal "Chesser power" now residing in my dog has been reincarnated in dog after dog. My theory is utterly foolish, but I can still persist with it and no one can really say that it's wrong. In my private imagination a relationship of ideas has been established that expresses a consistent experience of repetition. I readily admit that my example is far-fetched and strained, but the attempt is to make a very Humean point. Hume drew the astonishing conclusion that human imagination does not really allow for certainty in knowledge. There can always be something outside our awareness that accounts for our experience, and there can always be a different way, even an absurd way, to explain our experience. Hume asks us, however, what is more likely? Is it more likely that the orbit of the moon, its mass, and gravitational influence account for tides on earth or that the tides are caused by someone's dog being named Chesser? We must, in good conscience, answer that gravitational influence of the moon is the best answer. We must so answer because this is what best aligns our senses to the experienced repetition.

Somewhat similarly Hume considers the question of God. What is more likely, that God exists or that God is a creation of the human imagination? Here there is no avenue to repetition like there is with a natural phenomenon. God does not "repeat" for every human being but varies from culture to culture and from existence to non-existence. Not every religion has a deity. And for those that do, some have multiple deities and some have one. Then, even in religions with a deity, there are always dissident traditions in the religion that question the majority beliefs. Since human beings are exceptionally good at imagining fantastic things that do not exist and since fantastic things can be made as variable as we wish without consequence, what is more likely: that God is a human creation or that God is a real thing in the world? Hume supports the conclusion that God is a human creation.

It is the impact of Hume's thinking that brings us to the problem of religion persistent in our time. People still believe in God because the idea of God still appeals to the psychological need for stability in human experience. The legacy of God as order still has a hold on the human imagination. But "psychology" is not a physical sensation; it is a way of reacting to and re-imagining physical sensation in the relationship of ideas. Impressions, like happiness or sadness, constantly repeat throughout the course of one's life. The reactions to these basic emotions become imprinted upon us as habit. They become our lifestyle or the way we are comfortable with being in the world. Personal psychology emerges out of our biology, our impressions, both cultural and personal, and our way of putting these experiences together in thought and in language. Out of this complex multiplicity, human beings form living habits. God persists in human experience because the repetition of the idea of God continues to hold cache in human experience. The idea of God can comfort us, fascinate us, contribute to self-esteem, work as a cultural marker, and even get us singing. God works on the level of ideas where a complex fantasy called religion emerges from a history of impressions of repetition.

Through Descartes, Spinoza, and Hume, Christian theology moved from an era where God was a necessary explanation to a new era where God is the problem of human experience. For our time the question has moved even slightly further. Theology is no longer just the problem of God and human experience. It is now also, and even mainly, the value of God in human experience. In other words, the new question about God is really about whether God has a value for human beings and our collective future. The God of human experience displaces the old God of cosmic order, which means that even though God is not necessary to explain the world, perhaps God is still valuable to being human.

From the contemporary perspective, so greatly influenced by Descartes, Spinoza, and Hume, God is no longer a source of reason but accountable to reason. The stimulating challenge, then, is to think about religion and its future outside the tempting desire to introduce the authoritative God of revelation. To help with this I will introduce and contemplate the future of a God who, after the Enlightenment, "almost" is.

9

Religion and the God Who Almost Is

When asked whether or not God exists, what would it mean if you responded that God almost exists? To be "almost" is to be between something and nothing, to be partially there but not fully there. I almost arrived on time for a dentist appointment. When the dentist looked for me at 9:00 a.m. on Tuesday morning, I was nowhere in sight. I was an experience of absence and nothingness. But there was a message at the receptionist's desk, "I am running late today. I will be there by 9:10." So, at 9 a.m. I did not "exist," but there was a trace of my existence in my absence that promised my presence. There was a sign that I will be but am not yet; at the moment I am "almost."

God is good at being almost. Through religion God leaves a trace in human history and culture of being around but never really present. Lots of words and writings about God promise that God will show up. But God disappoints. There is a delay. Morning arrives and God is nowhere to be seen; there is an absence left in the notes that made the promise. Of course, God does not "really" exist. We know, do we not, that God is a human creation? Language about God and religions concerning God are signs made to stand in place of the absence of God. It is not God but words about God that remain like a promissory note. God resides in the regard to the heavens, the question of why, and the silent response. God is the emptiness of the fullness of it all.

If God was really the fullness and not the emptiness of things, there could be no question about God's existence. If God really did exist no one could ask whether God existed. If I were on time for my dentist appointment, the dentist could not question whether or not I would arrive. My absence has to occur before the question about my presence can be asked. That's one of the great ironies of life: we are aware of existence because in the background is non-existence. If there was no non-existence, then I could not be conscious of existing. Such irony, like many forms of irony, depends upon a gap or a separation between things: an emptiness. There is a gap between myself and others that allows me to know that I am not others. There is a gap between my existence and nonexistence which allows me to know that I do exist. There is a gap between my thoughts, the moments of my considerations, that allows me to hold different thoughts and be aware of my thinking. Is this gap the greatest irony of life and the main thing that made Socrates so wise? Maybe it is not the greatest, but the first. We only know things well when we know the gaps that compose our knowledge, the gaps that are our ignorance. Socrates knew his ignorance. He knew, and we know with him, that the wisest people among us are those who know when to keep silent.

The gap that makes wisdom possible also accounts for the existence of religion. If there was a God, there would be no reason for religion. Religion exists only because there is no God but an absence of God. If God were absolutely present, there could be no question about God, no yearning for God, and no belief in God. No one needs to believe in something that is present. It is only absence that raises the question of belief.

I do not need to believe in my partner to make her my partner. She is, and that is all that is required. To say I believe in her would mean to say that I believe she is telling the truth or that she is dependable or that I have faith she will reach her goal. But to say I believe in her as I might say I believe in God does not make the same sense, for she exists and I can hold her hand. The existence of God, on the other hand, requires belief because God is absent. What about people, you might ask, who say they experience God? This makes the point: we experience God in the yearning for God, which is the presence of the absence of God clinging to our hearts. In such conditions I must say "I believe, help my unbelief" (Mark 9:24). I believe because I have unbelief. My act of believing is against unbelief, against the consequence of the absence of God. So, believing is willfully taking a leap over the abyss of absence without knowing where one might land. Such is religion: it exists because God does not exist; it is the willfulness of being human. It is the act of leaping across unbelief. Like Søren Kierkegaard (1813–1855), the great founder of Existentialism, said, belief is the condition of uncertainty. Belief is about lying "constantly out upon the deep and with seventy thousand fathoms of water" underneath.[1] Such oceanic depth is Kierkegaard's metaphor for bottomlessness, for emptiness. God is not about certainty, and religion is not about God's exis-tence. Religion is about creating God while it awaits God. Religion is the "almost" of God; that is, religion is the record of beliefs that arise while waiting for the arrival of nothing. Religion is the trace of a God, culturally conditioned, who almost is.

In older times, as we have seen, the "trace of God" was taken positively into cultural forms of government, language, rhetoric, texts, and divine envoys. The trace of God held and holds still two significant forms in the Western tradition that I earlier called Covenant and Enlightenment theology. It was the case, when we reviewed these theologies, that while God was never present in antiquity any more than God is present now, there was neverthe-less an always powerful presentation of God. The Torah is given by God on the mountain to Moses; the Torah is not God, but it is that which makes God present in the absence of God. The Torah stands in place of the God who is not there. The covenant, in this way, is equally about absence. Covenant theology is the theological act of forming community, of creating the presence of God out of noth-ing. The biblical prophet as an envoy relates what God says to the

people, but here again the envoy speaks in place of the God who is
not there. The Prophet issues the warning about either what God
demands or will do in the absence of satisfaction. But the Torah, the
prophet, and the prophetic words are all there because God is not
there. All stand in place of God. All are a virtual God but none the
real one. Religion steps in for God and presents God in the absence
of God, and in so doing creates a God. Religion substitutes. That
is its basic act. Covenant theology is theology in covenant with the
creativity of doing theology. It is theology in covenant with the God
who almost is.

Similarly, God appears and disappears in the quest for enlightenment. Theology conceived as enlightenment is theology understood
as the quest for self-realization. Enlightenment theology is the quest
for the fullness of the self. The symbols of such fullness are given in
avatars, those figures or signs where the manifest qualities of God
are expressed. Angels are avatars in the sense that they represented
certain divine qualities. The Torah can also be an avatar in the sense
that the ultimate religious goal is to become the Torah in the flesh.
But God as God transcends all qualities and can never be only one
quality. A quality limits God to a characteristic and a definition. To
multiply the qualities and conclude that God has many or even innumerable qualities does not solve the problem, for God is still held
to definitions and characteristics. Religiously speaking, God cannot
have qualities like goodness because, even if nice sounding, qualities
limit God to a particular kind of being. On the other hand, if one
is seeking enlightenment through religion what else can be done?
The qualities of God bring forward the questions about God even
though the qualities, as such, stand in place of God as substitutes for
God. In relation to God, every human idea about God is as a partial
way of understanding God and not the whole idea of God. This is
the basic insight of Enlightenment theology. Only by removing all
the qualities that substitute for God do we begin to understand the
transcendence of the idea of God. In enlightenment the idea of God
breaks apart our egos, defeats our partial ideas, exposes our selfish

motives, and brings us before the true God who is not and can
never be. Theology is the enterprise of substitution. Enlightenment
theology, truly understood, is awareness of the substitutions for
God and awakening to the absence of the God who almost is.

Even Jesus as the Christ, who is Christianity's great avatar, reveals
and hides God simultaneously. He is at once the incarnation of the
divine second person of the Trinity and part of the mystery of God
that the Trinity seeks to present. The Trinity is that, or at least is
supposed to be that, which renders us silent before the mystery of
God. As the incarnation of the logos of God and yet as the mystery of God, Jesus understood as the promise of self-realization in
Enlightenment theology is doubly absent. In orthodox Christianity
he is absent once as the sign of God and absent a second time as the
sign of the sign of God. In the first case Jesus is like a doorway to
God, which is a favorite image in the Gospel of John (10:9). Jesus
is the incarnation of the logos or cosmic order. The particularities
of Jesus as a figure of history are lost in and irrelevant to the sign
that he is. The physical Jesus is not Jesus but the sign of the logos
not seen. Then, as if a second movement, in signing the logos Jesus
also signs the absence of the God who needs Jesus as the logos to
substitute presence. The problem is that God needs both presence
and absence out of Jesus, needs the flesh of Jesus even though the
historical person is of no value. This is the problem Christianity tries
to solve with the Trinity. In the Trinity every sign—the Father and
the Son and the Holy Spirit—is a sign of the other sign. In the attempt to present Jesus as the full and last sign, Jesus slipped away,
in the Council of Nicaea, into other signs that represent each other
and that substitute for the absence of God. Jesus is so important
in Christianity because Jesus does not matter, that is, because his
value is in substitution, in erasing himself, in being present to signal
the absence of God. This peculiar theological play in Christianity
keeps the mystery of God alive, but it is the mystery of a God who
almost is. It might be, despite common theological criticisms of
Greek thought, that Aristotle had a better idea. For Aristotle, God

is the unmoved and absolutely silent one. What we experience at the surface is the movement of orderly things that presuppose a God who is neither the things nor the order that arranges them. God is the Being who is not; and religion, the presentation of this silence.

In both ways that God has been talked about, as Covenant and Enlightenment theology, God is present because God is absent. Or, as I like to put it, the overwhelming silence of God invites words to substitute for the absence of God. This means, practically, that God is only present because of belief in God. Or, to again employ the simplest terms, God is a human creation. In the 2014 epic movie *Noah,* on several occasions the hero played by Russell Crowe looks to the sky with questions for God. But God never answers. Yet, in the empty sky Noah finds answers and acts upon them. In some cases his acts are just ones, and in some cases his acts are terrifyingly wrong if not mad ones. The difference is not in the silence but in the ways he reacts to the silence. Standing before the face of silence, he is capable of making God his vision and his monster.

In older times the two theologies played out in a different way. Because God and gods were so important to the order of things, the gods in play effectively defined cultural and political identity. Religion was overtly the way a culture created itself. This was its covenant expression based on the priority of the collective identity. One participated in a culture by confessing, that is, adhering to the collective expressions of belief. To be a participant in the Roman Empire was to confess the lordship of Caesar. The confession separated those who belonged to the empire from the foreigner, the barbarian, who was the threat to the empire. Even though the Roman Empire could dominate other nations with overwhelming force, Rome still felt the threat of the barbarian and still acted out of exaggerated fears. Inside the empire, the "unbeliever" stirred up equal fear. Those who disrupted the ideological motivations of the imperial economy were labelled criminal. The historical Jesus, in his lifetime, was in the Roman sense a criminal. He was an unbeliever, an atheist, who was perceived as a threat to the order. Roman belief, like everyone else's, was collective; it was not based on singular opinion.

At the level of individual enlightenment, it was the case that an individual could have doubts about the gods. The myriad of philosophical movements in antiquity express this fact very well. Some movements, such as Epicureanism, are comfortably called "atheistic" from the modern point of view. In antiquity, however, the necessity of the collective commitment to the order of the gods over individual opinions about gods remained foremost. Despite the schools of philosophy, when it came to economics and to the recognition of the imperial theology, no one raised a question about taking a "leap of faith." Such a question requires a situation in which one is free to engage or disengage from the religious setting. In ancient times, one was already and always in the religious setting because there was little difference between such things as religion, economics, and culture. The economic policies of Augustus Caesar were divine ones. The policies pervaded and embraced the empire like a blanket descending from heaven, to use an image from the book of Acts (10:11). To advertise this fact, images of gods were everywhere. As Paul Zanker reports, "Never before had [the viewer] encountered such an extensive, fully integrated set of images." Zanker underlines further, "even the uneducated viewer was indoctrinated in the new visual program."[2] When theology is spoken of in this context, enlightenment means a movement toward the collective presentation. Enlightenment is about realizing the order of things and about belonging to the order.[3]

In the contemporary world, religious beliefs are a choice, at least we like to think they are, that are in no way self-evident. Whereas in times past, religious and cultural practices were very nearly the same thing, it is no longer true in the West that a culture is explicitly defined through beliefs in a God or a set of gods. The Western gods are now the insidious ones like consumerism and the appeal of technology. To be anti-capitalist in the Western setting is something like "atheism" was in ancient times, a threat to the social order. The overt demand to confess a god, like the Nicene god, has fallen away. The new order of the day is based on the authority of personal beliefs over collective ones and the libertarian idea that individual needs are greater than the common good. Modern gods are everywhere in consumer societies demanding the expression of our desires and the allegiance of our money but without much concern about our religious beliefs or the common good of our planet. These modern, hidden gods no longer need the additional help of bigger sky gods to represent the collective and to be mixed into the world as its proper order. Consumerism likes multiple gods customized to individual desires. Behind the scenes, it is science and not religion that gives authority to technology without any extra help from theology.

Religion is no longer a "fact" like it used to be, and the forms of theology related to religion are no longer self-evident. Religion is no longer necessary to ensure that blessings fall upon a culture and a people. That old idea has been transformed. Religion remains a sign only of what used to be and what is now absent. Religion has moved from its authoritative past, when it could explain the nature of things, to a contemplative setting where it is a matter of choice. It belongs to private life where it might be engaged in an effort to overcome anxiety, to achieve self-acceptance, or to cultivate family identities.

Nevertheless, even in the setting of a new libertarian culture of privatized religion, individual choices do not have to relegate the historic value of religion to a museum. Religion still expresses the artistry of life. It still expresses elements of wonder about life and still inspires acts of human compassion. Religion defines a culture's history and expresses its inherited orientation in the world. No culture or nation today would perceive the world as it does without the background of its history with religion. What troubles most people who are serious but not literalistic about religion is finding ways to be without "God"—without the old beliefs in supernatural things—but still be with religion in the artistic sense of valuing life, history, and the expression of beauty. For this, where does one turn? How does one have "God" without God? How does one be in the world with a God who almost is?

There are two elements that make what was old new again. The two are human autonomy and human wisdom, contemporary ways of expressing Covenant and Enlightenment theology. Human autonomy is the legacy of the dramatic age of the Enlightenment (seventeenth to nineteenth centuries). It forms the basic understanding of the self. Even though in postmodern thought the self is understood to be a complex of many different and simultaneous factors, including biological, sociological, and psychological elements all mixed together in political, historical, and cultural ways, nevertheless the modern self as autonomous—and thus as citizen holding human rights—remains a fundamental base of Western law. We owe this to writers like Jean-Jacques Rousseau and the famous book *Emile*, which was at the time a revolutionary way to understand education. Rousseau gave us the image of a child educated by self-motivation, self-discovery, and by trusting the innate qualities of reason. This vision of education turned its back on models of external discipline to exalt self-actualization in the act of discovery. It laid a foundation for modern values based on the autonomous self. It was coupled in philosophy with the rise of the authority of human reason and with the idea that nature (including human nature), rather than God, is the only direct source of our knowledge. In Rousseau we see the extension of philosophy from Descartes to Hume into the social body. In Rousseau we have not only one of the first expressions of natural psychology but also of natural theology. Rousseau did not need to refer to God to explain human nature nor to uphold moral ideals. He could assume that what used to be called God was actually the heart of our true selves. Therefore, he could propose that the political vision of a just society ought to be built on the natural equality of human beings.

We could argue that Rousseau was rather simple in his conclusions. He was, no doubt, overly optimistic about the promises of reason and seemingly ignorant about the stark realities of human nature. He never recognized that reason also operates within a culture and, when set as the savior of human ills, does not see its own prejudiced assumptions. Reason needs to be held under the critique of reason, and Rousseau's enthusiasm overlooked such realism. From the perspective of today, the remarkable achievements of reason expressed in advanced technology contribute to the environmental crises of our time. The gift of reason is not automatically a good thing. Nevertheless, the astounding new ways of thinking that marked the Enlightenment period still lay the foundation for modern social thought. To advocate for social justice is to appeal to the equality of persons, and this equality rests on the inherent dignity of life. Such respect is rooted in the recognition of human autonomy where an individual is seen not collectively as a class but specifically as a citizen of equal rights.[4] Even further, the idea of autonomy in the contemporary world extends to other life forms and to nature itself. Animals of the earth have a right to dignity as do the many vibrant ecosystems of the earth. James Lovelock and his Gaia hypothesis extended the sense of Enlightenment autonomy to the complex and interwoven ecology of the planet as a single organism. So autonomy, even though rightly subject to criticism, remains at the heart of the modern sense of both human and natural rights.

Autonomy, then, is one key to developing religion without God. Whatever religion can mean for humanity, it must mean at least the development of the idea of the dignity of life in all its forms. A religion without God can be about providing community dialogue, about learning how to hold respect for difference, about how to engage in creative debate, and about how to value the social aspects of being human on the foundation of equality. Especially in a technical age where virtual reality can isolate individuals from their living surroundings, these minor values of religion may prove to be no small matter. Religion remains fundamentally community centered, and in this respect it remains counter-intuitive in a libertarian age. Religion offers a collective value because it is about a community covenant. God is not necessary when we value religion as covenant. It is the community that effectively displaces God and that consequently creates God in the activities of its being. The God who almost is can be in a community where the positive values of autonomy recreate and revalue the ancient idea of covenant.

Wisdom is a second value from old religion that is new again. The teaching of wisdom is found throughout the world in the heritage of religion. What makes wisdom an easy companion for the God who almost is, is the way the teaching of wisdom rarely requires confessions about God. In wisdom teaching "God" remains sidelined. God is at the edge but never the center of wisdom. Wisdom places the human imagination on the edge of what is and what is not. The parables of the historical Jesus hold this quality in spades. The parables are not about God, and God is not present in any parable. The parables are secular theology, which means theology acted out in the world. They concern a vision called the *basileia* of God, which is something like the activities or happenings of God within a realm. The Greek word *basileia* is from the world *basileus*, a monarch. The property of the monarch is the *basileia*, which can refer to the palace, the realm, and the laws of the realm. In English the word Basilica is derived from the Greek root. As the New Testament authors record, when Jesus speaks of the *basileia* of God, we know the reference is to a place where God is supposed to be. However, if you do walk into a Basilica, you will notice that it is mostly empty. That is essentially the experience of a parable about the *basileia* of God. The parable is empty of God. Like a Basilica, it feels like a place where you might meet God, but God is absent. In God's absence you have to create God out of nothing through imagination. The parables of Jesus are not really about God. They are about creating a vision that can be called the way or the happening of God in a counter-intuitive *basileia*.

The historical Jesus parable of the Prodigal Son is an excellent example. Here, the number two son, who cannot inherit the larger portion of the family wealth, takes what portion is his due and goes off to enjoy life. As a young Jewish man in first-century Palestine, we can imagine that "enjoying" life means going to Roman baths, participating in symposium banquets, and indulging in theatre. He lives among gentiles as a profligate, but surely it is a lot of fun. However, the day comes when he has no money and he, a Jew, ends up in the most embarrassing position of feeding pigs to survive. Rather than be a slave on a gentile farm, he decides he is better off being a slave on his father's estate. So he goes back home. Now the comedy begins: he is welcomed home by his father, he is given the householder's mantle, his father thrusts upon him the signet ring, and a fatted calf is slaughtered for a feast in his honor. He even sits at the head of the table. The hearer of this tale must wonder, has this peculiar father taken the main inheritance away from the older son and given it to this second-born loser? That at least is what the older brother thinks. This second-born is apparently a Jacob figure stealing the birthright away from the older Esau. This time, though, the father is handing over the birthright and shunning his eldest son, or so it seems. The elder son sends a servant into the banquet honoring the younger. He wants to know what is going on, and he is rather upset that this younger son who blew his inheritance should be celebrated like a visiting dignitary or perhaps a newly ap-pointed heir. The father comes out to the eldest son, and we might expect bad news for the older brother. But the news is ordinary. The father reassures his heir that in fact he gets everything. This younger son is being celebrated only because he has come home, but in no way does he get any part of the older son's rightful inheritance. This younger son will be under the lordship of the older son. The father only asks his heir, are you going to see this person as my son or are you going to see him as your brother? If he is your brother, should you not celebrate, too?

The question about the prodigal son is twofold. One is, what is being celebrated at the conclusion? The answer is "nothing." There is no party here for re-acquiring one's inheritance. There is no promise here for the replacement of money spent. There is not even any assurance that the younger son will not be a laborer under his older brother. There is no victory for this younger son but only a momentary party about being present in the family again. What will happen after this moment passes is anyone's guess, including Jesus'. Meanwhile, throughout the story, there is no God present. The banquet is not a worship service. The thanksgiving is about the son's return and not about God's providence or mercy. There is no indication that the characters in any way invoke the name of God. This parable, like many of the Jesus parables, is about life—a certain dynamic or incident in life—where the activity of the characters conveys a vision or intention about a different kind of reality. We know the parable is not really about a dysfunctional family. We know it is about something else, but there is nothing in the story, aside from the characters, to grab onto. We know it is not a story about a family but at the same time there is only the family story to deal with. There is something there that is not there. There is something attractive in the parable created out of the absence of an explicit moral, teaching, or statement of faith. We, the reader or the hearer, have to create something in the emptiness of the parable in order for the parable to have meaning for us. We have to take advantage of the God who almost is in order to create meaning in the story. We have to use our autonomy, our own minds, to effectively create something out of nothing.

We could say that wisdom in religion involves the act of creating value out of nothing. This, we might even further venture, is the way Enlightenment theology continues in our time as a truly religious act. Enlightenment theology is the bringing forward of a vision that recreates the value of life as a kind of leap of faith. It is not a leap based on physical evidence, but neither is it purely speculative fiction. It is a value created as a vision of what life can mean. In the prodigal story, the younger son does not get his inheritance back. He does not get anything out of the deal of returning home except that his father welcomes him home with a banquet. We do not know what he will get from his older brother, and there is no mention of a mother. We don't even know why his father should celebrate his homecoming as he did. There is so much not given in the parable, so much absence in the parable, that we have to fill in the background to create some meaning. This is the nature of wisdom teaching: to bring us to nothing so that we can wake up to the possibility of creating something. We can wake up to a leap of faith. Wisdom as this generous opening to life is a most basic religious act.

To bring us to nothing so that we can see something is the value of Enlightenment theology. As a religious act, ironically—and what is wisdom without irony—it has nothing to do with religion. We do not have to be religious to understand wisdom. Neither does one have to believe something to hear in religious language the presence of human wisdom. When the Apostle Paul wrote that "I am crucified with Christ; nevertheless, I live" (Galatians 2:20),[5] we do not need to be religious or even to believe in Christ to understand what Paul is saying. His ego-centrism has been crucified. He has died to his former way of being. He has overcome whatever caused him to harass the early followers of Jesus. But he still lives. It's not that he is physically dead. It is that he sees life in new ways. The image of being crucified but still living is the image of coming to see emptiness in what was but, in this, awakening to the great possibilities of many new things. That younger son in the prodigal story is, in a way, crucified. He lost everything. Somehow the father says, "Nevertheless, you live." The older brother is going through a type of crucifixion as he sees in the younger one only a profligate who makes him jealous. His jealousy is over the banquet. Nevertheless, looking upon this nothingness, in place of seeing a rival he might now see his brother. He could know that the very nothingness he is experiencing is the chance to see things in a new way. He is offered a moment of reflection. He has a chance to change. We do not know whether he will take it. We are left standing with him in the story, at the edge of the abyss, gazing into the banquet of nothing, and waiting to see if he and we get it. That is the value of religion as enlightenment. It has nothing to offer us except everything. It gives us no God, but in not handing over God it does give us the possibility of life. Out of nothing religion creates life. That is its artistic skill, its hidden promise, its value, and its vision. That is the wisdom of religion, but, necessarily, it is religion without God. It is wisdom with a God who almost is.

Learning to understand and then to value religion without God requires getting over Christianity. For traditionally, despite Jesus, Christianity attempts to give us God. In the Christian parable of the Prodigal Son, the tradition is to take the story allegorically where the father is God and the son is a lost soul who finds forgiveness and acceptance in God. This is the gospel writer Luke's interpretation, which we can read in the verse preceding the parable where we are told "there is joy before the angels of God over one sinner who repents" (Luke 15:10). For Luke, there is no abyss here to stare at, and there is no question about creating something out of nothing. Rather, it's all there. God, the sinner, repentance, and the forgiveness. It is, to be sure, an effective interpretation, but it opts to place into the story what is not truly there. It opts to have the assurances of the arrival without the quest of the journey. Traditional Christianity is not about the God who almost is but about the God who brings everything that is to a close. Traditional Christianity places an insistence not only on God but more precisely on what God does, which is to spell out the order, purpose, and final conclusion of the universe.

With an emphasis on order comes the focus on authority, and this might be why traditional Christianity had a lot of trouble with the rise of individual autonomy and the birth of science as the new authorities in our age. Traditional Christianity upholds that only God as the authoritative father can have the final word in the story, which means that only the church can ultimately state what is true. The Church traditionally invested its authority in structures that supposedly represent permanence, and it has traditionally struggled to revise those structures even when desperately needing to do so. It is as if the Church developed the habit of thinking that when the day of judgement finally arrives, if it can manage to hang on, Jesus will return to put the world back in order and to say to the church "well done." In traditional Christianity, the evil people go one place and the good another, and in each place there is a hierarchy of beings from God to angels to saved people and then on to Satan, demons, and the damned. To its credit, the Roman Catholic tradition surmised that perhaps there is some wiggle room here, so we do have purgatory. But finally, the day of judgement arrives, the apocalypse happens, and the motion of all things comes to an end. Nothing further changes. There is no longer the lively "becoming" of autonomy to recreate covenants nor the wisdom of enlightenment open the challenges of an alternative vision. There is now only the static being of subservience. And this supposedly is the good news.

Perhaps, outside such an apocalyptic scenario that shuts down history with the hope of a static and unchanging ending, there is a chance today for alternative visions and even an alternative Christianity. In the prodigal story the older brother acts out of habit. He expects everything to be as unchanging as ever. He was the responsible older son who stayed home and worked, not the younger wasteful son who took his money and ran. The universe is supposed to be just; the rewards should fall on the good. Perhaps this parable, among its other dimensions, indicates that the possible is possible only when the inevitable is not inevitable. Christianity, in its history, has been like that older son, waiting for the apocalypse and its just reward. But what if there is no apocalypse? What if, like the older son, the Church waits outside the banquet of life only to find that the banquet holds no threat to our existence and no sign of ending with a bang. It only invites. What, then, becomes of Christianity, and of God, and of the human future?

10

Saving
Apocalypticism

Apocalyptic theology is that form of theology committed to holding
the last card in the deck of human history on the last day of the cal-
endar of cosmic time. Apocalypse means unveiling, from the Greek
compound *apo*, away, and *kalumma*, veil. To reveal hidden contents
is the apocalyptic act. In traditional Christianity the unveiling at the
end of time consists of the final judgement when all the nations will
be gathered before Jesus, as the writer of Matthew liked to imagine
it, and "he will separate them one from another as a shepherd separates the sheep from the goats" (24:32). In this last act of revelation
the unrighteous are deservedly exposed and punished while the
hereto now unrecognized righteous receive their reward.

When it comes to God in the Bible, unveiling the hidden contents of the apocalypse is not always good news. A lot depends
on two things: which God and which theologian are involved.
When the theologian is the author of Isaiah, the apocalypse can be
welcomed since the God of Isaiah is the God of compassion who
unveils peace on earth in the final days. When the theologian is the
author of the book of Revelation, the apocalypse is, ridiculously,
about revenge and a gleefully God of destruction. In relation to the
apocalypse the problem for the Church historically has been answering the question about which God and which theology should be
involved. The historical Jesus does not seem to have an apocalyptic
vision, but if he does it is given in parable. Since God is more or less
absent, or at best "almost" present in the parables, this source is not
a very good one for defining an apocalypse. The Church, though,

has other options. Gospel writers like Matthew enjoyed adding apocalyptic elements to stories both about and by Jesus. Images like lakes of fire and the gnashing of teeth are climatic additions that provide end time content to the confession of the Church. At the end of time Christ shall return. As the Catechism of the Catholic Church puts it, "God's triumph over the revolt of evil will take the form of the Last Judgment after the final cosmic upheaval of this passing world."[1] There is no "almost" about God when it comes to the Church's version of "unveiling" truth at the end.

How do you take a parable-telling wisdom teacher like the historical Jesus and turn him into the hero of an apocalypse who shows up as Lord of the Last Judgment? How do you take the openings of wisdom and close them with apocalypticism? How do you silence wisdom? The first act in doing this, which Augustine taught us in chapter 7, is to turn parables into allegories. The second act of the same play is to convert the new allegories, through philosophy, into the doctrines of the Church. Let us try to break down and understand this process.

A parable is a story involving characters. An allegory is a story in which the characters involved become the symbols of a second story. In chapter 7 I used Augustine to exemplify how the Jesus parable involving a Samaritan character can be interpreted as an allegory about Christian salvation. But Augustine was not at all the first to understand (or misunderstand) that a parable can be read as an allegory. He was not the first to see in one story a second, hidden story. The gospel writers beat him to it by several centuries. The second story introduced into the parables through the hands of the gospel writers concerns the nature of Jesus Christ and the nascent faith of the Christian movement. Only as an allegorical symbol can the father, in the parable of the Prodigal Son, be for Luke the Christ figure who welcomes home the lost, and only as an allegory can the Samaritan be, again for Luke, the enactment of the Christian call to love one's neighbor. Neither of these points belongs to the two parables. As we have seen, the prodigal story is about choice in the face of resentment and the Samaritan story is about our enemy pouring uninvited loving kindness upon us. In the gospels such stories slide from their original setting into the concerns of emerging Christianity. Then, in the history of Christianity and through figures like Augustine, this initial slide becomes full permission for the Church to conceive Jesus as the essential figure of apocalyptic warnings and judgments.

The use of Jesus' parables as allegories about Christian identity, Christian beliefs about Jesus, Christian attitudes toward Jews, and Christian confessions about Jesus being the end time judge is exactly what we see in the rise of Christianity.[2] Indeed, we might venture to say that in the Christian gospels, the historical Jesus is used as an allegory for Jesus Christ.

With Jesus established as an allegory for Jesus Christ, a second act follows which consists of transforming the allegory, with philosophy, into doctrine. The Christian gospels having set the precedent, later Councils like Nicaea could easily extend the allegory of Jesus Christ into the philosophical category of substance to form the basic doctrines of the Christian confession. Jesus is not Jesus but a second Jesus, the allegory of Jesus Christ, who is of one substance with God. It is in this great and final act that Christ, the second and, for the Church, "true" story of Jesus, becomes the God who will bring time itself to a close.

When taken literally, as is often the case in our times, the apocalyptic scenes of biblical and catechetical proportion fail to rise above absurdity. No amount of belief can turn imaginary allegories into factual events. No theologian, however determined, can turn the symbolism of Christianity into evidence-based conclusions about time and the cosmos. But of course theology is not science, and the Bible is not a set of books about conclusions drawn from evidence. It is only modern literalism about the Bible that leads the Bible, the "books," to this dead end. Is there a way to avoid such delusions with the Christian tradition and not demand from it an uncompromising, if not absurd, truth? Is there a way to reshape the covenant tradition of theology such that apocalypticism can usefully describe experiential metaphors rather than confessional truths? The difference is important. Experiential metaphors are about life and how to imagine it; confessional truths are about supernatural beliefs and how to hold them. To recast this step as a question, can the silencing grip of apocalyptic beliefs be reimagined such that Covenant theology can find a voice of value for our time?

Apocalypticism, despite the exaggerations of modern literalism, remains the essence of Covenant theology, for the covenant is about the foundational purposes and values of community. One cuts a covenant in order to seal the promise that certain practices will be observed. The covenant is a social bond, broadly understood, that seeks to answer questions about our destiny as humanity and define the purposes of our community. In this sense, the idea of the covenant is visionary and apocalyptic, that is, the covenant is driven by the question of our common destination. But we know that apocalypticism runs away with itself and can, if unguarded, turn the covenantal spirit of community into a wrath-filled body of believers set against perceived enemies and various non-believers. Christianity has been as capable as any other religion of producing in its midst apocalyptic groups so defined. Obbe Philips experienced and wrote about the apocalyptic community of the Melchiorites in the sixteenth century, "They could suffer neither the love nor benefit of another who was not of their belief, sect, opinion, and who did not say yes and amen to all their enterprises and onslaughts."[3] Apocalypticism in its worst forms, and the Church has known many such forms in its history, is about insiders with a second and true story set against outsiders with a false one. The allegories run unchecked among the insiders and usually involve, as Phillips noted, the recasting of outsiders as threatening and demonic. But there is an antidote, if we can imagine it this way, which consists of not allowing the allegories to be the final words about the parables. The value of apocalypticism is its concern for a common vision involving communal destination, which is the hallmark of Covenant theology. Apocalypticism can be positively cultivated if the allegorical temptations to divide and conquer remain under the humble spell of the parable.

I mean here not that every allegory, especially those intentionally recorded, is in reality intended to be a parable. There are allegories written to be allegories. The writers of the Christian gospels do intend to tell some allegories and do recast some parables as allegories. Gospel writers do add "second stories" to the first ones with their commentary and elaborations. A parable of Jesus can be converted into an allegory by a gospel writer to express the gospel writer's convictions, or secondary beliefs, about Jesus. This is to be expected, and part of understanding the Bible is to become good at recognizing exactly this. What I do mean, though, is that an allegory need not be overwhelmed by the ultimate claims of apocalypticism such that apocalypticism should hold Covenant theology in captivity. Instead an allegory can be converted by the spirit of the parable such that every allegory is opened as theological speculation rather than closed as end time or final claims. Insofar as apocalypticism remains fundamentally part of the spirit of Covenant theology, this seemingly minor change to the allegory or second story is significant.

When the gospel writer Matthew tells the parable of the Marriage Feast at 22:2–14, Matthew does indeed mean this to be an allegory. Matthew is taking the earlier Great Banquet parable recorded in Luke 14:15–24 and rewriting it as the allegory of the Marriage Feast. The parable as it is found in Luke comes from the Q Gospel, which is a source gospel for both Matthew and Luke. But unlike Luke, Matthew changes the story dramatically. In Matthew's version, it is a king who gives a marriage feast, and the feast is for his son. The king's servants go out to escort the invited guests to the banquet, and just like in Luke's version the guests refuse the invitation. However, Matthew elaborates. Not only do guests refuse the invitation, they also beat and kill the king's servants. In response, Matthew continues, the angry king sends an army out to destroy the city of the invited guests. Matthew's allegory improves only slightly from here. The king invites a second set of guests but notices one is not properly dressed. This poor soul is bound hand and foot and cast into the outer darkness where there is weeping and gnashing of teeth. The pattern of Matthew's theology riddles this once-upon-a-time parable now converted to an allegory. To Matthew, the Jewish prophets invited the Jewish people to the banquet of Jesus the son, but the Jewish people refused the invitation. To ensure we understand this, Matthew employs the image of Jesus crying over Jerusalem as the city that killed the prophets (23:37). After the death of Jesus, Matthew has the risen Lord announce that the gospel is now for the nations. However, not all the people of the nations take it very seriously. The undeserving among the nations, like the improperly dressed person in the allegory who apparently did not care, will be cast into darkness or worse thrown into an eternal fire (25:41). Consequently, even though the writer tells the story as if it is a parable, Matthew definitely intends the Wedding Feast to be an allegory. On the surface the allegory involves beaten and killed servants and a cast out guest, but there is a second story involving Jerusalem's treatment of the prophets and the fate of the nations. Matthew takes what was once a very different parable and uses it to inspire the writing of an allegory. The movement Matthew employs is from parable to allegory, and this movement generally describes the same movements of traditional Christian theology. But what if the historic move of the Church was reversed? What if allegories were interpreted in the spirit of a parable, thus reversing the usual pattern of revising parables in the spirit of an allegory?

This reversal requires some explanation in order to present Covenantal theology as a continuing value of religion, which is my intention. It is particularly necessary to distinguish between the spirit of an allegory and that of a parable. I call the spirit of an allegory, resolution. An allegory seeks to reveal a second, hidden story within its narrative. The desire is to use the second story to explain or resolve the true meaning of the first story. An allegory wants to state that within the puzzling and often contradictory experiences of the world, there is a second, underlying intention to all that happens. It is the secondary intention, which is the hidden intention of God, that resolves the primary, contradictory situations of life. So, the gospel writer Matthew can reveal in allegory that though the primary situation is the destruction of Jerusalem, the secondary resolution is found in the divine intentions associated with Christ. Jerusalem refused the invitation of the prophets to the banquet of the son. The "king" is justified in seeking destructive revenge. So, the historic siege and destruction of Jerusalem during the First Jewish War is resolved for Matthew, who writes several decades later, in allegorical Christian theology. The primary situation for Matthew also includes the fact that not all people from among the nations who presume to follow Christ are necessarily righteous. Matthew here again can explain that even among those who received the gospel, some will be too casual and will be thrown out from among the righteous. Matthew's allegory is explaining that the underlying intentions of God will be fulfilled despite appearances to the contrary. In the unfolding of history, Matthew believes there is a second story being told behind the scenes. It is the secondary imaginary, the allegorical story, that resolves the problems of the real world, the primary or actual experiences in life. An allegory aims to uncover a hidden solution. A parable does not hold this intention. Even though a parable, like an allegory, is a fictional story, it actually creates rather than solves a puzzle. The parable opens up a question and leaves to the hearer both the task of interpretation and the question of relevance. The parable of the Good Samaritan does not resolve the question about who is my neighbor, as Luke believed (10:29), but opens the problem of enmity and creates a situation of discernment. The hearer of the Samaritan parable may well dismiss it. Precisely due to the influences of existing enmity, the hearer may be unwilling to face the problem of enmity. In any case, the Samaritan parable does not solve this problem. It plays with it.

The spirit of a parable is one that disrupts the desire for resolution. Whereas the allegory seeks to uncover the truth in a given situation, the parable seeks to play with the given situation to uncover a question. The conviction of truth gives to an allegory its spirit of resolution, but the problem of life gives to a parable its spirit of questioning. Matthew, in the allegory of the Wedding Feast, does not see a problem in the way things are going because it will all end up before the judgement of God. Jesus, in the parable of the Samaritan, does see a problem with the way things are going. Though he has no definite solution to offer, the problem is brilliantly raised. The hearer of the parable is challenged to confront his or her own prejudices. Distinct from the allegorical spirit of resolution is the parabolic spirit of questioning.

To bring this to bear on Covenant theology as a continuing value of religion, it is now important to restate how an allegory is apocalyptic in style and then how that style is recast in parable. Since the allegorical spirit is resolution, an allegory is a natural vehicle for delivering the real experiences of human history to a secondary story about the final end. The spirit of the allegory is to find at the end of time the ultimate resolution to the problems of the present age. In the book of Revelation there is the vision of the new Jerusalem (21:2) that descends to the earth from above as the expressed recreation of the earth according to the intentions of God. Like the garden of Eden, the new Jerusalem holds a flowing river of life and a tree of life (22: 1–2). Placed at the end of the Christian Bible, the book of Revelation, despite its many vengeful and torturous images, returns history at the end back to its beginning. Northrop Frye called this the "U" shape of a comic act. Effectively Frye looked at the seriousness of the apocalypse in Revelation as a comic metaphor. He interpreted the insistent apocalyptic allegories in Revelation as a parable. We start on top of the world in a good place, he indicated, and move down a slope to lose it all, and then revert and climb back up to fullness. In the Christian Bible, Frye wrote, humankind starts with but "loses the tree and water of life at the beginning of Genesis and gets them back at the end of Revelation."[4] The allegorical spirit concerns the act of getting back to what God intends, and it does so by presenting the present struggles as a hidden test of faith and a divine promise of vengeance to those who persevere to the end. In allegory, those who can see the secret of history will get their reward at the end of history. But if we add the idea of a parable to counteract the resolution sought in an allegory, something like Frye's sense of comedy enters the scene. It is possible to express that the important thing about an apocalypse is not its blast of trumpets at the end but its comic relief in the now. What we can consider here is how the spirit of a parable will not allow for a hidden allegorical resolution. The parable, in other words, will not transpose present history into a disguise for theology but rather will transpose the will to resolve history into the question of the present time. It is this transposing or feeding back that we can understand as the comic relief of the parable. It is "comic" in the sense that the parable releases—drops, lets go of—the closing desires of an allegory in order to retrieve in the present the struggle of Covenant theology. The Samaritan parable, again, does not resolve the problem of enmity but raises the problem in a supremely artistic expression as the current question. It is a comic act because it retrieves the apocalyptic vision of community peace that is present in Covenant theology as the challenge of the actual situation. The spirit of the parable understands this present struggle as a type of gift to life, not that the specific struggle with enmity is "good" but that the struggle awakens a transformative vision in the here and now. It energizes the value of theology as the task of translating the covenant in the present as a significant question. The apocalyptic element in the parable of the Good Samaritan is the vision of a world where there is no enmity, not even between Jews and Samaritans. But this vision does not come alive as an end time resolution. It is not delayed until later or deferred to the end. It is not awakened in vengeance. It comes alive in the situation as the question at hand—the theological question, we can say, about how the covenant lives now.

Thomas J.J. Altizer recently extolled the apocalyptic elements in the thought of Paul Tillich. In so doing Altizer, perhaps unintentionally, upholds Tillich as one example with whom the Christian apocalyptic temptation to desire final resolutions is turned by a parabolic spirit into the immediate ethical questions of our time. In this way, Tillich's theology is a Covenant theology. Altizer starts by asking whether Tillich was an apocalyptic theologian. He means in this question to ask whether Tillich embodies the hope of a final transformation of all things. Then, Altizer answers his question. "Tillich is seemingly closed to all apocalyptic worlds and all apocalyptic vision, but he was, nonetheless, in quest of an absolutely new Christianity and an absolutely new Christ."[5] Even though Tillich rejected apocalypticism in a literal sense, and is thus very much closed to it, Altizer emphasizes that, nevertheless, Tillich's quest is the immediate transformation of Christianity. Tillich saw the need for this transformation as the question now. We might say, and indeed we are reminded of this in the early Tillich's *The Socialist Decision*,[6] that a radical commitment to the transformation of society is the character of Tillich's form of apocalypticism. It is essentially apocalypticism transformed by parable into the encounter with the problematic world. For Tillich, and so for Altizer, theology is relevant insofar as it addresses the present cultural setting. In his later work, Tillich specifically highlighted existential philosophy, the modern problems of disintegrating communities, and personal angst about overpowering capitalism in an age of technology as the questions of our time. In the midst of such challenges Tillich offered the image of the New Being as a present form of reunification with the divine in the world.[7] Though this is highly religious language, we can see Tillich's point. The power of religion is transformational but not necessarily specific. Religion draws on its ancestral vision but gives that vision to the world as a comic turn to the present questions.

Altizer, to my mind, summarizes this nicely when he explains that in the context of rising secularity coupled with reactionary fundamentalism, Tillich did not offer an exit from culture but rather became "our most influential theologian, giving us a theology that could truly address this new world, and address it as could no other theology."[8]

We may not always agree with Tillich and exactly how he chose to go forward, but we can uphold his thought as an example of tipping Covenant theology away from allegorical temptations with the spirit of the parable. Tillich finds in the finite experience of being human the questions that arise out of our cultural condition. In ways like the historical Jesus Tillich draws his language from the contemporary world. For Tillich it was the language of human experience, which he found in the existential language of the twentieth century, that identified our version of the Samaritan issue. The issue for Tillich was estrangement: the alienation from genuine community by the automating effects of technology. Christ is Tillich's parable of "a personal life which is subjected to all the consequences of existential estrangement but wherein estrangement is conquered in himself [or herself] and a permanent unity is kept with God."[9] This is Tillich's way, I am proposing, of using the parabolic spirit to transform the allegorical Christ into the questions of Covenant theology today.

The temptation of the Church is to silence the open parable by giving a higher value to the allegory and its final resolutions. The Church prefers a delayed, futuristic, and second story to the immediate questions now. Kirsopp Lake held this very perception in 1925, and it is hard to deny that what he saw has largely come to pass.[10] Lake observed first that there would be an exodus of what he called "experimentalists" from the Christian church. The experimentalists are those who, somewhat like Tillich, are eager to revise if not revolutionize Christianity in light of modern breakthroughs in history and science. Such eager people, though, are judged to be idealist and effectively discover that there is no room in the inn for revolutions. Lake argued that this left-leaning body would move out of the Church. What remained would be the liberal orthodox and the fundamentalists. The liberal orthodox accept the consequences of nineteenth-century critical biblical studies and even accept that science today opens humanity to a very different understanding of the universe. Still, the intention of the liberal orthodox is to preserve the tradition, which means that all the effort is given to re-stating traditional doctrine. Meanwhile, the fundamentalists want neither the results of biblical criticism nor the information from modern science. Indeed, doctrines are not even that important in fundamentalism. What is important is confession. Belief and subjectivity trump history and tradition. In Lake's speculations from 1925, these two groups would move the Church steadily to the right where, finally, fundamentalism would define it while the orthodox, who remain, would tolerate fundamentalism so long as the doctrines continued to be confessed. Meanwhile, the left-wing of the Church would disappear. To elaborate Lake's observation, not only was he basically right but we can also say that his orthodox and fundamentalist groups rose to dominate the Church by silencing the parabolic spirit of Jesus. At the dawn of the twenty-first century, across many denominations and on any given Sunday, the Christian gospels seemed inevitably to be about a second story that will one day unfold in God's heaven. The actual setting in life, especially on the right side of the political scene, became as it were an apocalyptic stage on which to play out the allegorical significance of the present with end time ultimatums, violence, privileged and prejudiced policies. But Lake might have missed one point, which perhaps we are witnessing today. Though the experimentalists, who might also be called the parable keepers, find little or no room in the Church today, they have found recently that they do not actually need the Church. What is needed is community, the basic element of Covenant theology, in which progressive and independent understandings of Christianity can be pursued. Lake did not see the irony in his observation. Though the experimentalists would indeed leave the Church they would at the same time recreate the Church but outside the Church. They would become the anti-Church, which one could argue is more authentically Christianity. After all, if the "Church" is the community of Jesus, then its parabolic foundation is precisely about the experimentation needed to enact the covenant within the issues of today.

The challenge for progressive forms of Christianity and generally for progressive religion today is to reverse the tradition of allegorical apocalypticism with the spirit of the parable. This means recasting the point of religion—its true apocalyptic intent—not with the closing but the opening of time. In the Western tradition, the sense of history has been honed in allegories as closed apocalypticism: that is, history understood as hiding a second story about the end of time. Reversing this form of thinking without losing the basic heart of the covenant, which is the act of living intentionally in community with vision, requires a different sense of what religion is about. This can be found in that theological style, which I have called Enlightenment theology. If Covenant theology can, through the parable, reverse apocalyptic intentions to bring hope and new vision to the surface now, Enlightenment theology can answer the question about why religion as such is still a basic human value.

11

Theology and the Opening of Time

Covenant theology is the communal emphasis of theology; it is theology's move into the community situation and its concern for society. Enlightenment theology is related to the individual, the quest for meaning, and the value of a religious tradition in the act of seeking self-actualization. In the covenant tradition, theology has the ability to bankrupt its own heritage by investing all its wealth in a fictional apocalyptic time to come that displaces the move into the time that is now. In Enlightenment theology the act of bankrupting the tradition comes in the form of avoiding the question of meaning through popular theologies, which I will the call confessional, sacred, and salvation forms of theology. Each turns the potential value of religion for humanity into something substantially less. These three forms of theology close the transformational promise of enlightenment. They do so by seeking from the experience of time an ultimate expression of theology and thus an unchanging divine norm. Similar to how the allegory silenced the value of Covenant theology, the three forms above appropriate time as a closed, that is, predetermined system.

It is worth stating as a reminder that as I use the word "theology," I mean art. Theology is not about the technical achievements of science. Theology can certainly be informed by science, but its subject is the question of meaning in human existence. It is easy enough to conclude that human existence has no meaning whatsoever, that inside a universe that unfolds endlessly with no obvious purpose, the human experience counts for very little. The

theological task is not to decide how much meaning the human
place holds in the dynamics of the cosmos. There is no answer to
that question on an objective scale other than the obvious answer
that human life is only a momentary flash in the unlimited history of
the cosmos. Rather than voicing ultimate answers, on the enlightenment side the theological task is to ask how, in the moments of
fleeting life and changing history, human experience can hold value.
To address such a question on a factual basis with a definitive yes
or no answer fails to understand the kind of question asked. Giving
meaning to an experience is an interpretive act. Using experience to
evaluate one's life and to creatively become something more than
one was is the enlightenment task. Religion can be a resource in the
enlightenment task like the paint brushes of an artist or the lyrical
expressions of a poet. But no piece of art and no poem is understood if viewed simply as a fact. Like religion, they are understood
as an interpretation, an expression, and an experience.

Life expressed as art consists of standing before the abyss of
the threatening, curious, unknown, amazingly full, and amazingly
empty nature of the cosmos and saying yes to it all. The yes is not
due to scientific facts; it is due to hermeneutical acts, that is, to
acts of interpretation that create meaning and value as the art of
being alive. The supreme hermeneutical act in religion, as Paul
Tillich famously expressed it, is to stand before the abyss and say
yes to the courage to be. Tillich understood this resolute yes to be
a joyful expression in theology. "Joy is the emotional expression of
the courageous YES to one's own true being," as Tillich put it.[1] If
someone can stand before the abyss, can grasp the vast nature of the
question of meaning, can answer yes to the question with courage,
and can find in this act that a religious tradition helps give form to
life dynamics, that person can be the kind of artist we commonly call
a theologian. That yes, we might also say, is the heart of theology in
its enlightenment expression.

Understanding life as the challenge of finding meaning in the
emptiness of the universe is not at all foreign to the Bible. The

writer of Ecclesiastes speaks of a vanity of vanities. The writer refers to momentary vapor that fades to nothing like a frosty breath on a winter's morning.[2] This is why I am saying that the theological act of enlightenment is fortitude, a somewhat wild but certainly creative affirmation of meaning. Affirming meaning is an act, a human-creating act, where religion is like a resource of poetic expression. Such acts place the focus on qualities like forgiveness, loving beyond enmity, and overcoming egoism with compassion to create a sense of human value in the midst of vanishing temporality. Each act can be called religious, for each is about relationships formed beyond the natural limitations that our families or our cultures place on our perspectives. Each act, in this sense, is "open"; each is about confronting the question of life with a certain attitude of trust. Christianity, as a historic religion, has always held elements of enlightenment in this way, but equally it has always closed this narrative with final judgments about time and final statements about doctrinal truths. Christianity, like many other religions, has always tended, if not even preferred, to address genuine questions with closed options. A closed answer is one that allows no further point of debate, which is a simple way to avoid the hermeneutical task of religion. When I review the confessional, sacred, and salvation forms of Christian theology, I am reviewing those propositions intended as enlightenment that actually close the hermeneutical questions and end the task of religion. As I review these three forms, I will review them in their philosophical expression, but the reader may well be capable of translating these into other kinds of expressions like dogmatic, biblical, or historical theology.

The confessional form of theology holds its philosophical foundation in the medieval cornerstone of God as a necessary being. It repeats, in a modern style, the medieval logic that a primary being must be a perfect (unchanging) being and, as such, a necessary being. In the Middle Ages, a perfect being provides stability to all other forms of being and is therefore the presupposition of all forms of being we see physically in the world. A perfect being like perfect heat is necessary or pre-given to fire. Perfect heat qualifies the status of a given fire here on earth, and the fire on earth holds a lower status than the fires of the stars in heaven. This form of argument is called the ontological argument because it involves arguments based on the perfection of beings, the order of beings, and the necessity for a perfect, absolute, and immovable being who is God.

Contemporary philosophical theology no longer upholds the ontological argument as it was expressed in the Middle Ages. In place of claiming that God is a necessary being, it is more popular to propose that God is a reasonable assumption within the experience of being. In other words, reason cannot prove that God exists but reason can prove that it is not possible to prove God does not exist. It's like using the back door of the same house that the theologians of the Middle Ages entered through the front. In place of concluding God is necessary, the conclusion is that God's possibility is reasonable. I call this a confessional argument in theology because the argument attempts to force human reason into admitting that God's existence is entirely credible.

A contemporary expression of this theology uses modal logic, and a contemporary philosophical theologian who uses modal logic exceptionally well is Alvin Plantinga. The word "modal" refers to the "mood" or tone of a logical premise. In place of "if" and "then" arguments found in basic syllogisms, modal logic employs degrees of probability that reflect the moods of the predicate (explanation) of the premise. A classical argument could be expressed as *If dogs bark, and the sound I heard was a bark, then I heard a dog*. The mood of that argument is definitive, that is, it concludes without qualifying statements or modal conjunctions. Modal logic, in contrast, expresses degrees of probability and holds in this sense moods that add tones to the argument. Nevertheless, the attempt remains to demonstrate that a premise might not necessarily be true, but it is more reasonable than its contradiction. In modal logic I might say that *I heard a bark and that every bark potentially comes from an actual dog. But it is not necessarily so that every single dog barks.*

So what I heard was more probably a dog than not a dog. In this way of stating the argument, my conclusion expresses a probability that is strong but not absolute. The probability is strong enough that I can call it a basic premise. A basic premise means that I can accept the premise without further questions, so whenever I hear a bark I am justified in accepting at a basic, virtually instinctive, level that the sound is from a dog. If we change our dog argument to a God argument, modal logic can be used in the attempt to demonstrate that the existence of God is a reasonable and most basic premise.

Plantinga offers a difficult argument in this spirit. In place of medieval perfections, Plantinga talks about maximal greatness and leads us through a series of subtle arguments to the conclusion that it is possible there is a being of maximal greatness. Such a being of maximal greatness must also be one of maximal excellence, for excellence is defined as the quality of greatness. Such a being would be necessarily all powerful, all knowing, and a morally perfect being. Plantinga states that it is possible there is a world where such a being exists, but if this is possible then such a being, in order to be maximally excellent, must exist in every other world (otherwise it cannot be a being of maximal greatness). This argument does not prove that God exists. The mood of the argument is based on the language of probability. What Plantinga wants to show is that the argument establishes the "rational acceptability" of theism or belief in God. We could as equally start the argument by saying that it is possible no being has maximal greatness, and we could as easily conclude the argument with the statement that no being of maximal excellence can exist in any given world. It's the same reasoning and the same use of modal logic, but Plantinga's point is that since both arguments employ the same style of reason, both theism and atheism are equally reasonable.[3]

Though many might object that Plantinga's argument is built out of thin air, for it is purely suppositional, my point is that the argument is structurally closed. By this I mean that it is actually based on confessional beliefs rather than modal logic. The attempt is to put atheism and theism on the same footing, but this means theism and atheism should be set in the same playing field of modern, evidence-based reason. This act reduces the argument to yes or no (affirmative or negative) statements. Even further, the argument assumes that theism and atheism use the same kind of reason to reach identical, though opposite, conclusions. One is that God exists and the other is that God does not exist, but both are based on identical forms of logic. However, surprising as it is, before the advent of modern science, theology rarely supposed that belief in God is the same kind of reasoning as natural or logical reasoning. Even the quintessential theologian Thomas Aquinas, the theologian who symbolically represents all theologians, never held that natural reason proved the existence of God. Aquinas thought that reason can lead us to the edge of this conclusion, but the type of thinking involved in belief is of a different order. As stated above, the better way to describe the type of reason involved in belief is artistic rather than natural reason. Aquinas called this altered form of reason, revelation. It is the kind of reason that is not necessarily reasonable but that does count as genuine insight. Since the Middle Ages, philosophical theologians have been less likely to talk about revelation and belief in God. Belief no longer expresses what theology is about. Instead, the words trust and faith are more appropriate. Theology, as we saw with Covenant theology, is about trusting the story of humanity and investing hope in the human story. Theology opens up a vision of life, as a parable, that inspires a present confrontation with the question of life. Though this is far removed from medieval attempts to explain something about a necessary being, the act nevertheless shares with the Middle Ages the basic idea that when it comes to theology, technical reason—reason employed to understand nature—is not the same kind of reason that defines the theological task. To speak about meaning in life, the kind of reason involved is artistic or parabolic reason.

The problem with attempting to prove that the existence of God is as factually reasonable as the denial of God's existence involves subordinating the hermeneutical value of the question of God to the factual question about God's existence or lack of existence. The act of closing down the question, or reducing it to factuality, is a hidden form of confessional orthodoxy. It removes God from the stage of hermeneutics where interpretation rules supreme and isolates God purely as an assertion with which the faith tradition can continue confessing truths about God—God's power or God's perfection or God's nature—in safety. The factual question deletes the faith element, which is risk and artistic achievement rather than supposedly factual assertions conceived in natural reason. To persist in the effort to prove that God as a thing exists in the world or is at least as probable an option as any other, recasts the persistent hermeneutical struggle for meaning into a final claim of fact. The claim that there is a God may draw from me the assent or rejection of my reason but ironically does not draw me into faith or what I would otherwise call the poetry of life. The trust question is interrupted by the factuality question. In this form of argument, the only option for the participant is to affirm or deny that God exists, and the only option for God is to be the all-powerful deity or nothing at all. Theologically speaking, the all-powerful deity is a dead God. It is a God that cannot disturb my question about meaning, cannot be the problem concerning trust, and cannot make much difference to my personal existence. There is no quest for meaning with a God who cannot be anything but factual or non-existent.

With Enlightenment theology God is not an answer or a claim but an open question that concerns a vision, and "vision" is used not to mean something abstract and distant but something through which one might find orientation in life. A parable, we can remember, does not solve a problem but raises it creatively and offers, in its hearing, not the final word about an issue but the opening words about a debate. Inasmuch as confessional theology seeks to close the question with a final claim about the reality of God—without ever raising the problem of God as a human value—it remains subtlety an anti-enlightenment, indeed, anti-theology form of theology.

The same contrary spirit is evident in a second way of silencing the open spirit of enlightenment: sacred theology. At first it might seem that sacredness should be the center of theology since the word depicts the sanctity of God and "God's creation." Teilhard de Chardin (1881–1955), a gifted Jesuit Priest who, among other things, was also a physicist and paleontologist, made the idea of the sacred a centerpiece of his theology. In his autobiographical book, *The Heart of Matter*, Teilhard recounts how he came to conceive the heart of Christ as the heart of the cosmos.[4] In these two metaphors he joined sacredness to matter and attempted to see the whole of the cosmos as something like a theater of the sacred. It is not my intention to downplay this fascinating, mystical expression, but it is important, nevertheless, to point out how the idea of sacredness can be used in a contrary way to lead theology astray to a closed expression.

The idea of sacredness assumes in ritual acts a division between the sacred and the profane. In fact, as we reflect on this, the common idea of sacredness is actually opposite to Teilhard's attempted integration. In place of integration, sacredness divides space devoted to God from secular or profane space in the world. The division means that there is a special kind of sacred time and location distinct from the regular times and places in the world. What is the nature of that special kind of time and space? It is time experienced within Christian liturgy as space reserved for God. In the confines of that sacred space, time stands still as language separates itself from nature to become the Word of God. This liturgical act is quite fundamental and key to the critique here proposed. Liturgical language is not just any kind of language. It is language reserved for a special or sacred location, whether that be a physical building or a significant natural setting. The language metaphorically causes time to stand still in the location. It does not, of course, literally do so, but as metaphor the intention of liturgical language is to signify in "other speak," that is, in special language for the occasion, the presence of the divine and unchanging world. In this way the sacred stands against the profane as the other world. And this other world comes into the present as "other speak," which in Christianity is called the Word of God. The act of making the sacred, of bringing the sacred into the present in religious ceremony, is the act of making time stand still. It is the act of creating in space and in time the experience of the other.

In many ways the language used in sacred ceremonies moves across the common human experience, like the spirit of God over the waters of chaos, to create out of certain spaces holy locations now separated from the profane as the other. To be sure, sacredness is alluring. It is the outside. And it is the authoritative voice breaking into the common world of existence. Theologians belonging to the movement called Radical Orthodoxy love the sacred and describe it, as John Milbank does in *Theology and Social Theory*, as the true and rightful voice of an original space that has been corrupted in modernity through the rise of nineteenth-century secularity.[5] The sacred, though, is not really a pure and original time later altered by the secular. The sacred is rather a mimicry of time, a duplication of time that seeks to create from the duplicate a special kind of time in which rituals are metaphors for timelessness. Since humans are wholly in time, the sacred is sacred because in this mimicry time and space become exactly what is not human, which is divine timelessness. Often "enlightenment" is mischievously presented as the act of being mystically united to timelessness. To be sure "timeless" is attractive, for it most certainly is the dream of finite existence, but there are two failures here as well. One is the obvious failure to see sacredness as a human invention. It arises from the initial act of mimicry. When the sacred becomes separated from the act of human creativity, it functions as a delusion. It creates a false self out of the same act of mimicry that created a false time. The second and subtler failure is the inability to grasp enlightenment as the affirmation of being human rather than the act of seeking to exit from the problem of being human. The act of seeking an exit, of seeking to be timeless, poses enlightenment as a transcendental solution that belittles the human experience of time. There are many examples in Christian history of ways to belittle the physical world of time, from fanatical beliefs in an imminent apocalypse to overly enthusiastic mysticisms that regard the physical world purely as temptation. These two forms of enlightenment failure, the one in which enlightenment is posed as timelessness and the one in which it is posed as anti-physical, close theology—bring its task to a halt—with final solutions for the human struggle. But in truth the task of Enlightenment theology is not to get out of time or beyond the flesh. The task is to get into the world. The task is to raise contemporary problems in world affairs and community dynamics and to be in solidarity with such problems that define the struggle to be human. The parables of Jesus place the problem of life before the hearer for debate. The parables do not solve anything; they problematize things. This, not escapism, is the basic act of Enlightenment theology. This, not timelessness, is a value theology can hold in the larger picture of the human enterprise.

If a theologian can navigate around the closing acts of the confessional and sacred forms of theology, there is still the temptation to turn to salvation. It seems, after all, that salvation should be the point of theology. The Gospel of John is popularly quoted to reduce Christianity to the belief in Jesus as savior. Our present culture of commodity fetishism popularly turns salvation into the marketing product of Christianity. We do not need to travel very far into Christianity today to get the message that Jesus died for our sins. Historically, however, Christianity is more sophisticated than this popular mantra. Salvation is the act of restoration. It means healing or returning to a healthy state. On the cosmic scale it is about returning to the Garden of Eden, the mythical state of perfection. In historic Christian expression, the role of Jesus is to be the divine and absolute witness in this present life to the perfection to come. Jesus is so because, as the incarnation of God, he is God's perfection in human flesh. The Nicene Council, as we have seen, is the paramount expression of the theological claim that the fully human Jesus was simultaneously identical in substance to God. In various ways philosophical forms of Christianity continue to preserve the idea that salvation is the lingering knowledge of a primordial perfection that persists in this life, and that of which Jesus is the absolute sign. Wolfhart Pannenberg (1928–2014), a respected, conservative apologist for Christian doctrine, rested his theology on this very element. In human memory, accordingly to his metaphysical speculation, an originating consciousness of the wholeness of creation forms the foundation for the present anticipation of salvation. Our partial experience of life signifies and anticipates the promise of a fullness yet to come. In this way Pannenberg represented a very determined Christian theology that, while open to speculation, is driven to the end of speculation in the closing act of the saving eschaton.[6]

Inasmuch as historical Christianity has upheld salvation as a vision of the final completion of creation that lingers in human memory as anticipation of the end, the tradition of salvation theology problematically assumes that the meaning of theology therefore lies in its invocation of the end. In simplest terms, the trouble with salvation theology is its reduction of theology to speculation about a supernatural world. On the popular scale, it ceases to value theology as the question concerning our humanity in the world and temptingly redirects theology to the question about getting out of the world. In more sophisticated forms, it converts the parabolic task of being in the world to the doctrinal task of believing in another world. Among the texts in the Nag Hammadi library discovered in 1945 is a tractate given the title of *The Discourse on the Eighth and Ninth*. It relays the striking idea that special knowledge is needed to transcend the spheres of the lower powers (the first seven spheres) to reach the divine eighth and ninth spheres. The first seven spheres are physically represented by the sun, moon, and the five then-known planets (Mercury, Venus, Mars, Jupiter, and Saturn).[7] The next two spheres, beyond the limits of the seven known spheres, approach the bliss of divinity. Reaching these higher realms is a question of knowing the unity of the mind with all things. Though this image of attaining salvation in the form of blissful unity with the divine is embedded in ancient cosmology, we can note that the pattern of separation from the divine as a problem and unity with the divine as a solution is the general pattern of salvation theology. Even in mainstream forms of Christianity the pattern holds true. A Christian service of worship is essentially set on the basic acts of confessing separation from God and engaging rituals of reunification with God.

The objection I raise against the salvation form of theology is its implied reduction of theology, especially in exaggerated forms, to ultimate, cosmic solutions that displace existential, living questions. Salvation is helpfully understood as healing, but this initial promise is translated as the aim of human enlightenment and, by extension, the endpoint of history itself. This inevitably means that history serves a purpose only for God. History ensures that God has a platform upon which to solve problems and the means, in human beings, to work them out. Once God is finished, history comes to an end. If not for human beings and their separation from God, there would be no point to this exercise. In effect, it is as if God needs the historical existence of human beings so that God's problems about salvation can reach a conclusion. The value of human existence is tied to God's destiny, and without God there can be no purpose. The problem of being human is given over to humanity's chief creation, which is God. In such abstraction the question concerning meaning escapes into the heavens as that which concerns only God.

In each of these theologies—confessional, sacred, and salvation—God's existence is tied to necessity: God is needed for credible expressions of reason or for the establishment of sacred space or for history to reach its proper conclusion. Each theology is a closed enterprise. The struggle to be human is exempted by confessional yes and no answers, by liturgical attempts to mimic timelessness as the Word of God, and by the reduction of history to God. Can there be ways to struggle with the problems of theology today that resist these classic moves to closed theology? Can there be daring, contemporary ways to open theology and to see this task as theology's new enlightenment expression? There can be such ways provided theology is willing to work against the grain of its historic commitments with some frank and overdue admissions: 1) that God's existence is unnecessary; 2) that God is a human creation, and 3) that the future of God is a human future. If, with God, theology is trying to break open the present with a resolute choice for the now, then one can say that God's future and the human future are the same thing. This ought to mean that God and theology are a continuing value, and even a central value, in the experience of being human.

The claim that God's existence is unnecessary no doubt seems like a strange postulate for the start of a new theology. Theology is supposed to be the "study of God." The claim, though, is not nearly as foreign to theology as one might think. It is not even a radical claim. We have already seen that in the Middle Ages it was comfortable to hold the position that God does not exit. The meaning in the Middle Ages was that God is the presupposition of existence, and this meant that God was outside of and before existence. So, to say "God exists" is to place God in time and make God subject to change. This idea was absolutely not comfortable for most theologians in the Middle Ages. Nevertheless, God was still the presupposition necessary for anything at all to be. So, while God did not exist, God pre-existed what does exist and gave to existence its stability, order, and purpose. In the Middle Ages, though God did not exist, God did "super-exist," that is, God existed as the necessity of existence. God was necessary.

In theology today, to say God's existence is unnecessary is to contradict the heritage and continuing presence of the Middle Ages in two ways. One is the affirmation of the new religious reality. The new reality, as I mean it, is the affirmation that God is a literary figure in human history created by human beings, arising from social histories, and a product of cultural proclivities and languages. This is both a significant shift in the history of theology and an honest admission in light of knowledge today. It is affirming that God is neither the necessity nor aim of existence. On both levels, that of origin and destiny, God no longer functions in our thinking as a needed primary principle. God survived as the universal principle of order until the end of the Middle Ages, but the reality of our time makes this old God a non-answer for questions about the universe today.

The second way that God is unnecessary in contrast to our heritage is the way in which God is "almost being" as opposed to being the "fullness of being." It is as the "almost being" that God is a literary figure. God accompanies human history as that other party who never shows up for the appointment but always leaves a promissory note. It is not easy to answer the question of why this "promissory note" called God persists in hanging around, in one form or another, in our history, and unfortunately for the immediate purpose this question is too complex to address.[8] Presently, I will hold to the assumptions of modern cosmology that there is no one out there whose name is God. However, this assumption does not hinder the work of theology, for is it really the point of theology to say that there is a being named God?[9] Is it really the nature of theology to seek a demonstration for the reasonableness of belief in God? One might say that this very literalism about God is a practical demonstration of why God is unnecessary. When God becomes a simple question about assenting to the reasonableness of belief, the poetic task of struggle deflates. The parable once again becomes the allegory because the struggle of theology once again ceases to be the question by becoming only a response. Thinking again of the Good Samaritan, here the parable opens the question of enmity, but the allegory that Augustine used turned the persistent question of enmity into an end time vision of the Kingdom of God and the glory of the Church. Allegories dilute problems and defer them to transcendental locations. They belie the parable by creating out of its rhetoric a supernatural claim. Whereas the parable is about the shape of reality, an allegory is about its nature. Shaping reality is a creative act; focusing on the nature of reality is a descriptive act.

A parable tells a story about human beings and raises the question of how to imagine a situation differently. The proper subject of theology, in what I have called the enlightenment form, concerns this creative act in which the experience of life can be shaped differently. To convert this concern of the parable to the abstraction of an allegory, so that theology as a work of art becomes theology as a description of beliefs, is to move theology outside the creative realm of time.

The claim that God is not necessary and is a human creation rests on a third insight, which consists of a distinction in the postmodern understanding of language: a distinction between what is called linguistic realism and non-realism (which I will describe here only in the simplest terms). Linguistic realism states that language directly indicates an existing thing. At a fundamental level, there is no interpretation involved in the act of identifying something. When I say dog, in other words, I mean dog. This basic understanding of language is natural and is largely what defines how language is commonly understood in a technical society. The word simply identifies the operating thing over there. Postmodern understandings of language are non-realist because they do not accept a basic one-to-one correspondence between a word and a thing. Instead, the word creates a relationship to a thing, and one word on its own never signifies just one thing. Practically speaking, I can have many relationships to one thing, and the word I use to indicate that thing has a complex history and diverse meanings. I look to my side and I see a telephone. Let the games begin. The word "phone" means sound in Greek, but in Latin it can mean reporting. Its Latin cognate *fama* (talk) is related to the English word fame. I can see in the simple phone the slippery and complex history of an everyday word. But the word also signifies other things. It signifies a positive feeling about communicating with distant friends, a negative feeling about being tied down to this desk, a liberating feeling about having only a cellphone and no land line, or a feeling of no escape in a never ending network of communication. I could work for a phone company, but I could work for another company that seeks a technology to end the era of the phone. The telephone maybe a simple illustration, but even this everyday object demonstrates a postmodern understanding of language. The word I use is always in context, always referring and deferring its meaning, always becoming a new meaning against its history of meanings, and always related to me not merely as an object but as an interpretive relationship to the world.

While it is not the case that words create the world in postmodern thought, it is the case that words create a relationship to the world. Or, words create the interpretive frame of any given experience. So, effectively "words create the world" in the sense that without language there is no relationship.[10] Seeing that words are slippery in this way, that is, that words are contingent, multivalent, and transitional, defines the major premises of linguistic non-realism and its claim that language creates the world or the context of experience in the world.[11] When this insight is brought to bear on God, the problem of theology is no longer the question of God's existence. The question is not whether there is a one-to-one correspondence between the word God and a reality out there that holds this identity. The problem concerns what relation to the world is created in God language. The question is how is God created, and even how should God be created? The struggle of theology, unlike traditional dogmatics, concerns the relationship to the world created in the language of God and not the linguistic realism of God-language. Even further, theology engages struggle specifically to avoid linguistic realism. The struggle of theology today involves changing the existing relationship to the world; it is about a parabolic relationship to the world. Robert Funk, who founded the Jesus Seminar and deeply influenced contemporary understandings of a parable, once claimed that "God is the oncoming future." We can see in his comment that the struggle of theology is about the re-evaluation of the present. It is about inviting an undetermined vision into the thinking of the now. It is about opening the trouble of life to the promise of a different option. In other words, to Funk, theology is a parable.

To expand these statements in practical examples, we can consider how theology can be used as either an invocation or an invasion of the future into the present. Each way is a rhetorical maneuver designed to recast the experience of the moment differently, but whereas the first is a critical recasting, the second is a crisis recasting. To distinguish these two meanings in a popular way, consider incidences from the presidencies of Franklin Delaware Roosevelt and George W. Bush. Granted, the two make an awkward paring, but the distinction between critical and crisis rhetoric lies in their differences.

President Roosevelt was at Mount Rushmore in September of 1936 to witness the unveiling of the sculpted face of President Thomas Jefferson. At that ceremony Roosevelt gave an unscripted speech in which he imagined how a future generation of Americans ten thousand years from now would gaze upon the great monument. There was little doubt for Roosevelt that there would be an America ten thousand years in the future and that those future folks would hold the same patriotic spirit he so deeply expressed. Roosevelt, in other words, confessed a destiny for America, and this evident conviction added to his great popularity. He expressed a belief in a destiny for America through employing a delay of meaning—in this case a ten-thousand-year one. Down the road, ten thousand years from now, Roosevelt believed that the great monument would hold even greater meaning. But when Roosevelt said this, his rhetorical move was not really about the future; it was about how the American people saw the present value of their work. Roosevelt invited the future into the present to re-value the experience of the working American. The delay in meaning was used critically to feed into the present, to re-experience the present, in an alternate way. In Roosevelt's rhetoric the "critical" element is not a criticism of the present age. It is critical in the sense that it momentarily opens the present to an altered vision that can feed into the moment as the question of the immediate value of experience. In this sense Roosevelt was attempting to enlighten his audience, to awaken in the present a reconsideration of events. By displaying his rhetoric as a critical recasting of the present, the whole scene at Mount Rushmore can be called parabolic. It was a simple situation in life but Roosevelt was able to recast the simple situation as "the oncoming future," the re-evaluated present.

The administration of President Bush also employed rhetoric that used the future to recast the present, but in this case it was crisis recasting. It was rhetoric that author Naomi Klein describes as "shock doctrine."[12] Klein defines with this expression how a political administration can dig out from a disaster an apocalyptic element that enables the administration to defend specific policies as non-negotiable. The Bush administration made the case for the invasion of Iraq with the rhetoric of crisis recasting. The shock of weapons of mass destruction, which in the end never existed, was used to create a crisis invasion of the future into the present. What this means is that a vision of a disastrous future composed of emerging fascism and heightened terrorism was used to narrow present decisions to one option. The option for the Bush administration was the invasion of Iraq, which was presented as an absolute necessity. The rhetoric was not critical rhetoric but shocking rhetoric, and by taking this route the present situation was not recast as a time to act differently but as a time to reinforce existing fears so that actions could be exactly the same. Whereas a parable changes the experience of the present, an allegory reinforces the experience of the present. Whereas the Roosevelt administration, we can say, was about parable, the Bush administration was about allegory. One invokes a future to alter the experience of the present; the other invokes a crisis to reinforce an uncompromising destiny for the present.

The two types of rhetoric exist in religion. Both use the rhetorical device of delayed time to impact the future on the present. One form of religion is to employ the thinking style found in allegory such that present experience is cast into a future heaven that comes back into the present as a shock. The religious decision is a crisis decision affecting one's eternal destiny. Time is closed because it is fixed absolutely on the end. The second form is the parabolic understanding of what I have presented as Enlightenment theology. The same technique of delay and reversal is used. The parable paints a picture out of everyday life, but as a story the parable happens in the imagination. It unfolds at the side of one's immediate experience of life. The parable, too, brings that future initially at the side into the present as its question, but here there is no reduction to a single destiny. Instead the parable opens to display the problem of life and in that precise moment is the risk of seeing the world differently. There is not one choice and not one path. Such reductions are both too suspicious and too convenient. The future in parable recasts the present as an alternate world. The Samaritan lives an alternative without enmity, and the hearer of the parable is invited momentarily to that side, but the parable does its work when it re-enters the hearer's life. The question is will the critical recasting of the present be a path taken up by the hearer or will the "shock" of a Samaritan being present in the parable act to seal in the hearer a destiny of hate?

I imagine an enlightenment theologian who knows that a parable critically recasts the present, and I imagine this theologian facing the allegories of shock created by the Bush administration. I imagine such a theologian would tell a parable. It would be about a servant who asked forgiveness from a master to whom the servant owed a great sum of money.[13] With the forgiveness granted, the servant then fails to forgive a friend who owes the servant only a trivial amount. In place of forgiving, the servant throws his friend into prison until the debt is paid. Now the master hears of this and takes revenge on the servant who failed to forgive. The master throws the unforgiving servant in jail and he will stay there until every last cent is paid. For the theologian, such a parable would demonstrate how the world turns to violence even when there are initial efforts for peace. It raises the problem about why we must succumb to violence even though we exhort peace and occasionally act accordingly. It asks, do we choose the road to peace in spite of violence or do we value peace only so far as it goes? Now, before the righteous and great power of the political administration that spoke of peace but advocates war, our theologian asks if righteousness is only occasional? Is the righteousness both a way of life and a committed path? Is it a true alternative? In telling such a parable, what the theologian has done is taken a metaphor about being righteous out of the language of the administration and returned it to the heart of a government as a question about its very identity. Does the government know that to boast about peace also means to be committed to peaceful actions?

We can note that the theologian does not offer a solution. The theologian raises the question. From the political point of view, the theologian is surely exasperating. The government might caricature the theologian as a "seditious, half-naked fakir," as Winston Churchill so portrayed Mahatma Gandhi.[14] From the theological point of view, this matters little. The parable has done its job. It has raised the problem for debate. It has awoken the enlightenment task by moving the question into the heart of our humanity and has asked for a covenant response with the persistent question about how we might act differently.

Religion and God can be a value to humanity if the metaphorical act of theology is genuinely the act of awakening the future to critical vision now. In such an act, and in such a parabolic spirit, God has a future. It is a human future. God as a metaphor makes religion, as poetry, a call to our humanity. Collectively, as the human family, we need great acts of poetry to place ourselves fully in time, and, strange as it may seem to some, we still need "religion" to awaken such poetic acts in the struggle to live now. This is the value of religion. This is the opening of time. This is God's human future.

Epilogue

Theology as a subject and a discipline, like philosophy, is always capable of great abstraction but little concrete address. My own attraction to theology was its abstract nature, especially hermeneutical questions about language, interpretation, and meaning. The path I took into theology was through continental philosophy. I state this not in the spirit of self-defense but as an indication of the concern I hold for finding ways theology can be a central and important voice in the world today.

In the writing of these pages, the two ways used to talk about theology are called Covenant and Enlightenment theology. They express the social and personal relevance of theology. I attempted to show how the two aspects of theology have been part of Christianity through its history and equally part of the Western experience of religion generally. However, it is unlikely that one can find something out there called "Enlightenment theology." There is, of course, lots of information about theology and the enlightenment, but not very much about theology as the task of enlightenment. Covenant theology is a more popular term used by different authors, often from the Reformed Christian tradition, such as Michael Horton in *Introducing Covenant Theology*. I did not take the term from this context, and I do not intend the same thing. Instead of trying to talk about God as the fundamental thing that has different covenants with humanity, my aim was to talk about the social nature of theology and how, historically and today, that social aspect can be talked about as theological intention. Whether these two terms work as effectively as I hope remains in the judgment of the reader.

In the two kinds of theology examined, part of my conviction is that both "create" God as a human value. It is not automatically the case that the "value" is a good one. Nevertheless, both ways of thinking about God are human acts of creating God, though it is hard to identify this since the concept of God is so closely knitted to human cultural history and language. To admit that God is a human creation does not mean to conclude that theology as a subject holds no value. Quite the opposite is the case. Because God is a human creation, theology holds a lot of value in both positive and negative senses. The negative value is obvious in extremism where theology becomes a form of literalism that makes ultimate claims about the nature of reality and how one should live. Regretfully, the positive value is not often noticed behind the much louder sound of religious extremism. There are positives to highlight, though. These include how theology can be about the task of re-thinking the world, how the inspiration to think is popularly available through religion, and how theology is, finally, not about God but the way in which human beings create God in expressive forms of hope, dreams, transformations, and the call for justice. What I hope, through the reading of these pages, is that between the gaps of expressed extremism in religion there will be a chance for the progressive good news about religion to surface as a value for humanity.

My final word concerns the critique I received when my initial chapters were proposed. The critique addressed my skepticism about whether the cosmos holds any discernible meaning. I subsequently modified the presentation of this line of thought in an effort not to be misleading. The skepticism, though, so far as we can understand, is justified based on contemporary knowledge of the universe, but it is also justified based on the worry that human beings hold the propensity to project their experience of the world onto the horizon. For Nietzsche specifically human values such as holy origins, purposes, and morality are projects that the human will casts upon the natural world as its content, intention, and meaning. To prevent this deceiving transfer of human values onto the cosmic order, a healthy skepticism is necessary.

In addition to guarding against projection, skepticism is also valuable for such things as community, language, questions of value, or ideals of peace. Each of these qualities requires a separation between things that enable relationships. Skepticism is the act of separating or creating space between things. It is the act of opening up space for inquiry, which is essential to dialogue in community. Inasmuch as it is often the case that human beings hold a desire to articulate the ultimate meaning and thereby to conform members of a community to a single identity, this natural desire can be counter-productive. In fact, a community needs it skeptics. Skepticism en-ables the capacity to open dialogue and thereby to hold the promise of transformation. It is theologically correct to value skepticism above belief as the energy of social transformation.

To address strictly the question about meaning or lack of mean-ing to the cosmos, a second element of skepticism involves how the idea of meaninglessness is not, theologically speaking, disappoint-ing news. Meaninglessness awakens the call to creativity and to meaning-making, and both of these tasks are basic theological tasks. When I presented Enlightenment theology, especially in chapter 11, I wanted to show how this theology works against the background of meaninglessness or nothingness. If not for this background the-ology could hardly be about creativity. Rather, it would be princi-pally about description, and it seems clear to me that understanding theology as the act of describing the world—the act of conceiving theology as positivism—is a dead end. There is nothing in this act that adds to our knowledge of the world. It rather detracts from, if not even sidetracks, contemporary knowledge. Instead of engaging such distractions, the value of theology is really found, I am uphold-ing, in its capacity to reimagine the world.

I am inclined to name this capacity to reimagine, joy. It is joy because in the unfolding of a cosmos that has no apparent pur-pose there is the gift of skepticism, which is the liberty of human thought. This liberty of skepticism is, in religion, the parabolic act.

It expresses the joy or gratuity of life in the midst of it all. Skepticism is challenging, playful, and creative. We call something that is challenging, playful, and creative a work of art. In religion, we call it a parable. As a theology we can call it one of joy.

Notes

Introduction

1. It is debatable whether the Hittites of the Bible are "these" Hittites of the PIE tradition in ancient Anatolia (modern Turkey). More likely, to my mind, the Hittites in the Bible are an ancient Canaanite population similar to the Israelites.

2. In this book, Boman distinguishes dynamic thinking, which he relates to Hebrew thought, from static thinking, which he relates to Greek thought.

3. In the Babylonian Talmud, Tractate *Baba Mezi'a* (59b) is the famous debate about whether a constructed oven is clean or not. Both Rabbi Eliezar and God thought the oven clean, but the majority of rabbis ruled against both. In this Tractate God laughs at being overruled, and God can be overruled because God already gave the Torah and is thus subject to its interpretation according to the majority. Though this story comes from centuries later than the originating writers of the Torah, nevertheless the story indicates the way the Torah as covenant is mutual between the divine and human participants.

Chapter 1: What Is the Bible?

1. The New Revised Standard Version more accurately translates this passage as, "May her breasts satisfy you at all times," replacing the older RSV puritan-like translation of, "May her affection fill you with delight."

2. One could argue in this instance that the dishonor falls on Tamar's father-in-law who failed his obligation to give her to his son (Genesis 38:26), but of course is Tamar's action the right way to address such problems? Matthew is counting on the reader's discomfort with Tamar's solution.

3. A sincerely excellent demonstration of this point is found in Miller, *Born Divine.*

4. The reader who would like to think further about families and sexuality in the Bible may wish to seek out Knust, *Unprotected Texts.*

5. Though the Bible is frank about Moses giving misleading information to Pharaoh, it does not even approach the problem of colonialism involved in forcefully taking land from indigenous people.

6. Thucydides lived approximate 460 to 395 BCE and composed, in the *Peloponnesian War,* one of the greatest works of history from ancient times. But of course it's not "really" history: it is fiction-history in which a

modern reader has to be critically aware of the information before presenting it as a fact.

7. John Tyndall (1820–1893) was the first physicist to prove that at-
mospheric gasses like carbon dioxide have a "greenhouse" effect on earth,
making our planet warm enough to sustain life. Unfortunately, as Naomi
Oreskes and Erik Conway point out in *Merchants of Doubt*, too much of a
good thing is a bad thing. The industrial production of carbon dioxide is of
such magnitude as to influence the climate on earth and change the experience of life here. "Merchants of doubt," which is the phrase I am borrow-
ing for use in the context of biblical scholarship, are those interested parties
whose ideology (and wealth) depend upon fabricating lies. It is a disturbing
problem in science and, unfortunately, a well-known problem in religion.
See Oreskes and Conway, *Merchants of Doubt*.

8. The E source refers to the writer called the Elohist because this writer
refers to God (in Hebrew) as Elohim. Some other sources identified are
called J (the Yahwist writer), P (the Priestly writer), and D (Deuteronomist
writer who edited the books from Deuteronomy to 2 Kings). A good, in-
troductory book covering these sources and other questions about the compilation known as the Hebrew Bible is Coogan, *A Brief Introduction to the
Old Testament*. I will refer to the Elohist writer later in this book.

9. The story about the origin of using Q to symbolize the common
material in Matthew and Luke is not absolutely certain. The German scholars who first identified the common material, which is largely "sayings of
Jesus," called it "L" (from the Greek *logia* or oracles). In English scholarship the word "source" was used for the material, and it came to be called
"Q" presumably from the German *Quelle*.

Chapter 2: What Is Religion?

1. Derrida's *Of Grammatology* is a difficult but significant text that
opened postmodern philosophy to the decentering (anti-logocentrism) of
words and their meaning. Difference is an interesting example because it
really means "no reference" but in the history of language has moved flex-
ibly to many varied meanings. Derrida never raised the example of an au-
tomobile and "differentials" that mechanically transfer engine power to the
wheels. Nevertheless it's a good example of a meeting place where things
that do not directly refer to each other get connected, coordinated, and
combined.

2. In Islam a free choice in religion is utterly central, for no one can be
Muslim without freely choosing to submit to the will of God. Anything
less is not submission but compulsion. As the Qur'an states, "Let there be
no compulsion in religion" (2:256). This makes sense. To be compelled to
believe by threat or other worries means that the individual so motivated is
not acting from a pure heart. What is religion if the individual involved is
not motivated by reasons of the heart?

3. Søren Kierkegaard made this point in several ways in his *Attack on
"Christendom"* where he stated that "the whole thing [Christendom] rests

upon the assumption that we are all Christians, which is precisely the knavish way of doing away with Christianity." In his lifetime, Kierkegaard felt that to say one was a Christian was a meaningless statement, so he claimed that he was not a Christian in order, paradoxically, to be a Christian truthfully. Bretall, *A Kierkegaard Anthology*, 447.

4. The linking of *religare* to religion is a longstanding tradition, as note 17 below indicates. It is often used by default in popular writings and blog posts. Joseph Campbell advocated this association in books like *The Power of Myth*, 268.

5. Augustine got his definition from Lactantius (240–320 CE), a Christian who was also the Emperor Constantine's religious advisor. It is not at all certain how *religio* originated, and it may be best to say that the word is a mystery—strangely religious in its nature. The Bible does not have a single word for religion. Rather, religion is used to translate several different words in Hebrew and Greek.

6. Cicero in ˌOn the Nature of the Gods 2.72, 107 explains "religion" and its meaning in this way: "But they who diligently pursued and, as we say, read or practiced over again all the duties related to the worship of the gods were called *religiosi*, religious, from *relegendo*, reading over again or practicing." Carl Jung, in a Letter to Gunter Wittwer, 10 October 1959, related religion to *religere*, which is to observe and thus means conduct.

7. I will leave to the side two big questions which involve the extent to which Hinduism can have a central teaching and the extent to which Buddhism can be called a religion. From the Western perspective, these traditions have historically been called "religions," and it remains true on a general level that the major emphasis of Hinduism is set upon the Vedanta school of Adi Shankara (usually believed to have lived in the eighth century CE).

8. Here, I am not being literalistic with Aquinas but suggesting that in the Medieval context he actually shows remarkable agreement with Schleiermacher and the spirit of liberal theology.

9. I cannot, of course, do justice to these great, modern, cosmological theories, and my bracketed comments are meant to be minor, if inaccurate, orientations. For a more accurate and perhaps troubling picture of the universe, see the popular Krauss, *A Universe from Nothing*.

10. Perhaps there could be a "flat" option in religion, which I will not pursue. Some of the work in process thought in relation to theology and contemporary understandings of the universe might be interesting to some readers. For example, see Keller, *Cloud of the Impossible*.

11. Warren, *A Purpose Driven Life*.

12. This is not an exact translation of Luke 17:33 // Matthew 10:39, but it is close to (and influenced by) the way the translators put it in Borg, Powelson, and Riegert, *The Lost Gospel Q*, 92. The saying in its simplest form is considered "authentic" (something clearly in the spirit of the historical Jesus) and is found, in altered forms, in all the canonical Christian gospels.

13. Nietzsche, *On the Genealogy of Morals*.

14. To read further about the idea of a weak God and weak theology, and to realize its radical implications, see Caputo, *The Weakness of God*.

15. By Corinthian correspondence I am referring to Paul's letters to the early Christian community in Corinth and their letters of response to him. We have no idea how many letters were sent and received (or who started the correspondence). The Christian Bible holds at least five letters of Paul that were edited and combined into what is now 1 and 2 Corinthians.

16. Nietzsche, *On the Genealogy of Morals*, 39.

Chapter 3: Enlightenment Theology

1. *Republic*, Book II, 379, is where Plato refers to theology as "the pattern or norms of right speech about the gods." The phrase, "right speech about the gods" is how the Hamilton and Cairns edition (1961) renders the single Greek word (plural) *theologias*.

2. Plato goes so far as to propose a law stating that poets and other public speakers must conform to the principle that God is not the cause of all things but only good things (380c).

3. The term "meme" identifies cultural customs that spread across the human family or link identifiable traditions to their past by way of imitation (from the Greek verb *mimeisthai*, "to imitate"). The term was coined by Richard Dawkins in *The Selfish Gene*.

4. Most scholars today are very cautious when using the word "Gnosticism" and some, like Karen King, hold that the word is not a valid analytical category. See King, *What is Gnosticism*. I agree with King, but at the same time the history of the use of the word often makes it hard to avoid.

5. There is not necessarily a malicious intent in the use of the word gnostic. Historians have simply found the word convenient. I made the error of using this word too conveniently in *Embracing the Human Jesus*. We might note, too, that today there is a Gnostic Church, and so there is indeed an appropriate way to use "Gnosticism" in reference to this form of Christianity.

6. The writer of Ecclesiastes takes the guise of King Solomon, the supreme figure of wisdom in the biblical tradition. The writer indicates that the very idea of eternity makes it impossible for human beings to know purpose. The writer blames God for this innate state of ignorance (3:11).

7. Etymologically, avatar is the root "tr" (across), related to the English "through," and the prefix "ava," which is the movement downward or across. This Sanskrit word does not occur in the Hindu Vedas. It became popular only after the time of the grammarian Panini, who lived in the fourth century of the Common Era.

8. The story of Vishnu as Rama composes the great Hindu epic, *Ramayana*.

9. The writer John may have taken the image of the Word not from Greek philosophy (or not only) but from Proverbs where Wisdom often

speaks. At 8:22 Wisdom proclaims, "The Lord created me at the beginning of his work, the first of his acts of old" (NRSV). In other places, Wisdom indicates that she is the order of the cosmos, such as 3:19, "The Lord by wisdom founded the earth; by understanding he established the heavens" (NRSV).

10. E identifies a writer or editor from northern nation of Israel. After the fall of Israel to Assyria in 722 BCE, northern traditions, like this creation narrative, were woven into the writings of southern Judah. E is therefore found in fragments in the first four books of the Bible. The second story is compiled by the J writer or Yahwist, who is from the Southern nation of Judah. The J narrative consists of the Garden of Eden story found at Genesis 2:4b–3:24.

11. *On First Principles*, Book I, 6.3. In somewhat complicated and hard to follow prose, Origen indicates that all manner of intellectual beings, whatever sins they have committed and by whatever road necessary, will again one day return to the invisible and eternal realm of heaven. Naturally the church, and many people today, did not and do not like this Enlightenment theology of compassionate understanding. At the Council of Constantinople in 453 CE certain of Origen's beliefs, including this one, were declared *anathema*.

12. This idea appears in many dialogues of Plato and is usually called the Doctrine of Recollection. It holds that when we grasp an idea we are really remembering it, not gaining it as new knowledge. The *Meno* dialogue (especially section 81a–d) is perhaps the most straightforward expression of the idea of recollection. Sometimes Plato is taken too seriously and we can see this in the way people call his metaphor of recollection a "doctrine." What Plato is after is a way to explain why human beings commonly recognize things despite their individual differences and even when they have never met each other.

13. This is certainly the great critique if not worry of Reinhold Niebuhr in his seminal work, *The Nature and Destiny of Man*. One of the great points that Niebuhr makes in this two-volume work is that in what I am calling Enlightenment theology, there is no final reconciliation between the individual and the State. Rather, the relationship is one of tragedy, which is why theology will always carry in its reasonings an aspect of political struggle.

Chapter 4: Covenant Theology

1. It is generally thought today that the populations composing ancient Israel and Judah arose from existing Canaanite populations. Thus, "Canaanite" is a generic category identifying various but closely related people.

2. Lloyd Geering describes the traditions of ancient Israel in four paths or forms that he calls the Torah tradition, the Kingdom tradition, the Prophetic tradition, and the Wisdom tradition. These four are a more accurate breakdown than my intended generic term of Covenant theology.

To defend myself, my aim is to find a feature or model that substantively influenced Western theology without pursuing more complex dynamics. See Geering, *Such is Life*, 5.

3. An example of this act is in Genesis 15:9–10, where God instructed Abram to bring out a heifer, a goat, a ram, a turtledove, and a fledgling and cut them in half. This act binds God to the promise of liberating the Jewish people from Egypt after four hundred years of slavery. Another example of the same act outside the Bible is a text that records the covenant between Ashurnirari and Mati'ilu. In this case a lamb is used to cut the covenant, and the severed head of the lamb represents Mati'ilu's head should he break the covenant with Ashurnirari.

4. The origins of this interesting ceremony are not easily traced, but it is reasonable to assume the ceremony relates to the sharing of blood to form a bond. That a weaker party might break a covenant and thus be subject to bloodshed is not explicitly the nature of the ceremony but it is certainly an implication of it.

5. Jehud first designated a Persian Province created by Cyrus the Great when Jews were granted the liberty to return home after the Babylonian Exile (though many stayed having made new homes in Babylon). The Greeks translated Jehud as Ioudaia and the Romans as Judea (in all cases I am using English equivalents).

6. A covenant could exist between equal parties, which is called a Parity Covenant. An example would be the bond between Israel (King Pekah) and Syria (King Rezin) against Assyria (Tiglath-Pileser III). The resulting war meant the fall of Israel to Assyria and a new Suzerain Covenant for Judah (the non-combatant bystander in this affair) with Assyria (in which Judah would have recognized the superiority of the gods of Assyria).

7. Micheal D. Cogan offers some good, general, commentary on covenants in the Ancient Near East in his *A Brief Introduction to the Old Testament*, 101–4, 155.

8. There are, of course, always exceptions, and the Egyptian Pharaoh proved to be one of them.

9. The Hebrew word *hesed* is not easy to define in English. It does involve love, especially God's love for Israel. It also involves loyalty, and in some ways love is the expression of loyalty. The quality of loyalty is why faithfulness seems like one of the better translations. Jack Miles indicates that *hesed* is more like a word of diplomacy than one of personal relationship. Jack Miles, *God: A Biography*, 121–22.

10. The critical relationship of the book of Ruth to the book of Ezra is expressed with great care and erudition in Crossan, *The Power of Parable*.

11. James Barr defended this position in "The Problem of Fundamentalism Today," *The Bible and Interpretation*, Vol. 2, 497.

12. In the case of Islam, variant readings of the Qur'an were destroyed during the Uthman Caliphate in an effort to standardize the text. However, variant readings do remain extant, such as the find at Yemen in 1972 of the Sana'a manuscript.

13. From today's point of view, Justin is condescending to other traditions in the way he judges their integrity on the assumption that Christianity is the final and ultimate expression of truth. In other words, while it was okay to be Socrates or Moses, it would be even better if Socrates or Moses were Christians.

14. See Justin Martyr, *First Apology*, Chapter 46. The text is available online as part of the Christian Classics Ethernet Library (www.ccel.org).

15. *Dialogue with Trypho*, Chapter 32. My brief quotation is from Hanson, *Justin's Dialogue with Trypho*, 31.

16. The Damascus story is from the book of Acts, which is not widely considered to be history. Acts is like a novel that could better be called, "The Adventures of the Apostles." What would happen if in church we announced readings from the Book of Adventures?

17. See Scott, *The Real Paul.*

18. Traditionally the authentic letters of Paul are seven, though some of the seven, like 2 Corinthians, are several letters combined later as one. The authentic letters of Paul are Romans, 1 and 2 Corinthians, Galatians, Philippians, 1 Thessalonians, and Philemon.

19. See Brandon Scott's excellent description of this scene in *The Real Paul.*

20. Gaston, "Paul and Jerusalem" in *Paul and the Torah.*

Chapter 5: Jesus the Teacher of Nothingness

1. In the notes of the late Robert W. Funk I read the following: "In rediscovering the historical Jesus, we stumbled into a deviant reality imagined by Jesus in his parables and aphorisms." These notes were kindly made available to me by Char Matejovsky, and in them I found, in thoughts such as this, the inspiration for this chapter.

2. These are the two ways the parable of the Dinner Party is interpreted by Luke (14:12–24) and Matthew (22:1–14).

3. Jülicher, *Die Gleichnisreden Jesu.*

4. Crossan, *In Parables*, viii.

5. Technically, "allegory" is from two Greek words. One is *allos*, which means different, and the second is *agora*, which means "assembly area" (and later was also "the market place"). Accordingly, the word means something like "to speak differently" or "to speak of another (place)." The "speaking" part of the definition is from the "agora" part of the word, for one spoke out in an assembly. The "different or other" part of the definition comes from the way one chooses to translate *allos*. The word comes to us in English through the Latin *allegoria*, and the Latin is a transliteration of the same word in Greek. Commonly an English dictionary will define allegory as symbolic language.

6. Scott, *The Trouble with Resurrection*, 2–3.

7. At the time of this writing, Ricky Gervais' monologue on Humpty Dumpty was available on YouTube.

8. As Scott says, "what we finally learn from Jesus' parables is how life can be imagined." Scott, *Re-Imagine the World*, 6.

9. The phrase in Greek is *basileia tou theou* with the word *basileia* referring to the realm in which the laws of the *basileus* (king, emperor, or leading aristocrat) are in effect. Since Jesus lived in the Roman Empire, the translation "Empire of God" is most effective even though traditionally in English the translation has been Kingdom of God. We might also note that when used as a noun *basileia* means Queen. In this subtle way to modern English ears, the lands or holdings of God (*basileia*) are inclusive.

10. This translation is the Scholars Version taken from *The Five Gospels*, 54.

11. In the Hebrew Bible Cyrus the Great is the first "Anointed" (Messiah in Hebrew and Christ in Greek) of God. He is so because in the imagination of Isaiah God used Cyrus to carry out a mission to liberate the Jewish people. This is what "anointed ones" do: like the characters in the Blues Brothers film, they carry out a mission from God. If ever Jesus got into a discussion about Babylonian Exile and God's doings in relation to it, he could have referred to Cyrus in this way (Isaiah 45:1).

12. This is Scott's translation, *Hear Then the Parable*, 343.

13. Taussig, *Jesus Before God*, 12.

14. Taussig, *Jesus Before God*, 12.

15. Scott, *Hear Then the Parable*.

16. Foucault, "Truth, Power, Self: An Interview with Michel Foucault October 25, 1982," *Technologies of the Self*, 9.

17. The full statement attributed to Hillel is found in the Talmud, "Sayings of the Fathers" (*Pirkei Avot*) 1:14. This famous statement fully expressed reads, "If I am not for myself, who will be for me? If I am only for myself, what am I? If not now, when?"

Chapter 6: Creating God in 325

1. I speak here ideally of the philosophers and not culturally of the Romans.

2. Though I have long understood that epilepsy was called the Sacred Disease and was sometimes treated by drilling a hole in the skull of the patient in an effort to re-balance the spirits (but often resulted in the death of the patient), I gained much in understanding the relationship between temple and natural medicine in antiquity from Todman, "Epilepsy in the Graeco-Roman World."

3. Marcus Aurelius, *Meditations*, p. 13. These references are drawn from Book 2.17.

4. Plotinus, *Enneads 1.1*, p. 121.

5. For Iamblichus the highest cosmic principle is the *monad* or One, and its primary guide is the *nous* or intellect. Immediately following the One is a second directive, which is the intellectual soul or *psyche*. It is a complicated system, but the point here is to see the common assumption that contrasted the purity of the intellect with the associated ambiguities of matter and flesh.

6. The song "Goin' Back" and its invitation to a "foreign land," which seems hauntingly like an invitation to engage history, appears on the 1978 album, *Comes a Time*.

7. Though in truth Rome had not been a Republic since the days of Julius Caesar (100–44 BCE), Diocletian liked to think that it was.

8. Eusebius, *Life of Constantine*, Books I, VII and XII.

9. *Life of Constantine*, Books IV, XXIV.

10. The record of Eusebius is naturally suspicious since he was Constantine's chief defender. Nevertheless, this fascinating biography is published as *The Life of Constantine*; the burning account is found in Socrates, *Historia Ecclesiastica* 1.8.

11. The Church addressed the Donatists controversy, similarly to the Meletian controversy, earlier and equally unsuccessfully at the Council Arles in 314. The Donatists also called their church the "Church of the Martyrs."

12. The dates for both Arius and Athanasius are not certain.

13. The dates for Donatus Magnus are unknown. He was disciplined by Pope Miltiades in 313 and presumably died in exile in 355 CE.

14. My remark here demands some extended comments in that the dilemma of the church at the time was extraordinary. Lapsed clergy, among other things, handed over names of people from their communities. The word "traitor" (Latin *tradere*: to deliver) is often thought to be rooted in the act of the lapsed clergy handing over names. If some of those names included, for example, your family members, related cousins, or best friends, it would be incredibly hard, following the time of persecution, to extend a forgiving spirit to such clergy and to be present when such a one celebrated the Eucharist or performed baptisms. The orthodox Church judged that after appropriate penance, depending on circumstance, such forgiveness could be extended. This judgment meant the invocation of a theology of sacraments that trumped the character of individual priests. With this theology, though, also comes the idea that God creates institutions. An institutional God then emerged in Christianity partly as an effect of a very difficult and morally fragile situation.

15. *Ex Cathedra* means that when a Pope speaks out of his office as the teacher and shepherd of the Church, upon the authority of his supreme apostolic position, and on the subject of doctrines of faith and morality, the Pope speaks "infallibly" such that the pronouncement is irreformable. The definition of *Ex Cathedra* can be read in the proceedings of the First Vatican Council, Session 4, Chapter 4.9. These proceeding are readily available online (see www.papalencyclicals.net).

16. St. Michael's Depot, proceedings from *The First Council of Nicaea—325 AD*.

17. Tillich, *A History of Christian Thought*, 71.

18. Quoting from Stevenson, "The Letter of Arius to Alexander, Bishop of Alexandria" in *A New Eusebius*, 346–47.

19. This being the likely text of the original Creed, though we have it in its present form from the Council of Constantinople several years later in 381.

20. Gregory of Nazianzus, *Epistle 101*, Letter "To Cledonius the Priest Against Apollinarius."

21. As an example, Colin Brown makes this observation in "Why Study the Historical Jesus," in *Handbook for the Study of the Historical Jesus*, 1412.

Chapter 7: Meet the New Jesus

1. Franz Kafka's parable is entitled "My Destination" and can be found commonly on the internet.

2. Ironically, if Augustine only knew, the Inns of the Roman Empire were (among other things) brothels, and the Samaritan paying for the needs of the victim may have included things we'd rather not imagine.

3. Augustine, *Quaestiones Evangeliorum*, 2. 19.

4. More specifically, the quotation is from the Preface of Friedrich Nietzsche's *Beyond Good and Evil* where he writes that "Christianity is Platonism for 'the people.'" See Kaufmann, *Basic Writings of Nietzsche*, 193.

5. As Huntington Cairns points out in his introduction, "the actual amount of space devoted to it [the theory of Forms or Ideas] by this name in the dialogues is scanty." Hamilton and Cairns, *Plato: The Collected Dialogues,* xvii–xviii.

6. We could argue in response that the consequences in Deuteronomy for not following the Torah are so unimaginably brutal that choice as such does not really exist.

7. Morrow, *Protest Against God,* discusses the tradition of lament in Judaism, which I have here called negotiation, and the deterioration of its value and presence in the history of Israel following the Axial age (that is approximately 500 BCE in post-exilic Judaism). Morrow's book is not definitive but does highlight current academic debate.

8. To Heraclitus (535–475 BCE), all things change; change is the nature of reality. Therefore, truth is change or at least exists in change. Nothing of the work of Heraclitus has survived antiquity except for scattered quotes found in other authors.

9. Paul inadvertently sets the Christian precedent for ignoring the historical Jesus with his comments at 2 Corinthians 5:16.

10. Joseph Bessler reviews these theologians who often represent the Neo-orthodox movement of the twentieth century and admirably clarifies the assessment the movement made of historical Jesus scholarship in *A Scandalous Jesus.*

11. Johnson, *The Real Jesus*, 142.

12. I quote Carter from Robbins, "Changing Ontotheology," in *Retrieving the Radical Tillich*, 165. Carter's original point is made in Carter, *Race: A Theological Account.*

13. The whole of Proverbs 8 is the instruction and happy praises of wisdom as if it were a figure of history. I use here the NRSV translation.

14. The writer is called Deutero-Pauline because the letter to the Colossians is in the spirit of Paul but written after the lifetime of the historical Paul. The writer borrows Paul's name presumably to add authority to the words.

15. Luther wrote *To the Christian Nobility of the German Nation* (1520). This work inspired the German peasantry to throw off their oppression, but as the peasantry engaged in this conflict Luther sadly wrote *Against the Murderous Thieving Hordes of Peasants* (1525), which justified as a divine right the violence the aristocracy poured upon the largely desperate and poorly armed masses. Though it is right to say that Luther did not cause the princes to act, as if they needed his permission, it is right to say that Luther approved of their acts with his usual flare for dramatic and severe words.

16. Leo obtained a decree from Emperor Valentinian III in 445 CE stating the primacy of Rome as the chief See among bishops based on the merits of Peter. This decree was issued in relation to matters in Gaul, but Leo took this decree as an assertion of his authority generally. In the Eastern Empire, which at the time was more stable than the Western, Leo asserted his will over that of Emperor Leo III with the appointment of Leo I's choice of Gennadius for bishop of Constantinople.

17. Scott, *Re-imagine the World*.

18. This famous and often cited reference is from Nietzsche's parable of the Madman, which can be found on the internet and in *The Gay Science*, trans. Josefine Nauckhoff, 119, section 125.

Chapter 8: When God Stopped Working

1. This is the day that Percy Bysshe Shelley was expelled from Oxford for publishing a pamphlet called *The Necessity of Atheism*. I have no idea what the weather was like on that day.

2. Gaunilo of Marmoutiers, an eleventh-century Benedictine monk, was a contemporary of Anselm of Canterbury (1033–1109) and wrote a response to Anselm's ontological argument based on imagining a most perfect island that cannot be surpassed.

3. This expression, from the height of the Middle Ages, means that every subject of the university curriculum was understood to contribute to theology as the fulfillment of knowledge.

4. David Hume, *An Enquiry Concerning Human Understanding*, 10.

5. Repetition is used in different ways in philosophy, and I think my form of use here is closer to Michel Foucault than other philosophers of the postmodern era (like Jacques Derrida). I also think this is close to what Hume meant by habit. Likewise, repetition is a key word for Søren Kierkegaard; he distinguishes repetition, as the act of going forward, from recollection, which is the act of going backward. I happen to (humbly) disagree with Kierkegaard on this point, but of course he was not concerned about the presentation being made here and he remains one of the key philosophers in postmodern thought today.

Chapter 9: The God Who Almost Is

1. Kierkegaard, *Stages on Life's Way*, 402.

2. Paul Zanker, *The Power of Images in the Age of Augustus*, 112.

3. Even though the image of the "body of Christ" can seem like

something arising from conservative Christianity, in fact this expression from the Apostle Paul is about a radically alternative collective, both economically and politically, to the collective of the Roman Imperial body.

4. The Universal Declaration of Human Rights (1948) begins its preamble on exactly this note, recognizing as its foundation the inherent dignity and the equal and inalienable rights of all members of the human family.

5. This translation is from the King James Version. The new Scholars Version (SV) of Paul's letters makes the following translation, "I was crucified with the Anointed. The person I used to be no longer lives."

Chapter 10: Saving Apocalypticism

1. The Catechism of the Roman Catholic Church is freely available online at www.vatican.va/archive/ccc/index.htm. The above quotation is taken from Article 7.677 and was accessed on October 15, 2015. A footnote ending the sentence refers to Revelation 20:12.

2. A classic example of a Jesus parable allegorized to express later Christian beliefs about Jesus is found in the Leased Vineyard parable at Mark 12:1–12. The writer of Matthew relays the parable at 21:33–39 and then in verses 40–45 aims threatening commentary explicitly at the Jewish representative. The original parable is lost, but the Gospel of Thomas 65:1–8 preserves the parable without commentary. The Thomas writer either does not know or writes earlier than emerging Christian anti-Judaism.

3. See Hunston and Mergal, *Spiritual and Anabaptist Writers*, "A Confession: Obbe Philips," 225.

4. Frye, *The Great Code*, 169.

5. Altizer, "A Homage to Paulus," *Retrieving the Radical Tillich*, 29. Tillich, *Systematic Theology*, vol. 2.

6. Tillich, *The Socialist Decision*.

7. Tillich, *Systematic Theology*, vol. 2: *The Courage to Be*.

8. Altizer, "A Homage to Paulus," *Retrieving the Radical Tillich*, 27.

9. Tillich, *Systematic Theology*, vol. 2, 135.

10. Lake, *The Religion of Yesterday and Tomorrow*. I owe many thanks to Lloyd Geering from whom I learned about Lake and about the significance of Lake's observations.

Chapter 11: Theology and the Opening of Time

1. Tillich, *The Courage to Be*, 14.

2. Ecclesiastes 1:2. The Hebrew word for vanity (*hebhel*) is vapor and breath. The translation of 1:2 can be expressed as "emptiness of emptiness. Everything is empty," or "temporality of temporalities. Everything is passing."

3. Plantinga, "A Contemporary Defense of Ontological Arguments," *Philosophy of Religion*, 342–52.

4. Teilhard de Chardin, *The Heart of Matter*.

5. Milbank, *Theology and Social Theory*.

6. Pannenberg, *Metaphysics and the Idea of God*, 98. Pannenberg attrib-

uted the idea of memory in Christianity to Stoicism. He helpfully points out how Clement of Alexandria employed the word *prolepsis* in a Stoic way. Prolepsis is a technique in rhetoric in which a speaker anticipates an opponent's criticism and answers it in advance. In Stoic philosophy this term was used to identify how a word, once employed, elicits presumed ideas. If I say "dog," the word raises in the hearer an idea about a "dog" that stimulates the mind. So, *prolepsis* is the act of stimulating anticipation in the mind through an uttered word. In Christianity, existential life, finite life now as we live it, anticipates in the same way the fullness of life to come. Many theologians from antiquity to the present continue with this basic idea. It was certainly present in the philosophy of G. W. F. Hegel (1770–1831) and was equally a feature in the foundational figure for modern liberal theology, Friedrich Schleiermacher (1768–1834).

7. Remember, the Earth is not counted because it was assumed to be the center of it all.

8. If the reader is interested, I tried once to answer this question in *Archives and the Event of God*.

9. Few progressive theologians think the point of theology is to name or describe beliefs in a supernatural being. Paul Tillich once suggested that to reduce theology to this claim is effectively to reduce theology to a form of blasphemy. See Tillich, *Theology of Culture*, 25.

10. I might add here that language in postmodern thought does not strictly mean speaking. Language is more about acts or responses to things that create context. For example, in the thought of Michel Foucault it is possible to see "language" diversely as a speaking-event, a seeing-event, and a gesture-event. In other words, like in *The Archeology of Knowledge* and *Discipline and Punish*, Foucault does not restrict language to words. Language is much more about the structural dynamics of culture and the manner in which a culture performs reality (holds its unique relationship to reality). Even though Foucault can be difficult to read, in fact he is what I would call a poetic philosopher. He consistently upholds the possibility of speaking the world differently and, consequently, upholds the radical hope for a different world.

11. Don Cupitt is really the creator of linguistic non-realism and it is a major emphasis of his writing. My initial considerations of Cupitt's thought came out of my reading of Cupitt, *Creation out of Nothing*. Cupitt is difficult to understand, and realist defenders come firing in voices that mistake Cupitt's intentions for the absolute nihilism of anything physical. Cupitt is subtle; he is about the liberty to be in the world differently. His is really a theology of hope. For a realist response to Cupitt (and I believe a misappropriation of him), see Clark's review of *Creation out of Nothing*.

12. Klein, *The Shock Doctrine*.

13. This is a paraphrase of the parable of the Unforgiving Slave found at Matthew 18:23–34.

14. This is a slight paraphrase of Churchill's reported words about Gandhi addressed to the Council of the West Essex Unionist Association on

February 23, 1931. Churchill's words and the response of Gandhi are recorded in a book of anecdotes about Gandhi now online, Prabhu, *This Was
Bapu*, 113–14. Churchill's actual reported words describe Gandhi as a "seditious fakir" who strides "half-naked up the steps of the Viceregal Palace."
Gandhi, who turned himself into a parable, was able to reverse the direction
of Churchill's critique when he responded, several years later, that he had
long been trying to be a Fakir and that the requirement of nakedness made
it even harder. Then he asked Churchill to use him as a vehicle of peace and
signed his response "your sincere friend." Churchill was the politician, and
Gandhi the theologian.

Bibliography

Altizer, Thomas J.J. "A Homage to Paulus." Pp. 23–29 in *Retrieving the Radical Tillich*. Ed. Russell Re Manning. New York: Palgrave MacMillan, 2015.

Augustine, *Quaestiones Evangeliorum*, 2. 19. A translation of this text appears in C.H. Dodd, *The Parables of the Kingdom*. New York: Scribners, 1961. Pp. 1–2.

Armstrong, A. H., trans. *Plotinus* (Loeb Classical Library). Cambridge: Harvard University Press, 1989.

Aurelius, Marcus. *Meditations, Books 1–6*. Trans. Christopher Gill. Oxford: Oxford University Press, 2013.

Barr, James. "The Problem of Fundamentalism Today." Pp. 474–94 in *The Bible and Interpretation, Volume II*. Oxford: Oxford Uni-versity Press, 2013.

Bessler, Joseph. *A Scandalous Jesus*. Salem: Polebridge Press, 2013.

Bretall, Robert, ed. *A Kierkegaard Anthology*. New Jersey: Princeton University Press, 1946.

Boman, Thorleif. *Hebrew Thought Compared with Greek*. New York: W.W. Norton and Company, Inc., 1960.

Borg, Marcus, Mark Powelson and Ray Riegert, eds. *The Lost Gospel Q*. Berkeley: Ulysses Press, 1996.

Brown, Colin. "Why Study the Historical Jesus." Pp. 1411–38 in *Handbook for the Study of the Historical Jesus*. Eds. Tom Holmén and Stanley E. Porter. Leiden: Brill Publishers, 2011.

Campbell, Joseph. *The Power of Myth*. New York: Anchor Books, 1988.

Caputo, John D. *The Folly of God*. Salem: Polebridge Press, 2015.

Caputo, John D. *The Weakness of God*. Indianapolis: Indiana University Press, 2006.

Carter, J. Kameron. *Race: A Theological Account*. Oxford: Oxford University Press, 2008.

Cicero in *On the Nature of the Gods* 2.72. Trans. Thomas Franklin. London: William Pickering, 1829.

Clark, Stephen R. L. "Review of Don Cupitt *Creation out of Noth-ing*." *Religious Studies* 27,4 (1991): 559–61.

Coogan, Michael D. *A Brief Introduction to the Old Testament*. New York: Oxford University Press, 2012.

_____. *A Brief Introduction to the Old Testament: The Hebrew Bible in its Context*. New York: Oxford University Press, 2009.

Crossan, Dominic. *The Power of Parable*. New York: HarperCollins Publisher, 2012.

_____. *In Parables*. Sonoma: Polebridge Press, 1992.

Cupitt, Don. *Creation out of Nothing*. London: SCM Press, 1989.

Dawkins, Richard. *The Selfish Gene*. Oxford University Press, 1976.

Derrida, Jacques. *Of Grammatology*. Baltimore: John Hopkins University Press, 1972

Eusebius, *Life of Constantine*, Books I, VII and XII.

Foucault, Michel. "Truth, Power, Self: An Interview with Michel Foucault October 25, 1982." Pp. 9–15 in *Technologies of the Self*. Eds. Luther H. Martin, Huck Gutman, and Patrick H. Hutton. Amherst: The University of Massachusetts Press, 1988.

Frye, Northrop. *The Great Code*. Toronto: Academic Press Canada, 1982.

Funk, Robert W., ed. *The Five Gospels*. New York: Scribner, 1993.

Galston, David. *Archives and the Event of God*. Montreal: McGill-Queens Press, 2010.

Gaston, Lloyd. "Paul and Jerusalem." Pp. 107–15 in *Paul and the Torah*. Vancouver: UBC Press, 1987.

Geering, Lloyd. *Such is Life*. Salem: Polebridge Press, 2009.

Gregory of Nazianzus, *Epistle 101*, Letter "To Cledonius the Priest Against Apollinarius." Christian Classics Ethernet Library (http://www.ccel.org/ccel/schaff/npnf207.iv.ii.iii.html), accessed June 8, 2015.

Hamilton, Edith and Huntington Cairns, eds. *Plato: The Collected Dialogues*. Princeton: Princeton University Press, 1973.

Hanson, R.P.C., trans. and ed. *Justin's Dialogue with Trypho*. London: Lutterworth Press, 1963.

Hume, David. *An Enquiry Concerning Human Understanding*. Indianapolis: Hackett Publishing Company, 1977.

Huntston, George and Williams and Angel M. Mergal, eds. The Library of Christian Classics, *Spiritual and Anabaptist Writers*, "A Confession: Obbe Philips." Philadelphia: The Westminster Press, 1957.

Johnson, Luke Timothy. *The Real Jesus*. New York: HarperCollins, 1997.

Jülicher, Adolf. *Die Gleichnisreden Jesu*. Freiburg: J.C.B. Mohr (P. Siebeck), 1888.

Kaufmann, Walter, ed. *Basic Writings of Nietzsche*. New York: The Modern Library, 1968.

Kierkegaard, Soren. *Stages on Life's Way*. Trans. Walter Lowrie. New York: Schocken Books, 1967.

Keller, Catharine. *Cloud of the Impossible*. New York: Columbia University Press, 2014.

King, Karen. *What is Gnosticism?* Cambridge: Harvard University Press, 2003.

Klein, Naomi. *The Shock Doctrine.* New York: Metropolitan Books, 2008.

Krauss, Lawrence. *A Universe from Nothing.* New York: Free Press, 2012.

Lake, Kirsopp. *The Religion of Yesterday and Tomorrow.* Boston: Houghton Mifflin, 1925.

Martyr, Justin. *First Apology.* The text is available online as part of the Christian Classics Ethernet Library (www.ccel.org).

Milbank, John. *Theology and Social Theory.* Oxford: Blackwell Publishing, 1990.

Miles, Jack. *God: A Biography.* New York: Vintage Books, 1996.

Miller, Robert. *Born Divine: The Births of Jesus and Other Sons of God.* Santa Rosa: Polebridge Press, 2003.

Morrow, William S. *Protest Against God.* Sheffield: Sheffield Phoenix Press, 2006.

Niebuhr, Reinhold. *The Nature and Destiny of Man.* New York: Charles Scribner and Sons, 1964.

Nietzsche, Friedrich. *The Gay Science.* Trans. Josefine Nauckhoff. Cambridge: Cambridge University Press, 2001.

_____. *On the Genealogy of Morals.* Trans. Douglas Smith. Oxford: Oxford University Press, 1999.

_____. *On the Genealogy of Morals.* Trans. Walter Kaufmann. New York: Vintage Books, 1967.

Oreskes, Naomi and Erik M. Conway. *Merchants of Doubt.* New York: Bloomsbury Press, 2010.

Plantinga, Alvin. "A Contemporary Defense of Ontological Arguments." Pp. 342–52 in *Philosophy of Religion.* Ed. Brian Davies. New York: Oxford University Press, 2000.

Prabhu, R. K. *This Was Bapu.* Ahmedabad: Navajivan Publishing House, 1954.

Robbins, Jeffrey W. "Changing Ontotheology." Pp. 159–77 in *Retrieving the Radical Tillich.* Ed. Russell Re Manning. New York: Palgrave Macmillan, 2015.

Scott, Bernard Brandon. *The Real Paul.* Salem: Polebridge Press, 2015.

_____. *The Trouble with Resurrection.* Salem, Oregon: Polebridge Press, 2010.

_____. *Re-Imagine the World.* Santa Rosa: Polebridge Press, 2001.

_____. *Hear then the Parable.* Minneapolis: Fortress Press, 1989.

St. Michael's Depot, proceedings from *The First Council of Nicaea* —*325 AD.*

Stevenson, J., ed. "The Letter of Arius to Alexander, Bishop of Alexandria." Pp. 346–47 in *A New Eusebius.* London: S.P.C.K., 1968.

Taussig, Hal. *Jesus Before God*. Santa Rosa: Polebridge Press, 1999.

Teilhard de Chardin, Pierre. *The Heart of Matter*. Trans. René Hague. New York: Harcourt, Inc., 1975.

Tillich, Paul. *A History of Christian Thought*. New York: Simon and Schuster, 1968.

_____. *Theology of Culture*. New York: Oxford University Press, 1959.

_____. *Systematic Theology*, vol. 2. Chicago: Chicago University Press, 1957.

_____. *The Courage to Be*. New Haven: Yale University Press, 1952.

_____. *The Socialist Decision*. Washington, DC: University Press of America, 1977.

Todman, Donald. "Epilepsy in the Graeco-Roman World: Hippocratic Medicine and Asklepian Temple Medicine Compared." *Journal of the History of Neurosciences* 17 (2008): 435–41.

Williams, George Huntston and Angel M. Mergal, eds. "A Confession: Obbe Philips." Pp. 206–25 in *Spiritual and Anabaptist Writers*. Philadelphia: The Westminster Press, 1957.

Warren, Rick. *A Purpose Driven Life*. Grand Rapids: Zondervan, 2002.

Wright Knust, Jennifer. *Unprotected Texts*. New York: Harper Collins Publishers, 2011.

Zanker, Paul. *The Power of Images in the Age of Augustus*. Ann Arbor: University of Michigan Press, 1990.

Index

Abimelech, 61, 62

Abraham, 10, 14, 20, 45, 52, 61, 62, 66, 68, 71–73, 112, 118,

Absence, 145–50, 155, 157, 158

Absolute (the), 13, 25, 26, 35, 55, 56, 57, 104, 106, 107, 127, 130, 133, 134, 150, 178, 184, 185

Augustine, 29, 30, 114, 115, 162, 163, 188, 201 n. 5, 208 n. 2 and 3,

Augustus (Octavian and title), 65, 96–98, 151

Akkad (Akkadian), 61, 63

Allegory, 4, 80–84, 162, 163, 165–69, 171, 175, 188, 189, 192, 205 n. 5

Almost (God), 4, 144, 145, 147–49, 153, 155, 157, 159, 161, 162, 188

Amos, 12, 53, 65

Ancient Near East (ANE), 1, 2, 61, 63, 65, 204 n. 7

Anointed, 65, 73, 83, 206 n. 11, 210 n. 5

Antichrist, 71, 72

Aphorism, 35, 89, 205 n. 1

Apocalypse (apocalyptic), 4, 34, 35, 41, 79, 92, 160, 161–65, 168–70, 172, 173, 175, 184, 192

Aquinas, Thomas, 31, 32, 120, 132–34, 180, 201 n. 8

Aristotle, 23, 56, 57, 120, 149

Arius, 101, 103–7, 207 n. 12

Assyria, 2, 61, 62, 64, 65, 111, 203 n. 10, 204 n, 6

Athanasius, 101, 207 n. 12

Atheism 44, 151, 179, 180, 209 n. 1

Autonomy, 137, 138, 153–55, 157, 159, 160

Avatar, vii, 1–3, 50, 51, 59, 92, 110, 117, 119, 148, 149, 202 n. 7

Babylon(ian), 61, 63, 67, 112, 199 n. 3 (re Babylonian Talmud), 204 n. 5, 206 n. 11

Barth, Karl, 118

Biographical writing, 13, 14

Bultmann, Rudolf, 118

Caesar (Julius), 65, 207 n. 7

Calvin, John, 9

Canaanite, 1, 45, 61, 199, n. 1, 203 n. 1

Carter, J. Kameron, 119, 208 n. 12

Closed/closure, 4, 33–41, 58, 67, 72, 75, 90, 92, 159, 162, 173, 175, 177–87, 193

Christ (body of, identity of, Jesus), 3, 37, 44, 50, 51, 55, 70–75, 83, 87, 88, 90, 92, 95, 99, 101–8, 114, 115, 118–23, 125, 149. 158, 162, 163, 167, 171, 182, 206 n.11, 209 n. 3

Church, 19, 38, 75, 80, 83, 87, 88, 92, 98–110, 113–16, 120–25, 159, 160–64, 166, 171–73, 188, 207 n. 14

Colossians, 119, 208 n. 14

Comedy, 22, 86, 156, 169

Common Law, 118, 123

Confession(al), 18, 24, 44, 75, 99, 104, 107, 108, 125, 150, 155, 162–64, 172, 175, 177–81, 184, 186

Constantine, 94–100, 105, 107, 109, 119, 207 n. 10

Constantius, 96, 97

Corruption (corrupt), 27, 50, 66, 102, 106, 183,

Cosmological Argument, 132

Crossan, Dominic, 80, 81, 88, 204 n. 10

Crucifixion, 72–74, 116, 158,

Cupitt, Don, viii, 211 n. 11

Darwin, 13

David (King), 8, 10, 67,

Descartes, Rene, ix, 135–38, 144, 153,

Deuteronomy, 8, 10, 14, 20, 21, 117, 220 n. 8, 208 n. 6

Diocletian, 47, 95–99, 101, 207 n. 7
Diogenes Laërtius, 117
Dogma(tics), 31, 38, 39, 89, 90, 92,
    102, 105, 177, 190,
Donatists, 101, 102, 207 n. 11
Duppi-Tessub, 63, 64
Ecclesiastes, 3, 8, 50, 88, 124, 177,
    202 n. 6
Elijah, 57, 58
Empire(s), 30, 47, 61–63, 65, 72, 73,
    76, 78, 82, 83, 85, 93, 96–100,
    107, 109. 111, 113, 114, 128, 141,
    150, 151, 206 n. 9
Emptiness, 77, 86–90, 145–47, 157,
    158, 176, 210 n. 2
Enemies (enemy), 8, 11, 39, 40, 45,
    78, 89, 90, 110, 113, 124, 125,
    139, 163, 164
Evolution, 22, 142
Exodus, 8, 10, 20, 21, 45, 67, 112,
    117, 171
Ezekiel, 3, 53, 54
Ezra, 67, 75, 204 n. 10
Fact(s), 9, 13, 14–19, 22, 25, 32, 68,
    72, 75, 76, 115, 118, 136, 151,
    152, 163, 176, 180
Forms (Theory of), 117, 208 n. 5
Fundamentalism, 69, 70, 171, 172,
    204 n. 11
Funk, Robert, 82, 190, 191, 205 n. 1
Galerius, 97, 98
Gap (necessary for irony), 146
Gaston, Lloyd, 75, 205 n. 20
Geering, Lloyd, viii, 124, 203 n. 2, 210
    n. 10
Genesis, 8, 15, 20, 118, 132, 169
Genocide, 10, 11
Genre, 13–15, 18, 19, 22, 76
Glory, 17, 81, 188
Gnosticism, 47, 48, 202 n. 4 and 5
God (read the book)
Golding, William, 51
Gregory of Nazianzus, 107
Guilt, 39, 46, 108,
Hebrew, 21, 50, 53, 61, 109
Hercules, 103, 104
Heraclitus, 118, 208 n. 8

Heresy, 49, 121,
Hero (heroic), 13–15, 35, 50, 51, 57,
    97, 104, 112, 113, 150, 162,
Hidden Treasure, The 88
Hierarchy, 98, 128, 129, 131, 160
Hinduism, 1, 31, 50, 51, 201 n. 7
Horizon, 13, 14, 36, 70, 79, 119, 196,
Hosea, 65
Human Nature, 33, 94, 97, 103, 104,
    108, 137, 153, 154
Hume, David, 135, 139–44, 153, 209
    n. 5
Iamblichus, 94, 206 n. 5
Idolatry, 68, 74
Imperfect, 56, 116,
Impressions (Hume), 139–42, 144
Incarnation, 2, 50, 59, 105, 106, 110,
    119, 122, 149, 184
Irony, 69, 112, 138, 146, 158, 172,
Isaac, 10
Isaiah, 12, 14, 54, 66, 73, 161, 206
    n. 11
Jacob, 10, 73, 156
Jehoram, 64
Jehu(d), 64, 67, 204 n. 5
Jeremiah, 73
Jerusalem, 63, 75, 99, 114, 116,
    166–68,
Judaism, 48, 72, 113, 115, 118, 208 n.
    7, 210 n. 2
Jezebel, 64
Job (book of), 3, 14
John (Gospel of), 16, 17, 51, 89, 149,
    184, 202 n. 9
Johnson, Luke Timothy, 118
Justice, 3, 12, 28, 39, 40, 48, 54, 56,
    66–68, 75, 102, 106, 140, 154,
    196
Kafka, Franz, 111
Land (of Israel and as metaphor), 10,
    20, 45, 63, 65, 199 n. 5
Legislative Law, 118, 119
Leo I, Pope, 121, 122, 209 n. 15
Levite, 112, 114
Literal(ly, ism), 13–15, 17, 22, 49, 63,
    68–71, 77, 163, 164, 170, 188,
    196

Logos, 46, 51, 54, 59, 71, 72, 93–95, 100, 103–5, 109, 116–19, 127, 149

Lost Coin, The, 78, 88

Lost Sheep, The 79, 88

Luke (Gospel of), 16, 17, 19, 79, 80, 159, 162, 165, 167,

Luther, Martin, 121, 209 n. 15

Lovelock, James, 154

Marcus Aurelius, 94

Mark (Gospel of), 16, 17, 19, 79, 82–84,

Martyr, Justin, 71

Mastery (of the self), 93

Matthew (Gospel of), 9, 10, 16, 17, 79, 80, 89, 161, 162, 165–68, 199 n. 1, 210 n. 2

Maximian, 96–98, 101

Maxentius, 97, 98

Meletius (Meletians), 101–3, 109, 207 n. 11

Metaphysics (metaphysical), 111, 114–16, 119–21, 137, 141, 185

Middle Ages, 22, 29, 30, 80, 116, 117, 120, 121, 125, 127–29, 131, 132, 135, 137, 177, 178, 180, 187, 188

Mind(set), 13, 14, 19, 43, 73, 89, 94, 136, 185

Morality, 88, 125, 196, 207 n. 15

Moses, 8, 10, 11, 14, 20, 51, 66, 98, 112, 116, 117, 147, 205 n. 13

Mursilis, 63, 64

Mysticism, 56, 57, 70, 72, 184

Narrative, 8, 12, 14, 15, 53, 57, 58, 117, 118, 167, 177

Necessary Being, 127, 130, 135, 177, 178, 180

Nicaea, Council of, 92, 95, 99, 101–6, 114–16, 119–24, 149, 163

Nicene Creed, 104

Neoplatonism, 94

New Testament, 16, 155

Numbers (Book of), 11, 15, 118

Ontological Argument, 132, 133, 178, 209 n. 2

Open/opening, 33–41, 58, 66, 75, 91, 92, 171–73, 180, 193

Origen, 55, 120, 203 n, 11

Orthodox(y), 47, 67, 108, 109, 181, 183

Pagan, 47, 98

Paley, William, 132, 133

Parable(s), 5, 8, 78–92, 108, 111–16, 120, 123, 124, 155, 161, 162–73, 180, 181, 184, 188–94, 198

Parable of the Sower, 79, 82–84, 91

Paul, 8, 9, 12, 36–40, 72–76, 91, 92, 113, 114, 119, 121, 158, 202 n. 15, 205 n, 18, 208 n, 9 and 14, 210 n. 3

Peasant(s), 4, 78, 83–86, 121, 128, 209 n. 15

Perfect, 4, 34, 52, 56, 57, 105, 106, 116, 119, 127, 128, 133–35, 137, 138, 177–79, 181, 184, 209 n. 2

Pharaoh, 10, 11, 199 n. 5

Philosophy, 3, 23, 25–27, 43, 44, 48, 55, 71, 72, 94, 109, 114, 117–20, 125, 129, 130, 135, 138, 140, 151, 153, 162, 163, 170, 195, 209 n. 5, 211 n. 6

Plotinus, 94

Plato, 23, 43, 56, 57, 71, 104, 116, 117, 120, 128, 129, 202 n. 1 and 2, 203 n. 12

Poem (poetry), 4, 5 12, 32, 77–79, 83, 84, 87–89, 91, 108, 123, 176, 177, 181, 188, 194, 202 n. 2, 211 n. 10

Priest(ly), 30, 58, 67, 112, 207 n, 14

Primary (being), 127–31, 177

Prodigal Son, 78, 91, 155, 159, 162

Progressive, 22, 38, 172, 173, 196, 211 n, 9

Projecting (a vision), 14, 15, 196

Promise(s of God), 11, 14, 68, 74, 105, 145, 149, 153, 169, 185, 204 n, 3

Prophetic, 12, 14, 53, 54, 65, 66, 75, 148, 203 n. 2

Psychology, 25–27, 32, 35, 40, 45, 114, 143, 144, 153

Q Document (Q Gospel), 16, 165

Qoheleth, 50, 88, 91, 92, 124

Qur'an, 31. 68, 69, 71, 200 n.2, 204 n. 12

Rabbi(s), 2, 91, 112, 199 n. 3

Reason (as principle), 93, 94, 127, 136–40, 144, 153, 154, 178, 180, 181

Repetition, 13, 21, 142–44, 209 n. 5

Righteousness, 45, 67, 71, 113, 117, 119, 123, 194

Rome, 13, 63, 74, 96–98, 122, 150, 207 n. 7

Rousseau, Jean-Jacques, 153, 154

Royal, vii, 2, 28, 53, 62, 64, 65, 117, 121, 124

Ruth, 10, 67, 204 n. 10

Sacred, 8, 10, 12, 51, 68, 69, 175, 177, 182–84, 186, 206 n. 1

Sacrifice, 10, 25, 37, 38, 62, 65, 102

Salvation, 9, 30, 43, 52, 58, 73, 95, 103–10, 114, 115, 119, 162, 175, 177, 184–86

Samaritan, 78, 90, 110, 111–15, 123, 125, 162, 163, 167, 169, 171, 188, 193, 208 n. 2

Science, 15, 19, 21, 33, 125, 128, 134, 135, 140, 143, 152, 159, 163, 171, 172, 175, 180, 200 n. 7

Scott, Bernard Brandon, 73, 80, 81, 85, 123, 205 n. 8

Severus, 97, 98

Sign, 17, 73, 80, 90, 93, 114, 145, 148, 149, 152, 185

Silence, 56, 59, 87, 88, 108, 150

Sin, 24, 26, 51, 55, 75, 101, 104, 107, 108, 110, 114, 115, 159, 184

Socrates, 7, 27, 51, 71, 86, 146, 205 n. 13

Source(s), 15–18, 68, 109, 139

Spinoza, Baruch, 135, 138, 144

Spirit (Holy), 32, 149

Suzerain, 64, 204 n. 6

Symbol, 10, 12, 14, 19, 20, 22, 24, 26, 27, 31, 32, 34, 43, 63, 64, 68, 80, 81, 82, 100, 116, 148, 162, 163, 180

Tamar, 9, 10, 199 n. 1

Technology, 13, 151, 152, 154, 170, 171, 190

Teleological Argument, 132

Temple, 63, 64, 67, 94, 112, 113

Tillich, Paul, 104, 170, 171, 176, 211 n. 9

Torah, 2, 3, 14, 54, 66, 68–70, 76, 112, 113, 116, 117, 147, 148, 199 n. 3

Typology, 46–49

Ugarit, 61

Universe, 3, 4, 13, 32–34, 36, 55, 71, 90, 132, 134, 137, 138, 139, 141, 159, 160, 172, 175, 176, 188, 196, 201 n. 9 and 10

Vision, 3, 5, 12, 14, 15, 36, 52, 54, 55, 59, 66, 70, 72, 77–79, 81, 82, 84, 86, 89–92, 96, 108, 111, 115, 120, 150, 153, 155, 157, 159, 160, 161, 164, 168–70, 173, 180, 181, 185, 188, 190, 192, 194

West(ern), 1–3, 7, 12, 13, 19, 21, 22, 25, 28, 30, 31, 39, 40, 41, 43, 46, 50, 52, 61, 71, 114, 118–21, 123, 127, 135, 147, 151, 173, 195, 201 n.7

Wisdom, 2, 7, 12, 14, 22, 23, 25, 36, 49, 50, 52, 54, 58, 72, 73, 86–88, 100, 119, 146, 153, 155, 157–60, 162, 202 n. 6 and 9

Wise, 7, 57, 73, 86, 113, 146

World Spirit, 93–95, 105, 117, 127

Yahweh, 58, 65, 112

About the Author

David Galston (Ph.D., McGill University) is a University Chaplain and Adjunct Professor of Philosophy at Brock University in St. Catharines, Ontario, Academic Director at Westar Institute, a regular speaker at the Quest Learning Centre, and academic adviser to the SnowStar Institute in Canada. He is the author of *Embracing the Human Jesus: A Wisdom Path for Contemporary Christianity* (2012) and *Archives and the Event of God: The Impact of Michel Foucault on Philosophical Theology* (2010).

CPSIA information can be obtained at www.ICGtesting.com
Printed in the USA
BVOW05s1141050616

450751BV00030B/467/P